RELATIONAL TRANSITIONS

RELATIONAL TRANSITIONS

The Evolution of
Personal Relationships

Richard L. Conville

PRAEGER

New York
Westport, Connecticut
London

Library of Congress Cataloging-in-Publication Data

Conville, Richard L.
    Relational transitions : the evolution of personal relationships /
Richard L. Conville.
        p.   cm.
    Includes bibliographical references and index.
    ISBN 0-275-93523-X (alk. paper)
    1. Interpersonal relations. I. Title.
    HM132.C628 1991
    302–dc20   91-4089

British Library Cataloguing in Publication Data is available.

Library of Congress Catalog Card Number: 91-4089
ISBN: 0-275-93523-X

First published in 1991

Praeger Publishers, One Madison Avenue, New York, NY 10010
An imprint of Greenwood Publishing Group, Inc.

Printed in the United States of America

The paper used in this book complies with the
Permanent Paper Standard issued by the National
Information Standards Organization (Z39.48–1984).

10   9   8   7   6   5   4   3   2   1

Acknowledgments

Mark L. Knapp. *Interpersonal Communication and Human Relationships*. Figure 2.1
reprinted by permission of Allyn and Bacon.

Richard L. Conville (1983). Second-order development in interpersonal
communication. *Human Communication Research, 9,* pp. 195–207. Selected passages
and Figure 4 reprinted by permission of Sage Publications, Newbury Park, California.

Richard L. Conville (1988). Relational transitions: An inquiry into their structure and
function. *Journal of Social and Personal Relationships, 5,* pp. 423–37. Selected
passages including Table 2 reprinted by permission of Sage Publications, London.

Contents

FIGURES   vii
PREFACE   ix
ACKNOWLEDGMENTS   xiii

1 The Ubiquity of Difference: They Saw a Game   1

2 Transition and Difference in Relationships: With New Eyes   19

3 Structural Analysis of Relationship Transitions:
   Similar Differences   41

4 From Description to Explanation in Relationship Transition:
   Repetitive without Repeating   59

5 Relationship Security: Fitting Relations   79

6 Relationship Disintegration: Taking Notice   93

7 Relationship Alienation: Still Life   113

8 Relationship Resynthesis: *Homo Relatio*   131

9 Prospect: *Via*   149

APPENDIX A: Helen Keller's Case   157
APPENDIX B: Diane's Case   160
APPENDIX C: Howard's and Judy's Cases   162
REFERENCES   173
INDEX   183
ABOUT THE AUTHOR   189

Contents

Figures

1.1 Knapp's Stage Model of Relationship Development   12

2.1 Chronology of Helen Keller's Account of Relational
     Transition   24
2.2 Analysis of Helen Keller's Account   25
2.3 Affective Oppositions in Helen Keller's Account   28
2.4 Diane's Analysis of Her Experience   31
2.5 Howard's and Judy's Accounts Analyzed   34
2.6 Episode Types in the Four Accounts Analyzed   38
2.7 Common Elements in the Four Accounts Analyzed   39

3.1 Howard's Account Analyzed   54

4.1 Dialectics and the Creation of a Social Domain   71
4.2 Structural Helical Model of Human Action   73
4.3 Structural Helical Model of Human Action   76
4.4 Structural Helical Model of Human Action   77

7.1 The Relationship between Turning Point Types, Their
     Involvement with Relationship Talk, and the Intensity of
     Their Effects   121
7.2 Turning Point Types, as Confirming or Disconfirming:
     Their Long-Term and Short-Term Effects, in Romantic and
     Organizational Relationships   126

8.1 Confirming and Disconfirming Messages   142

Preface

The theme of "process" is an enduring one in communication studies. Nearly 20 years ago Smith (1972) reminded us that a process view is necessary for an adequate understanding of the world in general (Whitehead, 1929) and of human communication in particular (Berlo, 1960). Change, however, comes slowly, and Duck and Perlman recently found themselves making the same recommendation (embedded in a prediction) for the study of personal relationships: "we believe strongly that future work will progress towards the view that relationships are processes." The particular process they selected as most important was "the cognitive transformations and representations through which partners come to perceive themselves as having a *relationship*" (1985, p. 13).

But "process" is a stubborn concept to implement, especially as "cognitive transformations and representations." Five years later personal relationship scholars were reminded, "relationships are unfinished business conducted through resolution of and dialog about personal, dyadic or relational dilemmas, through talk" (Duck, 1990, p. 9). Moreover, relationship researchers' conscientious efforts to engage in process thinking are plagued by a "human tendency" to conceive it "in terms of stages or easily characterized end-points of processes rather than the processes themselves" (1990, p. 19).

This book proposes answers to these questions: "How shall we conceive of relationships as processes?" "What shall count as data when we examine those processes?" and "How shall those data be interpreted?" Thus the book represents a move away from relational stage models, so common in the literature of personal relationships, and toward thinking that grants priority to the question of how relational partners move through those "transformations and representations" over the question of what those stages are.

This change in thinking is analogous to the change from alchemy to chemistry. Alchemy knew nothing of molecular structure whereas chemistry sees changes in molecular structure as common to all substantial changes. However, the invention of chemistry, with its emphasis on process at the atomic level, did not make stage models obsolete. Indeed, it brought along with it the periodic table, that display of elements in a sequence based on complexity of atomic structure. So, too, the process model of relational transition that I am proposing complements existing relational stage models.

Chapter 4 develops a structural helical model that is designed to focus attention on personal relationships as processes. Aspects of the model, moreover, are found to be implicit in current theories of relational change as well as in dialectical theory.

Chapters 1 through 3 establish a basis for the model. Chapter 1 develops the concept of Difference. Difference is both problematic and necessary in personal relationships. Adjudicating differences is the work of personal relationships. Stage models of relationship development rely upon Difference as do many common lines of research in interpersonal communication. Biology, biography, and the culture at large, I suggest, conspire to force us to come to terms with Difference. The concepts of *différance* and of dialectical differences enhance our understanding of Difference in relationships.

In Chapter 2 I argue for structural analysis as a procedure for interpreting personal narratives of relationship transitions. Structural analysis of three cases yielded three dialectical oppositions that were central to the subjects' relational transitions. The dialectical dimensions were time (past-future), intimacy (close-distant), and affect (positive-negative). Moreover, the kinds of episodes the subjects experienced provided a rough outline of the four phases of the structural helical model introduced in Chapter 4.

In Chapter 3 I provide an introduction to structuralism along with standard criticisms of it. For our purposes, the most telling problem is structuralism's failure to consider the individual, acting human being. Starting with the premise that human action may be usefully viewed as language-like, I elaborate on four cardinal points of structuralist theory. The solution that I propose to the absence of the human subject is to use personal narratives as the data for structural analysis.

Chapters 5 through 8 examine, one at a time, the four phases of the structural helical model: Security, Disintegration, Alienation, and Resynthesis. I show how the existence of each phase is substantiated in the literature of personal relationships and interpersonal communication and focus on key concepts that characterize the phase. In Chapter 5, I discuss Security, when relational partners feel comfortable, roles are complementary, and actions are coordinated. Partners are "in kilter," not "out of kilter." In addition, the three case studies are re-examined for their manifestation of a Security phase.

In Chapter 6 I take up the proposed phase of Disintegration. This phase is marked by the partners' noticing and questioning the relationship rather than merely taking it for granted. The literature confirms that such a period is common in personal relationships. Certain kinds of events intervene to increase partners' uncertainty about the relationship. Again, the cases are examined for their particular manifestation of Disintegration.

Chapter 7 takes up the phase of Alienation. Here, normal role-taking is attenuated; for example, one is unable to lay aside an undesirable role or assume a desired role. This phase is a cul-de-sac of transformation and is, thus, the pivotal step in relational transition. Relational partners experience turning points and pursue confirming messages, as indicated in the literature. The three cases are again examined for their display of an Alienation phase.

I examine Resynthesis in Chapter 8. Here, what it means to be "in relationship" is the key issue, as is the question of how to (re)build a relationship. Such issues are also common in the literature. Specifically, relational partners are deemed to be in this phase when they begin the process of deciding how to resolve the dialectical contradictions that confront them. Resynthesis is prompted by relational partners' pursuit of certainty, their need for human association, and their desire for unfettered role-action. The three cases are re-examined, this time, from the point of view of Resynthesis.

Finally, in the last chapter, I indicate ways in which the book presents an interpretive stance toward the human sciences. The structural helical model is an analytical tool and a thinking tool for interpreting the Difference that confronts us out of personal relationships. Further, the model is shown to generate interesting questions for research and to provide a fundamental structure for interpreting research in interpersonal communication and personal relationships.

Acknowledgments

I extend special thanks to Calvin Schrag of the philosophy department at Purdue University for his writings, for his personal counsel, and for his wise leadership of the 1986 Summer Institute for College Teachers at Purdue, sponsored by the National Endowment for the Humanities. In addition, I am grateful to Keith Erickson, chair of the department of speech communication at the University of Southern Mississippi for his encouragement and support. I am also indebted to the administration of the University of Southern Mississippi for a sabbatical leave during the spring term, 1986, and for additional released time for research. Finally, I thank my students whose challenging questions and inquisitive looks have shaped the ideas developed here. My work has been aided by these and many other generous facilitators, the chief of whom is my wife, Mozella.

RELATIONAL TRANSITIONS

1

The Ubiquity of Difference:
THEY SAW A GAME

On a brisk Saturday afternoon, November 23, 1951, the Dartmouth football team played Princeton in Princeton's Palmer Stadium.
Albert H. Hastorf and Hadley Cantril
"They Saw a Game: A Case Study"
Journal of Abnormal and Social Psychology

It was a classic confrontation, the last game of the season for both teams, bitter rivals. Princeton was undefeated and sported an All-American candidate in quarterback Dick Kazmaier. As recounted by Hastorf and Cantril (1954), the game was rough, marked by injuries and allegations of cheap shots and bad sportsmanship. Princeton won easily, but the game was replayed the next week in the respective school newspapers. Alumni got involved, and films of the game were angrily circulated about the country.

The ironic title of the case study is "They Saw a Game." "They," of course, did not see "a" game but, rather, two games, one seen through the eyes of Dartmouth fans, the other seen through the eyes of Princeton fans. In a survey of students a week after the game, 69 percent of Princeton students labeled the game "rough and dirty" as against only 24 percent of Dartmouth students. Moreover, 86 percent of Princeton students, compared to 36 percent of Dartmouth students, opined that Dartmouth started the rough play. In a controlled viewing of game films, Princeton students observed more than twice as many rules infractions on the part of the Dartmouth team than Dartmouth students observed

(Hastorf & Cantril, 1954). Conversations about the game between partisans of the two schools would have been difficult at best.

The investigators' explanation and extension of their findings regarding the game are instructive:

> the data here indicate that there is no such "thing" as a "game" existing "out there" in its own right which people merely "observe." . . . The "thing" simply is *not* the same for different people whether the "thing" is a football game, a presidential candidate, Communism, or spinach. . . . We behave according to what we bring to the occasion, and what each of us brings to the occasion is more or less unique (p. 133).

Difference is both inevitable and problematic in personal relationships. Nowhere is this more clearly demonstrated than in interpersonal communication. As Duck has observed, "Discrepancies of interpretation — even between close partners — are an inevitable part of everyday social life" (1986, p. 92). Face to face, our unique autobiographies often call out for adjudication, mediation, or refereeing.

But this is not always the case. Often Difference is what brings people together, as in curiosity or physical attraction, in which cases the Difference may or may not be problematic. Moreover, in easily replaced, impersonal relationships Difference is hardly an issue at all. But personal relationships generate Difference, and partners' selves are at stake (Wright, 1989). There Difference is both problematic and inevitable.

Therefore, the status of Difference in interpersonal communication is questionable. On the one hand, it is often considered self-evident. Hence, it is ignored or treated with the contempt of the overfamiliar. On the other hand, confronting Difference as problematic brings identity into focus and calls the relationship into question. Thus Difference, under interrogation, may prove to be a useful tool for thinking about interpersonal communication.

One line of research and theoretical formulation that has both spawned much creative and influential research as well as relied heavily on a presumption of Difference is uncertainty reduction theory (Berger, 1987, 1988; Berger & Bradac, 1982; Berger & Calabrese, 1975). Consider, for example, Berger and Calabrese's Axiom 3, "High levels of uncertainty cause increases in information seeking behavior. As uncertainty levels decline, information seeking behavior decreases" (1975, p. 103). The axiom presumes that Person One has less information about Person Two than she or he could have, that Person Two knows information about himself or herself that Person One does not know. Difference is the result. A need on the part of Person One to increase the predictability of his or her environment compels him or her to redress the difference in information between what he or she knows and what Person Two knows.

But the process works the other way as well. Actually redressing the difference between the personal knowledge held by relational partners about each other can increase uncertainty as well as decrease uncertainty (Planalp & Honeycutt, 1985; Planalp et al., 1988). Person One has X view of Person Two based on knowing A, B, and C. On finding out D about Person Two, Person One then views Person Two as X + D. Person One has thus experienced a Difference between what he or she first knew about Person Two compared to what he or she now knows and between how he or she views Person Two now and how he or she viewed Person Two before acquiring the new knowledge. Redressing one Difference created two others — an increase in knowledge and a consequent change in perception.

Difference, too, is the key issue in self-disclosure (Jourard, 1964; Nakanishi, 1986; Tschann, 1988). Its effects in interpersonal communication seem to depend upon the kind of knowledge about oneself that another does not have, one's willingness to share that knowledge (redress the difference in information) with the other, and once shared, whether the other will reciprocate, that is, redress the difference in the other direction.

Developmental perspectives on interpersonal communication also presume Difference. For example, developmental stages may be described in terms of the differences in language used by the relational partners, topics talked about, and message strategies employed (Knapp, 1984). In a possible scenario, when one partner wants the relationship to move to a less intimate stage, she or he may begin to talk about less intimate topics than they have been used to. If the other follows suit, that is, redresses the difference created by the other partner in topics talked about, then, implicitly or explicitly, they have struck a deal, and the relationship has been jointly redefined as less intimate.

Finally, several additional topics in interpersonal communication research will serve to illustrate the observation that Difference is the central presumption in much of the literature. Studies of interpersonal influence or compliance gaining require the assumption that the influencer holds a position different from the one held by the target of the influence (Witteman & Fitzpatrick, 1986). Studies of relationship repair presume a desired state of the relationship with the other that is not presently the case (Ayres, 1983; Stokes & Hewitt, 1976; Morris & Hopper, 1980).

Repairs are initiated to try to redress the Difference. Studies of conflict management likewise entail some manner of disagreement between relational partners, a Difference to somehow be managed or resolved (Hocker & Wilmot, 1985).

"How obvious!" you might say, like pointing out air. But what is obvious is also familiar and ordinary and even taken for granted. And that is the very point. A natural history of the ordinary takes one from the obvious to the taken-for-granted to the invisible. Many researchers in the field of interpersonal communication have peered directly through Difference and focused on other issues, a few of which I have named. Difference and its centrality to human interaction have become invisible. So here is a curious twist on the story of the emperor's clothes. Rather than trying to convince the well-heeled onlookers that the emperor has on no clothes, the naive onlooker tries to convince them that, wherever the emperor goes, the emperor has on the same clothes — Difference. He may vary his costume with color, texture, and shape (compliance, disclosure, uncertainty), but regardless of whatever else the emperor (interpersonal communication) wears, Difference is its essential garment.

My object in this chapter is to examine the assertion that Difference is both inevitable and problematic for interpersonal communication. Doing that will take our thinking in four directions: a consideration of the assertion that Difference is a given in human life; an exploration of several types of Difference that one may observe in relationships; an inquiry into the operation of Difference in relational stage models; and an investigation of the arenas in which Difference affects relationships.

DIFFERENCE AS A GIVEN

Difference is ubiquitous. Why would this be the case? First, there is, in Kenneth Burke's terms, "generic divisiveness." Burke calls it "common to all men, . . . a universal fact about them, prior to any divisiveness caused by social classes" (1950, p. 146). Persons live within physical boundaries marked off by the epidermis. I see that I am not the same entity as my neighbor. I see that we are different beings. I can borrow her ladder, but I cannot borrow her feet. I am *a* being, single and whole, and so is she; each one is distinct from the other. Thus is born the possibility of influencing others for collective action (Cushman & Cahn, 1985). About generic divisiveness, Burke has observed, "Here is the basis of rhetoric" (1950, p. 146), which in turn prompted Nichols's commentary: "communication is compensatory to division" (1963, p. 82).

Burke placed our physical separateness ahead of social class. However, social class is certainly powerful in accounting for the ubiquity of Difference, along with that host of other human characteristics over which we often have little control, that list of "givens" that falls under the head of "unique autobiographies." A person's special combination of gender, birth date, parents, schools, peers, locale — to name a few — generates a unique person. No one person traverses the world in exactly the same tracks as any other. Each of us writes a different story.

Thus biography and biology conspire to thrust upon us Difference. But there is another player. The rhetoric of our culture argues persuasively for the normality of Difference. Difference has turned into "radical individualism" for many, a phenomenon that is best understood in contrast to the nurturing community of nineteenth-century America.

> In Tocqueville's still-agrarian America, as indeed throughout the nineteenth century, the basic unit of association, and the practical foundation of both individual dignity and participation, was the local community. . . . Concern for economic betterment was widespread, but it operated within the context of a still-functional covenant concern for the welfare of one's neighbor. In the towns, the competitive individualism stirred by commerce was balanced and humanized by the restraining influences of a fundamentally egalitarian ethic of community responsibility (Bellah, Madsen, Sullivan, Swidler, & Tipton, 1985, p. 38).

In the late twentieth century, however, the typical American's experience is utterly different. "Clearly, the meaning of one's life for most Americans is to become one's own person, almost to give birth to oneself. Much of this process . . . is negative. It involves breaking free from family, community, and inherited ideas" (pp. 82–83). In the small town life of Laura Ingalls Wilder, young Laura was obliged to make the best of her relationships with the cantankerous shopkeepers, Mr. and Mrs. Olson (and they with her). But today I do not have to accept that kind of hassle. I can exercise my preferences and avoid troublesome relationships by taking my business to another shop, to another mall, or even to another city. I do not have to remain a part of the community. I can separate myself from it at will. Modernity has brought with it a vast array of relationship options and the permission to exercise them. The upshot has been to privilege the Difference (over the community) of the individual.

Other evidence of the normalizing of the individual as different is found in Allan Bloom's (1987) controversial indictment of U.S. higher education, *The Closing of the American Mind*. Bloom asserts, "Openness

— and the relativism that makes it the only possible stance in the face of various claims to truth and various ways of life and kinds of human beings — is the great insight of our times" (p. 26). This new openness, however, is not the benign openness of honest inquiry. Rather, Bloom contends, "Openness, as currently conceived, is a way of making surrender to whatever is most powerful, or worship of vulgar success, look principled" (p. 41). And further, "[Openness] now means accepting everything and denying reason's power" (p. 38). And finally, "If openness means to 'go with the flow,' it is necessarily an accommodation with the present" (p. 42).

A culture obsessed with openness of this sort obviously does not need the wisdom of the past or the advice of the community. As an individual one can see for oneself where the flow is going, what is successful and powerful, and indeed what there is out there to accept. Bloom concludes, "Our openness means we do not need others" (p. 34) — Bellah's "radical individualism" revisited!

Even if Bloom may have overstated his case somewhat, particularly when it comes to alternatives to relativism, he, nevertheless, seems to have accurately described a good deal of contemporary U.S. social and political terrain. One prevalent response to the growing pluralism of society in the United States is to accept all ideas and fashions as equally good. Is there more fertile ground for the growth of Difference? If one person's opinion is as good as another's, and if the past is passé, then each person is an atom, differentiated from all others by his or her peculiar, even accidental, constellation of opinions and experience. Difference rules.

DIFFERENCE AS *DIFFÉRANCE*

The concept of Difference is greatly enriched by reference to Derrida's use of the term. The context of his thinking (and necessarily of ours) is Saussure's *Course in General Linguistics*. This father of modern linguistics, Saussure, observed, "In language there are only differences" (1959, p. 120). This principle enjoys virtually universal acceptance among linguists and semioticians and will be amply illustrated in the next chapter. Briefly, it means that, in any language, what-one-says is distinguished from what-one-does-not-say (for example, one word distinguished from another) by a finite set of articulatory and acoustic features that are represented as polar oppositions. For example, when one means what /bil/ means in a sentence and not what /pil/ means, a hearer knows that because the first sound in "bill" has the feature voiced [+vd] (marked by the vibration of the vocal cords) and not the feature voiceless [-vd] (nonvibration). In other respects the words are heard as identical. The upshot is that we use sound differences (for example, voiced versus voiceless) to interpret the meaning of what we hear.

Derrida employs the neologism *"différance"* (spelled with an "a"; in French the pronunciation is the same, whether "e" or "a") to suggest, simultaneously, the two meanings, in English, of the Latin root "differre," to defer and to differ (Derrida, 1982). Thus in his analyses of texts, both literary and philosophical, Derrida has pursued the themes that what a text means can never be finally and fully decided, but, rather, definitive interpretations must be forever delayed or deferred; and that no text can be dominated by a single authoritative interpretation, but, rather, a multiplicity of different readings exists (Culler, 1982; Derrida, 1981; Michelfelder & Palmer, 1989). Defer, to Derrida connotes "the action of putting off until later, of taking into account, of taking account of time and of the forces of an operation that implies an economical calculation, a detour, a delay, a relay, a reserve, a representation" (1982, p. 8).

Perpetual deferral is the proper state of textual interpretations based on the second of the simultaneous meanings of *différance,* to differ. Readers differ among themselves on their interpretations of texts; they see different things in the same text. They differ. Those differences are, on the one hand, passive; they simply are. On the other hand, however, those differences are also active, and that is due to two features of texts: texts are interpreted by readers (that is, readers interact with texts), and texts contain intertextual references and largely depend upon them for their meanings (Culler, 1982; Derrida, 1981). Thus, just as the process of deferral is dynamic, so also differing is conceived of as a process. As Derrida has said, *"différance* refers to the generative movement in the play of differences" (1981, p. 27).

This "systematic play of differences ... by means of which elements are related to each other" is also a "generative movement" of differences (Derrida, 1981, p. 27) and constitutes the central focus of the critical movement known as deconstruction. Such analyses often begin with the critic's locating in a text polar oppositions of the kind Saussure (1959) referred to in the *Course* and the kind Lévi-Strauss (1963) often used in his cultural analyses, for example, speech/writing, silence/talk, raw/cooked, and high/low. Derrida's and his followers' typical critical program is to select a polar opposition that seems central to the text under consideration; argue that in fact it is a hierarchy, dominated by one pole of the opposition; and overturn the hierarchy by demonstrating ways in which the text itself subverts the hierarchy. Thus deconstructionists argue that a final determination of the text's meaning is successfully deferred (Derrida, 1981, 1982; Johnson, 1980). Broadening this view beyond the interpretation of texts, Caputo has proposed that the deconstructionists' agenda of "radical hermeneutics cultivates an acute sense of the contingency of all social, historical, linguistic structures, [and] an appreciation of their constituted character" (1987, p. 209).

Lest it appear that the deconstructionists' program is just another superficial relativism or militant nihilism, Derrida has made a revealing comment on the relationship of deconstruction to structuralism:

> the theme of *différance* is incompatible with the static, synchronic, taxonomic, ahistoric motifs in the concept of *structure*. But it too goes without saying that this motif is not the only one that defines structure, and that the production of differences, *différance*, is not astructural: it produces systematic and regulated transformations which are able, at a certain point, to leave room for a structural science. The concept of *différance* even develops the most legitimate principled exigencies of "structuralism" (1981, pp. 27-28).

The conjunction of deconstruction and structure is Difference. Difference enables the linguistic structure, hence the meaning, that deconstruction dismantles and reconfigures. *Différance* multiples Difference by locating textual differences in order to overturn them, thus deferring a final conclusion on the meaning of the text. Moreover, hearers and readers of discourse interpret by differentiation.

Having gone rather far afield, let us return to our main task — the elucidation of Difference as it seems to work in personal relationships. Having seen that Difference is a central presumption in much of the research literature and how Difference appears as a given in contemporary human interaction, our task now is to enrich our understanding of Difference in personal relationships by observing interpersonal communication through the lens of *Différance*.

The Difference that is presumed in research and given in interaction is Derrida's second reference of *différance,* to differ. For example, in the passive sense, two persons may simply experience a third person differently and establish different relationships with him or her; but, in the active sense as well, in the course of their conversations with and about the third party, their relationships may be altered, as in Derrida's "generative movement in the play of differences" (1981, p. 27).

But, as noted above with texts, the dynamic nature of interpersonal differences leads to the deferral of final or authoritative conclusions about the relationships in question. Whether one most appropriately relates to the third party as immature and thoughtless or as highly creative and often preoccupied cannot be answered in any definitive way. The passage of time, and continued interaction among our hypothetical threesome, will inevitably alter the relationships. Thus, a definitive "picture" of a relationship is necessarily deferred also, just as in the case of texts. Simmel has noted a quite similar dynamism in his own work. Interactions between persons give rise to "pictures" of one another, but their interactions are based on those "pictures" as well. "Here we have one of the deep lying circuits of intellectual life, where an element pre-supposes a second element which yet, in turn, presupposs the first" (1950, p. 309). Hence a final conclusion on the nature of the relationship must forever be delayed or deferred.

DIFFERENCE IN RELATIONSHIPS

If Difference is both inevitable and problematic in relationships and if Difference is both demanded by society and easily observed in human interaction, then proper understanding of interpersonal communication requires investigation of how Difference works.

Difference influences relationships primarily in the domain of definition. Viable relationships require that participants agree on what the relationship is (Morton, Alexander & Altman, 1976; Planalp et al., 1988; Wilmot, 1987). Without such agreement, participants experience uncertainty and take action to reduce that uncertainty (Berger & Calabrese, 1975; Berger, 1987), or they may move to explicit disagreement and on to dissolution (Duck, 1986).

Although the passage of time is often responsible for differences in relationship definition, the passage of time also permits the repeated encounters that are necessary for achieving consensus on the definition of a relationship. Morton, Alexander, and Altman's propositions about social relationships are instructive at this point, for example, "*As Relationships Develop, Modes of Exchange Tend to Expand and Diversify*" (1976, p. 109). The passage of time is not only necessary for a relationship to exist, but also brings about changes in the participants' communication. Biological maturation requires that parents and children widen their repertoire of talk. Parents who attended to their adolescent offspring in the way they attended their infant's every need would soon be alienated from their necessarily independent-minded teenager. Unforeseen and unsought experiences require coworkers and friends to expand their conversational domains over time. Business cycles, accidents, illness, new friends, and new ideas all thrust themselves upon persons. "These [new, expanded] domains are so varied, greatly expanded repertoires of communication modes and levels are required to attain mutuality of relationship definition" (Morton, Alexander, & Altman, 1976, p. 109), that is, for the participants to continue to agree that there exists such a thing as their relationship.

When that agreement ceases, there is a crisis. Enter Difference. Morton, Alexander, and Altman continue their analysis under the proposition,

> *Relationship Crises Entail Nonmutuality of Relationship Definition.* . . .
> Because both new and established relationships are characterized by expanding domains of interaction and diversification of exchange modes, frequent relationship redefinition may occur resulting in temporary or longer periods of nonmutuality, of relationship crisis (1976, p. 110).

Thus nonmutuality crises are to be expected, as are their concomitant process, relationship redefinition. The taming of "relationship crisis" is complete in the exposition by Morton, Alexander, and Altman when they conclude, "Relationship crisis, then, is a *transitional* process [italics added] associated with dynamic changes involved in the formation, expansion, and dissolution of social bonding" (1976, p. 110). Others have also suggested that relationship termination, as in divorce, may be seen as a transitional process (Masheter & Harris, 1986; Wilmot, 1987).

My concern here is not with trivial differences in a relationship, not whether to go to Wendy's or McDonald's or whether the peanut butter belongs in the cabinet or in the fridge. The crucial question is, "What Difference makes a difference in relationships?" or "What kinds of Difference lead to relationship crisis and redefinition?" One answer is that dialectical differences seem to bring about this kind of relationship reformulation or restructuring (Raush, 1981).

Dialectical theory has recently been employed by a variety of investigators in interpersonal communication (Altman, Vinsel, & Brown, 1981; Baxter, 1988, 1989, 1990; Bochner, 1976; Conville, 1988; Gergen, 1982; Masheter & Harris, 1986; Rawlins, 1983a, 1983b; Wilmot, 1987). Dialectical relationships are marked by the dual characteristics of process and contradiction (Baxter, 1988). Wilmot speaks of the "dynamic *interplay*" between dialectical opposites (1987, p. 167), a process brought about by the associated characteristic of contradiction. "Change . . . is caused by the struggle and tension of contradiction" (Baxter, 1988, p. 258). A relationship of dialectical opposition exists when polar opposites are found to stand in contradiction so that they depend upon each other for definition and existence.

For example, consider a hypothetical relationship that is in a nonmutuality crisis. The participants are past being uncertain about each other in the relationship and now agree that they disagree on their definitions of the relationship. Because they do not share a consensus definition of the relationship, they do not have between them that unseen but powerful third party in viable relationships — "our relationship." Rather, they have "his relationship" and "her relationship" (Fitzpatrick & Best, 1979). Let us further say that he defines the relationship as "longstanding, close friend," and she defines the relationship as "romantic: marriage a possibility." A given weekend finds her angry that he did not invite her out for an intimate dinner to mark the third anniversary of their first date and finds him dismayed at her emotions directed toward him when he returned from an overnight canoe trip with the Boy Scout troop he leads. Here we have a dialectical difference involving the oft-cited oppositional pair, intimacy (connection) and detachment (autonomy) (Masheter & Harris, 1986; see also Altman et al., 1981; Baxter, 1988; Wilmot, 1987). He sees their relationship as rather independent persons who occasionally enjoy each other's company but who otherwise go their own ways. She sees her decisions about how to spend her time to be tied to how he spends his time. She does not just enjoy his company; she wants it.

The reason this is a Difference that makes a difference is that intimacy and detachment stand in dialectical relationship. Each is defined by the absence of the other. This contradiction and interdependence are an unstable mass productive of change. One partner desires friendship, the other partner favors romance, and neither can be satisfied under these circumstances. The crisis they experience is due to nonmutuality of relationship definition.

The definitional disagreement is a crisis precisely because it affects important aspects of the self-definitions of the relationship partners (Wright, 1978). In our hypothetical romantic relationship, the man cannot be what he wants to be, a "longstanding, close friend," unless the woman will take the necessary complementary role of "longstanding, close friend." By the same token, the woman cannot be what she wants to be, his romantic partner, unless the man takes the necessary complementary role of "romantic partner." Each prevents the other from being who he or she wants to be in the relationship. Thus they experience a relationship crisis and probable relationship redefinition (see Cushman & Cahn, 1985, Chap. 6).

The differences that make a Difference in relationships are dialectical differences. Relational crises are precipitated when partners disagree about the definition of their relationship and when their respective relationship definitions (for example, labels, goals, and roles) are in dialectical opposition. However, relational crises seem to be associated with the normal processes of growth, stability, and deterioration of relationships. My object in the next section is to assess the operation of Difference in relational stage models.

DIFFERENCE IN RELATIONAL STAGE MODELS

Mark Knapp (1984) has proposed a model of relationship development that imaginatively depicts the growth and decline of intimacy in relationships (see Figure 1.1). In a relationship that moves up the left side of the staircase-like figure, relational partners are establishing ever higher levels of intimacy. Five stages mark that journey: Initiating, Experimenting, Intensifying, Integrating, and Bonding. Interaction at each stage is defined by characteristic language, conversational topics, and message strategies. The same characteristics mark the stages of relationship deterioration: Differentiating, Circumscribing, Stagnating, Avoiding, and Terminating. Partners in a relationship that moves through those stages down the right side of the staircase model experience decreasing levels of intimacy. The middle section of each stair step on the

FIGURE 1.1 — Knapp's Stage Model of Relationship Development

Bonding	Stabilizing	Bonding
Integrating	Stabilizing	Differentiating
Intensifying	Stabilizing	Circumscribing
Experimenting	Stabilizing	Stagnating
Initiating	Stabilizing	Avoiding
	Terminating	

Source: Knapp, 1984, p. 50; used with permission.

model allows a relationship to stabilize at a given stage. For example, at the Intensifying stage a relationship could "move" laterally to the right and stabilize there, or at the Circumscribing stage a relationship could "move" laterally to the left and stabilize there.

Partner Dynamics

Difference plays a key role in Knapp's and similar stage models of relationship development (Berger & Bradac, 1982; Cushman & Cahn, 1985; Goss & O'Hair, 1988; Levinger, 1983; Phillips & Wood, 1983; Wilmot, 1987; Wilson, Hantz, & Hanna, 1989). The process appears to work in two ways. First, one partner may place the relationship in the Experimenting stage while the other partner may place it in the Intensifying stage. They differ in relationship definition. This is problematic for the partners. They may signal this nonmutuality by their talk. Each one talks in a manner consistent with the stage in which he or she defines the relationship. In all likelihood both notice this Difference between utterance types — talk characteristic of the Experimenting stage and talk characteristic of the Intensifying stage. The Difference of scheme and utterance may also obtain. For example, the person who defines the relationship at the Experimenting stage would notice that the partner talk characteristic of the Intensifying stage does not fit into the scheme of rules that defines communication in the Experimenting stage. The Difference observed may then incite mutual persuasion in which they try to negotiate a satisfactory stage or definition for the relationship.

A second way in which Difference is at work in a stage model is within a single relationship partner rather than between two partners. He or she may experience a Difference between the stage he or she perceives the relationship to be in and the one he or she wishes the relationship to be in (Duck, 1986; Wilmot, 1988). Difference, yes, but intrapersonal, not interpersonal. Here the Difference of utterance and scheme would be prominent. What one partner wants to say (event) has no appropriate structure (scheme of rules or context) in which to be meaningful — the stage wished for. Conversely, the perceived stage (scheme of rules) is not a structure that furnishes a meaningful context for what the partner wants to say (event). Out of the internal dialogue prompted by a Difference of utterance and scheme may come conversations with the other partner aimed at resolving that discrepancy.

Stage models of relationship development neither take into account this intrapersonal dimension of Difference nor give the interpersonal dimension of Difference a prominent place. Typically, their designers have been content to focus on correlating types of communicative behavior with certain relational stages. Levinger (1980), for example, has reported two types of communicative behavior characteristic of couples in the Continuance phase of marriage, validation (in well-functioning pairs) and cross-complaining (in poorly-functioning pairs). Knapp (1984) has directed our attention to changes in relational partners' language, topics, and message strategies as evidence of their movement through stages of intimacy.

Partner Perspectives

Useful as they have been over the years as heuristic and teaching devices, there is another perspective that is normally missing from relational stage models: an "insider's" view (Olson, 1977) of Difference. Implemented, Differences would take the form of discrepancies between partners' own reported definitions of the relationship as well as discrepancies between a single partner's perceived and desired definitions of the relationship. Such a perspective would include as a corollary those "adverbial properties" of a move from one stage to another (Duck & Sants, 1983) — those properties that reveal how the relational partners themselves redefined their relationship.

A call for including participants' own (or insiders') views of relational transitions is not without precedent. Murray Davis (*Intimate Relations,* 1973) was among the first. Writing the same year as Altman and Taylor's *Social Penetration,* Davis concluded that

> Case studies of particular relationships should be collected. Something between personal biography and social history is needed. . . . focusing especially on such critical points as their origin, termination, transitions to higher and lower levels, outside influences, internal crises (1973, pp. 285–86).

Davis seemed to be calling for studies of nonmutuality crises (Morton, Alexander, & Altman, 1976) with "a focus on the phenomenology of relationship partners," as Baxter and Bullis (1986, p. 488) state in their study of relational turning points. Moreover, Masheter and Harris's study of the transition from spouse to friend via divorce employed a "viewpoint from 'inside' the relationship rather than the viewpoint of an 'outside' observer" (1986, p. 178). Finally, Conville (1983; 1988) has developed a method for analyzing insider viewpoints of relational crises that employs structural analysis of participants' own accounts. In later chapters these and other studies will be examined in detail, and means will be demonstrated for addressing the problems presented by relational stage models.

Arenas of Action

What relational stage models do well is to illustrate the relationship processes of growth, stability, and deterioration. However, a final perspective that is usually missing from the models is a distinction among the arenas in which this action takes place. An exception is Duck (1982; 1986). This distinction is exactly the one on which he has based his model of dissolving personal relationships. In his model Duck proposed three arenas of action (phases he calls them) in the deterioration process, the intrapsychic, the dyadic, and the social.

After a breakdown of some sort in the relationship, one partner decides that he or she cannot remain in the relationship and enters the intrapsychic phase of dissolution. Here the aggrieved partner focuses on the other's behavior, faces the dilemma squarely, and calculates the costs and benefits of leaving or remaining in the relationship. If the costs are high enough, the dyadic phase is next. Here the dissatisfied partner ordinarily, but not always, confronts the other (Duck, 1986), and negotiations are held regarding the possibility of reconciliation and the costs and benefits to both partners of dissolving the relationship.

Stage models of relationship development tend to limit our attention to the dyadic phase of communicative action. In that arena, relational partners' conversation is the focus and is the basis for characterizing their level of intimacy.

Moreover, there is a recursive element, not normally referred to, that is inherent in the application of stage models. At the boundary between each pair of stages, Duck's (1986) intrapsychic phase would again become relevant. There, a relational partner would, as before, engage in internal dialogue assessing the state of the relationship in that stage, in terms of Difference. It might concern a perceived difference between the partners' definitions (stages) of the relationship or a difference between the partner's perceived and desired definitions (stages) of the relationship. The structural helical model that is developed through this volume is an effort to capture this inherent recursiveness in the evolution of personal relationships.

Continuing with Duck's model of relationship dissolution, after the dyadic phase comes the social phase, that is, if the partners cannot negotiate a mutually satisfying redefinition of the relationship. Here the partners go public with their dissolution, assessing its effects on their respective social networks, getting the news on the grapevine in a face-saving manner, and negotiating a future relationship with the partner. The additional function of talk that Duck (1986) includes is "grave-dressing," participants' postrelationship storytelling that explains it all to onlookers. It too is "social" in contrast to "dyadic," and as such is better seen as a species of the social phase than as a distinct arena of action. Like the intrapsychic phase, the social phase is not addressed directly in typical stage models.

Duck's (1982, 1986) three arenas of communicative action, the intrapersonal, the dyadic, and the social, provide a clear and useful conceptualization of the deterioration of relational intimacy. However, I would suggest that his tripartite analysis of arenas of communicative action is also useful in conceptualizing the growth of relational intimacy as well. Differences in relational definition and preference can occur just as well in either advancing or receding intimacy. The three arenas of communicative action are relevant, moreover, in any consideration of Difference in relational transitions.

Difference may occur within a relational partner as a dissatisfaction with the present stage of the relationship (intrapsychic phase) or between relational partners, as in a disagreement over the definition of their relationship (dyadic phase); and Difference may occur as a discrepancy between relational partners' views of their relationship and that held by members of their respective social networks (social phase).

CONCLUSION

Difference is inevitable and problematic in personal relationships and occupies a significant place in the literature of personal relationships and relationship development. Moreover, cultural messages giving priority to Difference find resonance in both our biological nature and our personal histories.

Difference has a temporal dimension as well. *Différance*, the generative play of differences, makes relationships elusive (Derrida, 1981). Efforts to capture their essence are deferred while the process of differing continues unabated.

Differences of a certain kind seem to be necessary for the process of personal relationship, that is, dialectical differences (Baxter, 1988). Marked by attributes of contradiction, interdependence, and change, dialectical differences are central features in personal relationships.

Movement through existing relational stage models (Duck, 1986; Knapp, 1984; Levinger, 1983; Wilmot, 1987) presumes Difference: between a person's actions and the relationship stage occupied or between the relationship stage one is in and the one he or she desires to be in.

Relational stage models do not provide an adequate view of relationship transition. On the one hand, they do not give priority to relational partners' personal narratives whereas, on the other, they do grant priority to relationship dissolution (as opposed to growth) when placing relationships in the arenas of intrapersonal, interpersonal, and social interaction.

2

Transition and Difference in Relationships:
WITH NEW EYES

Life, insofar as she troubled to conceive it, was a circle of rich, pleasant people, with identical interests and identical foes. In this circle, one thought, married, and died. Outside of it were poverty and vulgarity forever trying to enter, just as the London fog tries to enter the pine-woods pouring through the gaps in the northern hills. But, in Italy, where anyone who chooses may warm himself in equality, as in the sun, this conception of life vanished. Her senses expanded; she felt that there was no one whom she might not get to like, that social barriers were irremovable, doubtless, but not particularly high. You jump over them just as you jump into a peasant's olive-yard in the Apennines, and he is glad to see you. She returned with new eyes.

E. M. Forster
A Room with a View

In E. M. Forster's 1923 novel *A Room with a View,* Lucy, the heroine, hitherto untraveled, visits Italy. The effects are profound. In the London of her upbringing, Lucy had been insulated from different others ("poverty and vulgarity"), even from Difference itself ("identical enemies and identical foes"). On her return from Italy, however, "she felt that there was no one whom she might not get to like." She saw the possibility of new kinds of relationships.

The Difference Lucy confronted in Italy was *différance,* which had two meanings: (to differ) she discovered important, even frightening, ways in which her upper class English upbringing was different from the ordinary Italian persons and events she experienced; and (to detour) that discovery sidetracked her view of herself and her relationships. She had settled such questions of who she was and how she should view others, but the difference of her Italian experience was unsettling, reopened those questions, and deferred the answers.

Investigators have taken note of experiences such as Lucy's and treated them variously as "turning points" (Baxter & Bullis, 1986; Bolton, 1961), "transition points" (Levinger, 1980, 1983), "problematic situations" of alignment (Morris & Hopper, 1980; Stokes & Hewitt, 1976), "critical events" (Planalp & Honeycutt, 1985), "second order development" (Conville, 1983), "relational turnover" (Wilmot, 1987), "thresholds" (Duck, 1982, 1986), "relationship rejuvenation" (Wilmot, Stevens, & Miller, 1988), "crucial transition phase[s]" (Masheter & Harris, 1986), and "relational transitions" (Conville, 1988). In each treatment Difference has played a key role. One may be exposed to different relationship alternatives, or one may experience a difference between present relationship and desired relationship. In either case the result is that the present is interrupted and the future is deferred while the relationship is redefined. *Différance* thus enters our thinking once again, this time as "the generative movement in the play of differences" (Derrida, 1981, p. 27).

The present chapter is an examination of three cases of relational transition. Particular attention will be given the role of *différance* in the cases: dialectical differences that seem to supply the energy behind the transitions and the resulting deferral of relational definitions. Of particular concern will be the question of how the transitions were accomplished, their process or structure. But first, the questions of structure and how it shall be used in discourse about relational transitions are considered.

STRUCTURE OF RELATIONAL TRANSITIONS

The study of language is the best resource for considering what comprises the "structural." When linguists describe the structure of a language, or its grammar, "It is a description of the principles that specify what strings of words are well-formed sentences of the language" (Langacker, 1968, p. 36). Those principles fall into two broad categories, systems of constraint and systems of relations.

I am suggesting that there is a structure of relationships and of relational transitions in particular, something like a grammar or set of principles, that specifies what constitutes a "well-formed" (i.e., actual or authentic) relational transition. Hypotheses of sentence structure have proved invaluable to advances in linguistics. Hypotheses of structure pertaining to relational transitions may prove equally valuable to advances in the study of personal relationships.

Structure considered as a system of constraint is exemplified by the linguistic fact that only certain sequences of sounds are permitted in English (represented here with letters). *Stug* and *slin* are possible English words, but they appear in no one's dictionary; *bnug* is not a possible English word (Langacker, 1968). The structure of the language permits some combinations and prohibits others, both within words and within sentences.

Any system of relational stages or phases is a system of constraint in that it specifies a particular sequence of events that is the standard, expected, or ideal version (Conville, 1983; Duck, 1986; Knapp, 1984; Phillips & Wood, 1983). Lee's (1984) study of romantic breakups is a particularly clear example. The author posits a five-phase process of Discovery, Exposure, Negotiation, Resolution, and Transformation as the basic model (well formed or legitimate). He then reports the observation of four variations on that ideal, based on omitted, extended, or repeated phases. The result is a system of variation within constraints, as is found in the study of language. By analogy, the basic model of the sentence in English is noun phrase plus verb phrase, but it is permissible to reverse that order to make questions or to omit the noun phrase altogether in conversational sentence fragments such as, "Could be."

When structure is taken in its other sense, as a system of relations, we can also point to some progress in the structural understanding of relational transitions. In linguistics, the significant relations are those of likeness and contrast. For example, English speakers do not distinguish the [t] in *top* from the [t] in *stop* whereas in both Chinese and Hindi, those two versions of /t/ are used to distinguish different words (Lehmann, 1972). Thus understanding any symbolic system comes from understanding the relations among symbols (as in sameness and difference), not from understanding individual symbols in isolation.

Such was the approach taken explicitly in Baxter's analysis of trajectories of relational disengagement. The 92 accounts she analyzed yielded six features whereby they could be distinguished at various points in their development:

(1) the gradual vs sudden onset of relationship problems; (2) the unilateral vs. bilateral desire to exit the relationship; (3) the use of direct vs. indirect actions to accomplish the dissolution; (4) the rapid vs. protracted nature of the

disengagement negotiation; (5) the presence vs. absence of relationship repair attempts; (6) the final outcome of relationship termination vs. relationship continuation (in transformed or restored form) (1984, p. 33).

She produced a flow chart following the notational conventions of computer programming. At appropriate points in the chart, the distinctive features were entered as yes/no options. The yes/no decisions on the flow chart were intended to model the behavioral options of the partners in the relational dissolutions and are analogous to the grammatical decision of an English speaker whether (yes or no) the [t] in *top* is the same as the [t] in *stop*.

The case is made in the present chapter that there are other structural features, systems of constraint and systems of relation, that characterize relational transitions. Students of personal relationships have noted the import of relations, in particular, dialectical relations, among relationship preferences, styles, or definitions. Recently Altman, Vinsel, and Brown (1981), Baxter (1989), Bochner (1976), Conville (1988), Rawlins (1983a), and Wilmot (1987) have argued for the utility of employing dialectical oppositions to better understand communicative action.

In order to raise the question of structural features (including dialectical oppositions) characterizing relational transitions, it will be useful to review and at points to reanalyze three previous case studies of relational transition (Conville, 1978, 1983, 1988). The qualitative case study has proved to be a useful alternative in investigations of relationship development (Masheter & Harris, 1986; Philipsen, 1982). The cases examined below, and included in the appendixes, are relationship partners' narrative accounts of their experiences of relationship transition. As such, these personal histories provide "a focus on the phenomenology of relationship partners" in which "partner reports of the events in their relationship are regarded as important in their own right" (Baxter & Bullis, 1986, p. 488).

Moreover, the narratives, apart from their content, are also considered to be texts per se and, therefore, are subject to, even demand, interpretation (Ricoeur, 1971; Scott & Lyman, 1968; Taylor, 1971). Schrag captured this hermeneutical perspective when he proposed:

> The textual model of hermeneutical theory . . . needs to be broadened in such a manner as to incorporate into its scope the spoken word as well as the written word. It needs to be extended to include the sphere of perception and its comprehension of the world as well as the transmission of ideational contents. It demands an inclusion of the reading of nature as well as historically delivered texts (1980, p. 98).

The interpretive procedure employed is structural analysis. Delia and Grossberg have argued that structural analysis is one among several critical interpretive approaches to the data of communication that are "most open to the originary character of the events of human communication and the fabric of social life created through them" (1977, p. 39).

The nature of the three cases is important because of their variety. The first is a text in the public domain, easily accessible, and not normally considered an account of relational transition. It is Helen Keller's recounting in her autobiography of her discovery of language. The second case is an account of a breakup of a college romantic relationship as told by one of the participants. This case is unique because the structural analysis was performed by the participant herself rather than by a third party "investigator." The last account has the unique feature of actually being two accounts, each one written independently by the members of a young married couple. So what we have before us is the opportunity to investigate the structure of relational transitions through the examination of three quite different cases. The presumption is that commonality among the cases in their structural features is a basis for confidence both in the method of analysis and in the findings.

STRUCTURE IN THE CASE OF HELEN KELLER

Relational transitions take many forms and occur in a variety of circumstances. An unlikely instance occurred between the deaf and mute Helen Keller as a child of seven and her newly arrived teacher, Anne Sullivan (see Conville, 1978; Stinnette, 1968). As told by Helen in her autobiography (1961), the story recounts Helen's anticipation of Anne Sullivan's arrival at the Keller home in Tuscumbia, Alabama, in 1887; Helen's frustration and anger in response to Sullivan's teaching methods; her experience of insight into the nature of language that came in a teaching session at the Keller family well; and finally Helen's elation over the world opened to her by her knowledge of language. The full text of this narrative is included in Appendix A.

Structural analysis involves, first, naming the episodes that constituted Helen's experience as she recounted it. By "constituted" I mean those pivotal events that drove the account toward its conclusion. The episode list presented in Figure 2.1 is based on my own reading of the narrative.

FIGURE 2.1 — Chronology of Helen Keller's Account of Relational Transition

---

1. Greeted by Anne Sullivan
2. Learned "d-o-l-l" fingerplay
3. Drilled by Anne Sullivan
4. Failed to associate objects with fingerplay-words
5. Anne Sullivan backed off
6. [#3 and #4 repeated here, then] Became impatient
7. Threw down the doll in anger
8. Went to the well-house with Anne Sullivan
9. Anne Sullivan placed Helen's hand under the spout while spelling "w-a-t-e-r" into her other hand
10. Discovered all things have names
11. Remembered the doll she had broken
12. Felt remorse
13. Relived the eventful day
14. Anticipated the next day

The second step in structural analysis is to arrange the episodes in a rows-and-columns grid (Claus, 1976; Conville, 1983, 1988; Lévi-Strauss, 1963, pp. 206–31). The purpose of the grid is "to reconstruct [the narrative] in such a way as to manifest thereby [its] rules of functioning" (Barthes, 1972, p. 149). This procedure preserves the temporal order of episodes while gathering together episodes of the same type. The rows of the grid (read left to right) present the sequential relationships among episodes and episode types; the columns (read top to bottom) present the types of episodes that comprise the narrative. Figure 2.2 presents the grid analysis of Helen Keller's narrative.

Construction of the rows-and-columns grid proceeds as follows. The procedure is based on differentiating the episodes of the account using the question of same-or-different. Consider the episodes in Helen Keller's account. Note the first two, and ask the question, "Are the two episodes quite similar or quite different?" Episode 1 is "Greeted by Anne Sullivan." Episode 2 is "Learned 'd-o-l-l' fingerplay." My answer is, "Quite similar." Both present Helen as happy and open to Anne Sullivan's influence.

Consider the next pair of episodes, episodes 2 and 3, and pose the same question, "Are they quite similar or quite different?" E 2 is "Learned 'd-o-l-l' fingerplay," and E 3 is "Drilled by Anne Sullivan." My answer is, "Quite different." In E 2 the game-like learning was quick and enjoyable, but in E 3 learning slowed, and the whole process had become quite dull. Therefore, while E 1 and E 2 comprise

FIGURE 2.2 — Analysis of Helen Keller's Account

Joy	Instruction	Frustration	Relief	Discovery: language	Discovery: self	Anticipation
1. Greeted by Anne Sullivan (+)						
2. Learned "d-o-l-l" fingerplay (+)	3. Drilled by Anne Sullivan*	4. Failed to associate objects (–),	5. Anne S backed off:			
		6. Became impatient (–)				
		7. Threw down doll in anger (–)	8. Both went to well house			
	9. "w-a-t-e-r" spelled into Helen's hand			10. Discovered all things have names (+)	11. Remembered the doll she had broken (–)	
					12. Felt remorse (–)	
13. Relived the eventful day (+)						14. Anticipated the next day (+)

*Repeat the sequence of episodes between colons until comma, then proceed to next episode after sequence.

the beginning of their own group of episodes, E 3 must go into a second, as yet unnamed group. So at this point two groups or classes (columns in Figure 2.2) have begun to be constructed.

Now consider E 4, and ask the question twice ("Are they quite similar or quite different?"), once comparing E 4 to E 3, and once comparing E 4 to E 1 and E 2 (as a group). My answer to both is, "Quite different." Here we have a turn in the story, Helen's first occasion to fail to learn with Miss Sullivan. Not only is she not enjoying the anticipation of Anne's arrival or simple, game-like learning, but also the drilling does not seem to be helping. Something is wrong. Episode 4 thus becomes the first member of the third group.

Thus one proceeds through all the important episodes in the narrative creating new episode classes or distributing episodes among existing classes (columns). Figure 2.2 presents the results of this procedure. The upshot of structural analysis then is a recasting of narrative episodes into a typology (the columns) while maintaining their temporal sequence (read left to right, line by line).

The third step in structural analysis is interpretation, explication of the "depth semantics" of the narratives as observed in the grids. The outcome of interpretation "is therefore actually a *simulacrum* of the object, but a directed, *interested* simulacrum, since the imitated object makes something appear which remained invisible, or if one prefers, unintelligible in the natural object" (Barthes, 1972, p. 149). The natural objects to which Barthes refers are the relationship partners' narrative accounts of their relational transitions. The grid for each is a simulacrum, or imitation, of the natural object, recast to reveal deep structures or underlying patterns latent in the narratives. Thus the grid depicts the structure of the relational transition that is recounted in the narrative.

Analysis of Helen Keller's account resulted in 14 episodes grouped together into seven types (see Figure 2.2): Joy, Instruction, Frustration, Relief, Discovery:language, Discovery:self, and Anticipation. The structural analysis revealed certain attributes of the narrative that shed light on Helen's relational transition.

Structure as a system of constraint is not evident in the narrative analysis. A grammar of relational transition is not available, but the structural helical model introduced below may be the basis of such a development. In contrast, structure as a system of relations is manifest in the narrative analysis. Relations of dialectical opposition seem to occur along three dimensions: time, intimacy, and affect. The dimension of time spanned two episode types, Joy and Anticipation (see Figure 2.2). Episode 13 was focused on the past, as Helen recalled her eventful day, and E 14 was focused on the future in her anticipation of the next day. "It would have been difficult to find a happier child than I was as I lay in my crib at the close of that eventful day and lived over the joys it had brought me, and for the first time longed for a new day to come" (Keller, 1961, p. 35).

The dimension of intimacy involved interplay among three episode types, Joy, Frustration, and Discovery:self. Baxter's (1988) dialectical opposition of autonomy and connection seems most useful here. In E 1 and E 2 Helen and her teacher were clearly in harmony — connected. Soon, however, Helen's frustration built in response to Miss Sullivan's persistent drills until in anger she dashed her doll to the floor and broke it (E 3–7). This act was particularly meaningful because the doll was a gift that Miss Sullivan had brought to Helen upon her arrival at the Keller household. Breaking the doll was a convenient way for Helen to express her autonomy, and clearly she enjoyed it. Their intimacy was broken. "I became impatient at her repeated attempts and, seizing the new doll, I dashed it upon the floor. I was keenly delighted when I felt the fragments of the broken doll at my feet" (Keller, 1961, pp. 33–34). In contrast, after the language-discovering experience at the well, and once back inside her house, Helen was reminded of her relationship with Miss Sullivan by her own remorse over having broken the doll (E 11–12). She sensed that her own feelings of remorse over breaking the doll and Anne Sullivan's feelings were somehow connected. "On entering the door I remembered the doll I had broken. I felt my way to the hearth and picked up the pieces. I tried vainly to put them together. Then my eyes filled with tears; for I realized what I had done, and for the first time I felt repentance and sorrow" (Keller, 1961, p. 34). Intimacy was restored by Helen's implied desire for forgiveness for her thoughtless deed.

A final dimension of dialectical oppositions that seemed to be at work in Helen's account was affect, her positive and negative feelings about episodes in the experience. Her oscillating emotions are found in episode types Joy, Frustration, Discovery:language, Discovery:self, and Anticipation. Positive feelings in E 1 and E 2 gave way to negative ones in E 4, E 6, and E 7. They returned to positive ones in E 10, turned to negative in E 11 and E 12, and finally changed to positive in E 13 and E 14 (see Figure 2.3). The structure of Helen's account is built in part on these four mood swings. Her frustration (–) at Miss Sullivan's persistent methods contrasted with her initial glee (+) at learning the nonsense, finger play spelling. That frustration (–) with learning turned to wonder and excitement (+) when she discovered the relationship between symbols and words and between words and things. But wonder (+)

FIGURE 2.3 — Affective Oppositions in Helen Keller's Account

<u>Episodes</u>

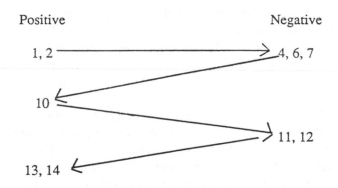

turned to remorse (–) when Helen recalled her destructive anger with the doll. Finally, joyful reflection and anticipation (+) replaced the sorrow (–).

The relational transition experienced by Helen Keller and her teacher Anne Sullivan seems to have been marked by dialectical oppositions of time, intimacy, and affect. Moreover, the dialectical oppositions pointed to the centrality of Difference as a driving force in the relational transition. Recall from Chapter 1 the observations that Difference is ubiquitous (biology, biography, and messages from the culture assure this); inevitable and easily observed in relationships and in relational transitions; and problematic in relationships when it precipitates nonmutuality crises and relationship redefinition. Therefore, in order to understand the relational transition experienced by Helen Keller and Anne Sullivan, one must understand the role of Difference in their relationship.

Regarding time perspective, Anne Sullivan anticipated a future in which Helen could function linguistically; in contrast, Helen was a prisoner of the present, unable to imagine herself having language. They brought a Difference in time perspective to their relationship.

The intimacy dimension also exemplified Difference. Misses Keller and Sullivan experienced connectedness in the first two episodes, very early in their acquaintance, and again on the occasion of Helen's feeling of remorse for having hurt Miss Sullivan by breaking the doll (E 11–12).

In between, however, in E 3–7, particularly E 7, Helen expressed her desire for autonomy in anger, marking her Difference with her teacher over the manner of her instruction.

Finally, Difference was apparent in the rapid cycling of Helen's moods between positive and negative affect. But Difference between Helen and Miss Sullivan on affect may not be so evident. However, closer inspection would suggest that Difference was at work in the category of episodes labeled Discovery:self (E 11–12). Helen felt remorse (–), but Miss Sullivan would have been glad of that (+), for it would indicate that Helen had the capacity for empathy, and more, that she cared what Miss Sullivan thought of her. This Difference in affect began the reconciliation that mended the tear in their relationship that had come in E 7 with the breaking of the doll.

STRUCTURE IN THE CASE OF DIANE

The case of Helen Keller was an account written by her, only one participant in the relationship, and analyzed by a third party. The next case is also an account reported by one member of a relationship, but, in addition, she performed the analysis following the procedures outlined above. Diane is a pseudonym. She wrote her account as part of a class project in interpersonal communication during the fall term 1977 at a large Southeastern university. The experience recounted took place during the previous academic year at the same institution. Diane's case is summarized as follows.

When she came to the university at age 18, Diane had been dating John exclusively her last two years in high school. As she recounted the experience, Diane pointed out three problems with their relationship: (1) John was nearly four years her senior; (2) they were not together much after he went away to college (two years before she went); and (3) what turned out to be the biggest problem of all, John was serious about marriage, and Diane did not realize how serious. They had discussed marriage, but it was always focused on the distant future when they were both out of school. It was like an exciting fantasy to Diane. Then, in December of her freshman year, John's best friend, also a junior, got married. John immediately began reassessing his finances, and decided that he and Diane could be married the following September. This frightened Diane. She simply did not want to be married so soon. But for fear of losing John she did not tell him how she felt.

Two months passed with John making arrangements for the wedding and for setting up housekeeping and with Diane frustrated and losing sleep and remaining silent in the face of her impending doom. Another month passed before she was able to break her silence on the subject. She told him she would not marry him the next September, but he would not accept it. The next two months saw John alternating between threatening suicide and begging Diane to change her mind. Needless to say, that brought on more frustration, lost sleep, and even lost weight on Diane's part.

In what turned out to be their last conversation, Diane was able to tell John how she had felt all along about marriage, that she had been too immature to consider marriage seriously so soon, and that she wished he would forgive her and be her friend. In Diane's words, "He couldn't, and I haven't seen him since" (Conville, 1983, p. 201).

Diane's analysis resulted in Figure 2.4: a chronological list of the important episodes in the account (episodes of her own choosing) with similar episodes grouped in the same column and a descriptive label at the head of each column. Moreover, the analysis was strictly an insider's view (Olson, 1977). My only part was in teaching Diane the rationale and procedures of the analysis. Diane first wrote an account of her relational transition, and from that she picked the most important episodes. They are presented in Figure 2.4 as she sorted them into five groups (columns), using the same procedure used with the Helen Keller account above, and labeled as she named them: Childish, Disrupted, Withdrawn, Dissatisfied, and More Mature.

Diane's construction of the grid revealed a part of the structure of her relational transition, structure as a system of relations. As in Helen Keller's case, three dimensions of dialectical opposition seem to be at work here, time, intimacy, and affect. First, there is the dimension of time perspective. For Diane, the temporal opposition was immediate versus distant, and it involved four episode types, Childish, Disrupted, Withdrawn, and Dissatisfied. Soon after Diane arrived on campus, marriage became an immediate possibility to John (E 2–4), but for Diane it remained a vague possibility far out in the distant future (E 5). ("In December of that year, John's best friend, Paul, also a junior in college, got married. Then John began evaluating his finances and told me that he had decided that we could get married the following September before school started. This really scared me because I felt I was too young and had too much I wanted to do before I settled down. On the other hand, I didn't want to say no and risk losing John for good; I said nothing at all.")

With regard to intimacy, Diane's desire for autonomy clashed with John's desire for connectedness (see Baxter, 1988). Before college they did not seem to exercise their potential for autonomy; connectedness was the norm. However, E 2–4 marked the beginning of Diane's distancing herself from John, a process that continued across all five episode types,

FIGURE 2.4 — Diane's Analysis of Her Experience

Childish	Disrupted	Withdrawn	Dissatisfied	More Mature
1. Entered college				
2. John got serious	3. John's friend's marriage	4. John plans wedding	5. Realized I didn't want to get married	
		6. John sent me roses		
	7. I got physically sick		8. Told John I didn't want to get married	
		9. John threatened suicide	10. John arguing and begging	
			11a. Friend's question, How could you have prevented this?	11b. Friend's question, How could you have prevented this?
				12. My reaction to friend's question
				13. Told John the whole truth
				14. John left for good

Source: Conville, 1983, p. 202; used with permission.

Childish through More Mature. To complicate matters there was not just this widening rift for them to deal with: within their separateness that resulted from their different views of marriage, there was also connectedness — in the self disclosures of E 8–10 and in Diane's finally revealing the truth of her feelings to John in E 13. ("I suddenly realized that if I had only been honest with John and myself from the start, the whole ugly situation might have been avoided. I had one final conversation with John and told him how I had felt all along. I explained that I had been too immature to have ever considered marriage, and I realized that it was all my fault. I asked if he could forgive me and be my friend.") So the structure of intimacy between John and Diane may be characterized in two ways: intimacy began to turn to nonintimacy with Diane's initial hesitation at the prospect of imminent marriage, and the period of growing nonintimacy was punctuated by two occasions of intimacy with Diane's self-disclosures.

Affect is the third dimension of structure as a system of relations observed in Diane's account. Like the intimacy dimension, the affect dimension involved all five episode types in the account, but it presented only one side of the dialectical opposition, the negative. Before the break in their relationship (E 2–4) Diane had been positively disposed toward John, but after the break, she was negatively disposed toward him. (Diane was "really scared" by John's hasty preparations for marriage.) Change the focus of Diane's feelings from John to marrying John, and we see that in E 3–13 (Figure 2.4) Diane was against marriage (–) while John was strongly in favor of it (+). (Near the end of the ordeal Diane reported, "I was nearly at my wit's end and was even considering marrying John anyway to put an end to the whole mess.")

Difference played a central role in John and Diane's relational transition. They held different time perspectives regarding marriage: he, immediate; she, distant. Regarding their intimacy, Diane's desire for autonomy grew throughout the account from an emphasis on connection to an emphasis on autonomy. At the same time John continued to desire connection. Moreover, during the period of battling over marriage, certain points of intimacy (self-disclosure and revelation) required a resumption of connectedness. Finally, regarding affect, from the start to the finish of the account, John continued to express strong affection for Diane and for marriage; but Diane moved quickly to expressing negative affect toward both John and marriage.

The variety and centrality of their Difference was a symptom of John and Diane's lack of consensus on a definition of their relationship. John and Diane's different definitions of the relationship precipitated the crisis that brought about the relational transition. When in E 8 Diane left the intrapsychic phase (Duck, 1986) and moved into the dyadic phase by sharing her hesitations regarding marriage with John, she and John were nevertheless unable to negotiate an agreeable mutual definition. The relationship was further resituated in a social phase with Diane's conversation with her friend that resulted in the question in E 11.

STRUCTURE IN THE CASE OF HOWARD AND JUDY

Finally, let us consider a case that derives from both partners' writing accounts of their relational transition. It presents the rare opportunity to have both participants' perspectives. Howard and Judy (pseudonyms) were married in 1976. He was 20, she was 19, and both were students. During their second year of marriage, they moved several hundred miles so that Howard could transfer to a large state university in order to meet entrance requirements for professional school. There, the relational partners wrote narrative accounts of their transition experience in separate terms of 1977 as part of undergraduate class requirements in interpersonal communication. In the case of each account, I devised a list of the most important episodes, then grouped them, with similar episodes in the same column, to form a rows-and-columns grid (see Conville, 1988).

The chronologies of significant episodes in Figure 2.5 give the outlines of their accounts. It is a story of a young couple's incompatible goals that they discovered only after a move of some considerable distance from their homes, their trial separation, and their eventual reconciliation. Howard's and Judy's narratives are found in Appendix C. The four terms, Anticipation, Separation, Discovery, and Reconciliation seem to accurately signify the episode types in the narrative. As such, they comprise one set of possibilities for the process of relational transition, in this case, for a relationship that successfully achieved regeneration. The structural analysis served as a discovery procedure for both kinds of structure.

With regard to a system of constraint, the most important evidence of structure in the relational transition was the episode types and their order that composed the accounts. For both Judy and Howard the episode types Anticipation, Separation, Discovery, and Reconciliation occurred in that order, with no recurrence. That is, in both analyses (see Figure 2.5), moving from left to right across the four columns, all episodes of a particular type (for example, Anticipation) occurred before episodes of

FIGURE 2.5 — Howard's and Judy's Accounts Analyzed

Anticipation	Separation	Discovery	Reconciliation
Howard's Account Analyzed			
1. Moved to Raleigh	2. Deterioration of H & J's relationship		
	3. H left	4. At seashore: a lot of remembering and setting priorities	
		5. "Rediscovered" J	6. H returned to Raleigh
			7. H & J reconciled
Judy's Account Analyzed			
1. Met "best friend"	2. Moved to Raleigh		
	3. Deterioration of J & H's relation-ship		
	4. Went to meet H's parents in resort town		
	5. Decided to sepa-rate for a while	6. J alone; decided to "find God"	
		7. Realized her "grasping depend-ency" on Tracy	
		8. Found God and a sense of "new me"	9. H returned home and they "knew the past was over"

Source: Conville, 1988, p. 430; used with permission.

another type began (for example, Separation), and none of the former type recurred. Therefore, I am suggesting that the two accounts share important characteristics of structure: the same episode types,

Anticipation through Reconciliation; and the same linear sequence of those episode types.

The two accounts share another aspect of structure, evidenced as a system of relations. Dialectical oppositions observed in the accounts of Howard and Judy were along three dimensions, time, intimacy, and affect. The dialectical opposition of time perspective involved past versus future, and it was observed for both Judy and Howard within the Discovery episode type. There they looked in opposite directions. Howard reported that his discovery focused on the past and took the form of a rediscovery of Judy. During a trial separation, he stayed at a quiet seashore campground (Figure 2.5, E 4–5). In sorting out his recent past, recalling good friends and good times, Judy invariably came to mind. (HOWARD: "I did a lot of reminiscing about good times, and I found myself rediscovering a lost sense of equilibrium. . . . Each time that my mind . . . glided across the waves with old friends, I was slammed back into reality with thoughts of Judy.")

But Judy's discovery was focused on the future (Figure 2.5, E 6–8). Remaining behind when Howard moved out, she decided to "find God." She tried to enter her best girlfriend Tracy's new life in Morehead (rather than recollect her old one, from before the move), and she acquired through it all a sense of "new me." (JUDY: "I gradually saw things with a new perspective and I felt absolutely wonderful. . . . I was anxious to get home to show Howard the 'new me,' to give him all the love he most assuredly deserved.") In Discovery Howard re-evaluated old experiences in the past, but Judy sought new experiences and moved into the future with enthusiasm. Thus appeared the first dialectical opposition, past versus future.

The second dialectical opposition concerned intimacy, and its poles were defined by the episode types, Separation and Reconciliation (autonomy and connection, Baxter, 1988). Unlike the first opposition, here Howard and Judy shared a common experience, of separation and reconciliation, but one that spanned three episode types. To Howard, separation (autonomy) came in two phases, first the deterioration of his and Judy's relationship after the move (Figure 2.5, E 2) and second his leaving, "to try to make sense of it all" (E 3). Judy's experience of separation was more complex. First, she was separated from familiar persons and surroundings when they moved to Raleigh (E 2); second, her relationship with Howard deteriorated after the move (E 3); third, that erosion turned to estrangement during a decisive argument while driving to visit Howard's parents at a nearby resort (JUDY: "We were screaming, crying, . . . confused as hell, and all I could think to do was

get away from Howard.") (E 4); and finally, separation for Judy culminated in her (actually their) decision to live apart for a time (E 5).

Both partners experienced reconciliation (connection) as well as
separation (autonomy). To Howard, reconciliation was marked by his
fearful return to Raleigh (E 6; Would she take him back?) and his joyful
reception by Judy (E 7). (HOWARD: "I arrived home and there was that
beautiful human specimen with the biggest grin and the most joyful tears
all over her face. She too saw our selfishness, . . . She too was able to
forgive, and I was no longer afraid to admit that I needed her.") To Judy,
reconciliation was in their happy embrace, knowing "the past was over"
(E 9). (Howard, on his return, made a surprise entry. Suddenly, JUDY:
"Standing two feet from me was my husband, . . . a smile stretching
from ear to ear, and most importantly, his arms wide open, ready for me
to climb into them. . . . We held each other and without having to say
anything, we knew the past was over; we knew everything was all right;
we knew we were hopelessly in love.")

Finally, both Howard and Judy experienced the affective dimension
of their relationship within the same episode type, Anticipation.
Howard's anticipation was a positive sensation, looking forward to the
freedom and challenge their move represented. Judy's anticipation was
wholly negative. In the context of having discovered at an early age the
joys of friendship and of having just recently found a "best friend" in
Tracy, Judy's anticipation of their move was one of loneliness and
insecurity. His anticipation was joyful; hers, full of distress. The third
dialectical opposition they experienced was positive versus negative
affect.

I have suggested that these narratives or partner reports of relational
transition are marked by common structural characteristics of constraint
(episodes of a certain type signifying Anticipation, Separation,
Discovery, and Reconciliation, and episode types in a certain order) and
by common structural characteristics of relation — dialectical oppositions
of time (past-future), intimacy (autonomy-connection), and affect
(positive-negative). Thus stressed by passing successively through four
different episode types and confronting three fundamentally different
dialectical oppositions, a relationship in one state or of one type was
redefined and became a relationship of another state or type. A relational
transition was accomplished.

The structural analysis of Judy's and Howard's accounts calls
attention to the role of Difference in their relational transition. Regarding
time perspective, Howard and Judy experienced Difference early in the
account (Anticipation phase) when Judy looked to the past while Howard

looked to the future. In the Discovery phase, however, their Difference was reversed: Judy looked to the future; Howard, to the past.

The dimension of intimacy was not a source of Difference between Howard and Judy. They did not disagree that things were going badly. However, before the move, they had apparently enjoyed a high degree of synchrony or connectedness. The move shattered this consensus as their separate autonomies came to the surface. Autonomous action increased with the deterioration of their relationship and culminated with a trial separation. The interlude of Discovery allowed for the ascendancy of their desire for connection in the Reconciliation phase of the transition. Both Howard and Judy experienced Difference regarding their intimacy, but in synchronous fashion, in the ebb and flow of their desires for autonomy versus connection.

The dimension of affect calls attention to Difference displayed in Howard's and Judy's attitudes toward the move to Raleigh. Howard could not wait to move, but Judy strongly resisted the move.

RELATIONAL TRANSITION: A PROPOSAL

The three cases of relational transition under consideration have been presented as having structure that is accessible to both the participant and the investigator. Structure was conceived of as a system of relations and as a system of constraint. I have further suggested that structures of the former type are composed of certain dialectical oppositions that point to the role of Difference in relational transitions. Difference, it was further noted, manifested itself in the relationships as dialectical oppositions of time, intimacy, and affect.

The question now remains whether structure of the second type — as a system of constraint — was at work in the accounts. Put differently, do certain episode types, perhaps occurring in a certain order, characterize these cases of relational transition? Observe in Figure 2.6 the variety of episode types or classes claimed to be in the four accounts analyzed above. With such disparate types of episodes observed in the cases, one would be hard pressed to fit them to a common mold. However, closer inspection reveals that there are yet some common elements in the accounts.

First, there is evident or implied in each analysis a time when the partners were secure in their roles. They were apparently happy and had consensus on the definition of the relationship. They were connected or in harmony. Such a time is explicit in Helen's case but is only implied in Diane's case and in that of Howard and Judy.

FIGURE 2.6 — Episode Types in the Four Accounts Analyzed

Helen Keller	Diane	Judy and Howard
Joy	Childish	Anticipation
Instruction	Disrupted	Separation
Frustration	Withdrawn	Discovery
Relief	Dissatisfied	Reconciliation
Discovery: language	More mature	
Discovery: self		
Anticipation		

Second, in each account there is a period of time in which relational partners take notice of their relationship and begin to question their commitments to it. In Helen's case, this process began with her frustration over Miss Sullivan's persistent drills. In Diane's case, John initiated the disintegration when he started pushing her for an early marriage. In the case of Howard and Judy, it began with their move.

The third element common to all four cases is a time of Alienation — when partners are prevented from assuming desired roles or are coerced into remaining in undesirable roles. For Judy and Howard, it led to their trial separation; for Diane, it was the period of battling over marriage; and for Helen, it was the period between smashing the doll and making her language discovery at the well house. In each case, autonomy instead of connection came to the fore; differentiation took priority; and relational partners put psychological, if not also physical, distance between themselves.

Fourth, each case is also marked by a process of Resynthesis or remaking the relationship in a new form. In Diane's case, for example, she redefined John-and-her-relationship in a way that excluded him. It came in episodes 8–13 when her resolve was growing that life without marriage to John was a necessity. Helen's relationship with Miss Sullivan was recemented when she felt remorse for having broken the doll (E 11–12). Howard and Judy reconstructed their relationship while apart and were confirmed in their decisions when they reunited (Judy, E 6–8; Howard, E 4–6).

Finally, each case displays, as an outcome, a new sense of Security. In each case the relationship-in-revised-form amounted to a new place from which to begin again, or a foundation on which to build a new relationship. Howard and Judy were reconciled, ready to make a new start, complete with new commitments. Diane redefined her relationship with John as ex-fiancee, an outcome she was satisfied with as necessary for her own peace of mind and happiness. And Helen was clearly eager to return to her drills the next day with Miss Sullivan, the one who had opened the door to language for her, and also the one for whom she cared.

Let us summarize in schematic form. Common episode types of the four cases analyzed are presented in Figure 2.7. In the cases examined, the structure of relational transition — as a system of constraint — can be characterized in the following manner. Episodes of these five types marked the relational transitions and occurred in this order: Security, Disintegration, Alienation, Resynthesis, and back to a new Security.

FIGURE 2.7 — Common Elements in the Four Accounts Analyzed

SECURITY$_1$	Comfortable role-action, mutuality of relationship definition, confirmation
DISINTEGRATION	Disruption, events that increase uncertainty, noticing and questioning the relationship
ALIENATION	Withdrawal, separation, nonmutuality, thwarted role-action
RESYNTHESIS	Redefinition, discovery, events that decrease uncertainty, confirmation seeking, coping with dialectical oppositions
SECURITY$_2$	Facilitated role-action, confirming messages, a comfortable redefinition

CONCLUSION

Linguistic structure may furnish a model for the structure of relational transitions. Systems of constraint and systems of relation (for example, same-different) may govern relational transitions as they govern language.

Structural features of relationships may be elucidated by interpreting personal narratives of relational transitions (Conville, 1983, 1988). Structural analysis is an appropriate hermeneutical procedure (Delia & Grossberg, 1977).

Relational structure is grounded in Difference. So is relational change. We interpret and redefine our relationships by differentiation.

Difference manifests itself as *différance*. Partners become aware of relationship alternatives or of discrepancies between present relationship and desired relationship. If the differences are important enough, the definition of the relationship is called into question, and its current status deferred, while it is redefined.

Difference also manifests itself as structure: structure as a system of relations (for example, the dialectical oppositions of time, intimacy, and affect) and structure as a system of constraint (the observed order of episode types).

In the cases examined, dialectical oppositions fueled the movement of the relationships through the four-phase model. Partner Difference of all kinds prompted the Disintegration of a Secure relationship; partner Difference led to Alienation; from thence the relationship was Resynthesized; and a New Security emerged.

3

Structural Analysis of Relationship Transitions:
SIMILAR DIFFERENCES

Order is seen as a matter of sorting and dividing.
But the essential notion in all sorting is that some
difference shall cause some other difference at a
later time.

Gregory Bateson
Steps to an Ecology of Mind

When considering the methods that could be chosen for investigating
the nature of relationship transitions, one starts by affirming two cardinal
attributes of personal relationships: they are dyadic, and they are
temporal. That is, two persons are the principal actors in a personal
relationship, and a personal relationship is a process. It "occurs" or
"happens"; it moves through time. Likewise, stories about personal
relationships are principally about the interaction between two persons as
it occurs over time.

Personal relationships and stories about personal relationships thus
display a congruency between the problem addressed (understanding
relationship transitions) and the data employed to engage the problem
(first-person accounts of relationship transitions). Along with MacIntyre,
Fisher, and others, I believe that "man [sic] is in his actions and practice,
as well as in his fictions, essentially a storytelling animal" (MacIntyre,
1984, p. 216). Fisher (1989) elaborated: "The narrative paradigm sees
people as storytellers, as authors and co-authors who creatively read and
evaluate the texts of life and literature. . . . Viewing human
communication narratively stresses that people are full participants in the

making of messages, whether they are agents (authors) or audience members (co-authors)" (p. 18). And further, "we experience and comprehend life as a series of ongoing narratives, as conflicts, characters, beginnings, middles, and ends. The various modes of communication — all forms of symbolic action — then may be seen as stories, interpretations of things in sequences" (p. 24).

Consequently, "Narrative history of a certain kind turns out to be the basic and essential genre for the characterization of human actions" (MacIntyre, 1984, p. 208). Further, a narrative perspective preserves "the interrelationships of the intentional, the social and the historical" (MacIntyre, 1984, p. 208), displays a trace of humanity, and glimpses the nuances of interaction normally invisible to conventional social science.

STRUCTURALISM

But what shall we do with these personal histories? How shall we read them? Delia and Grossberg have observed that structural analysis is one of several "critical-interpretive" approaches to social theory that has the advantage of preserving "to the greatest extent possible the pretheoretical meaning-structures of the original events" (1977, p. 39). Not only is structural analysis relatively unobtrusive, but also it has a substantial history of use in textual study and in analysis of social practices. Structuralist thinking has attracted attention across the social sciences as well as literary studies (Lane, 1970). Critics have been major importers of structuralist concepts for analysis of narratives (Culler, 1975; 1976). Structuralist methods have been widely used for analyzing literary and other kinds of texts starting in the 1970s and continuing to the present in the thought of deconstructionist and postmodern critics (Bannet, 1989; Berman, 1988).

Classical structuralism has come to us through the work of Claude Lévi-Strauss in anthropology and Ferdinand de Saussure in linguistics. Structuralism entered the academic world in the form of notes on Saussure's lectures of 1906–1911. Published in French by his students in 1915, they were put into English translation in 1959. The publication in French (1958) of Lévi-Strauss's *Structural Anthropology* (in English, 1963) cast the structural approach squarely into the middle of the social sciences.

A rash of brief commentaries on structuralism followed the publication of *Structural Anthropology* (1963). They included works by Leach (1974), Piaget (1970), Badcock (1975), Pettit (1975), and Hawkes (1977) as well as volumes of essays on sturcturalism, for example, *The Structuralist Controversy* (Macksey & Donato, 1972), *Structuralism* (Ehrmann, 1970), *The Structuralists: From Marx to Lévi-Strauss* (De George & De George, 1972), and *Introduction to Structuralism* (Lane, 1970). More lengthy commentaries followed, for example, by Glucksmann (1974), Clarke (1981), and Seung (1982). And continued vitality in the structuralist literature is signaled by such recent studies as *Structuralism and the Logic of Dissent: Barthes, Derrida, Foucault, Lacan* (Bannet, 1989) and *From the New Criticism to Deconstruction: The Reception of Structuralism and Post-Structuralism* (Berman, 1988).

The precedents for structuralist studies in communication are less well established, but clearly communication scholars, too, have noted the potential of the approach. Deetz (1973) has composed a useful introduction to the assumptions underlying its theory and method. Moreover, the number of published studies would indicate more than passing usefulness of the approach (Claus, 1976; Conville, 1978, 1983, 1988; Hopkins, 1977; Leymore, 1975; McGuire, 1977, 1982; Metz, 1974; Warnick, 1987).

THE PURSUIT OF ORDER

Structuralism presupposes an underlying order to society. By "underlying," Lévi-Strauss meant that that order may not be immediately apparent to an observer or a participant. Social structures, he argued, are "entities independent of men's consciousness of them (although they in fact govern men's existence)" (1963, p. 121). Or again, "If the structure can be seen, it will not be at the . . . empirical level, but at a deeper one, previously neglected." As McGuire has observed, "Structuralism is committed to the position that what is simply observable is rarely the whole truth" (1982, p. 2).

Warnick's application of structural analysis has been to texts. Her use of Ricoeur's work in rhetorical criticism led her to this observation: "Structural analysis generally uncovers internal relations among static elements in the text. Such elements might include recurrent patterns in the text's codes, cyclic themes in the narration, or internal transformations of narrative elements" (1987, p. 233).

Gellner has referred to the structuralist view as an "emanationist" view of causality, one that "explains the visible world in terms of entities and forces of another world," the only access to which "is through its alleged manifestation in this world" (1985, p. 131). Those codes, cyclic themes, and transformations to which Warnick referred are presumed to reflect fundamental order in reality, an order that is visible in certain cultural products, for example, rhetorical texts. The goal of structuralists, therefore, is to discover and reveal that otherwise hidden basis or deep structure of the objects of their study. Structural analysis, according to Barthes, is "to reconstruct an 'object' in such a way as to manifest thereby the rules of functioning . . . of the object" (1972, p. 149). Hopkins, while working in a quite different problem area, the oral performance of literature, has expressed a similar formulation: "The structuralist is not simply looking for structures, . . . is not describing any literary feature as a self-contained entity. Instead he is trying to discover and describe the rules that endow the features with meaning" (1977, p. 94).

The "otherworldliness" of the emanationist view is the basis of Gellner's (1985) criticism of structuralism. He questions the necessity of looking for explanations beyond what is simply observable. The competing view he labels positivist, a view characterized, in contrast with the emanationist, by its "reluctance to rely on inherently hidden, inaccessible entities for purposes of explanation" (p. 130) and its "reluctance to countenance experience-transcending entities" (p. 131).

The other sort of "otherworldliness" Gellner charged to structuralism is a tendency to retreat into a symbolic world where phenomena have meaning only "in relationship" to each other. In this view, the structure of culture is a closed system, a system that, according to Gellner (1985), "is assumed to have its central set of rules, which generates everything that can occur within it. Any relationship to anything outside, one might add, is almost accidental" (p. 137).

Gellner is thus making a kind of linguistic criticism of structuralism, for he uses as his two points of argument two cardinal attributes of language: (1) language is symbolic, or as McGuire has pointed out, "foremost among structuralism's assumptions . . . is that all human activities and objects 'signify beyond themselves'" (1982, p. 2) (this is Gellner's [1985] emanationist charge that structuralism relies on the invisible to explain the visible); and (2) language is systemic, or as Deetz has put it, "All meaning for objects and events comes from their relation to the particular system of which they are a part" (1973, p. 141) (this is Gellner's charge that structuralism loses touch with material reality). Structuralism is inadequate, Gellner seems to be saying, because it treats the objects of its analysis as if they were a language or a part of a language.

HUMAN ACTION AS LANGUAGE

When phenomena are viewed as language-like, the outcome of analysis is predictable. Those phenomena will be seen as signifying beyond themselves, or they will be seen as gaining their "meaning" from their positioning in relationship to other phenomena. Gellner is able to make the criticism he makes because structuralism presumes a fundamental analogy that he does not accept, that human action is language-like.

An excellent example of that presumption is found in Lévi-Strauss's essay, "The Culinary Triangle." There he briefly explained the vowel triangle, how the speech sounds [a, u, i] are distinguished by varying combinations among the acoustical oppositions compact-diffuse and acute-grave. Then he observed, regarding structuralist methods, "It would seem that the methodological principle which inspires such distinctions is transposable to other domains, notably that of cooking. . . . We will start from the hypothesis that this activity [cooking] supposes a system which is located . . . within a triangular semantic field" (1966, p. 937). That supposed "system" is, if not inaccessible, at least "experience transcending" and, therefore, anathema to Gellner's (1985) positivist alternative to structuralism.

Lévi-Strauss ended the same article with a glimpse at structuralist goals: "Thus we can hope to discover for each specific case how the cooking of a society is a language in which it unconsciously translates its structure — or else resigns itself, still unconsciously, to revealing its contradictions" (1966, p. 940). In the pages between the opening and the closing of the article, Lévi-Strauss deftly constructed the triangles of raw, cooked, and rotted and of roasted, smoked, and boiled, using oppositions such as nature-culture, close to-distant from (the fire), rapid-slow (cooking), and use of a utensil-nonuse of a utensil. Although the article is illustrated with seven photographs, there is no mention at all of actual cooking practices of individual persons. Such practices, when discussed at all, were always treated on the societal level.

Invisible Rules

The principle that human action is language-like, firmly embraced by structuralists, may be taken in several senses. First, following Saussure (1959), structuralists hold that language has an overt, explicit, and observable dimension (*parole,* speech) and a covert, implicit, and invisible dimension (*langue,* language rules). *Langue* is accessible only through instances of speech, and one's concrete experience of these rules is ephemeral at best. When I hear the sentence, "The cat hid the hat," the words are indeed overt, explicit, and observable, but the grammar or system of rules that makes possible the other's production of the sentence and my understanding of it, is nowhere to be seen, yet its presence is affirmed in our speaking and understanding. The distinction between speech and grammar is the emanationist position, which Gellner concedes in the case of language but which he cannot concede when applied to other domains.

But applying to other domains is just what structuralists do. They argue that a distinction like that between speech and language is "transposable," as Lévi-Strauss (1966) says, to other arenas of human action. There is an observable dimension and an invisible dimension. They believe that, in order to understand human action, they must discover and explicate the contents of this unseen dimension. What I can see, in other words, depends upon, or "emanates" from, something I cannot see. Social practices I observe and participate in come from a social structure, a system of rules that regulates and constitutes those practices. For example, the greetings we use with each other, in structuralist thinking, are not memorized routines that we utter by rote but, rather, are the results of applying rules that guide our selection of the appropriate utterance, rules that have us assess, for example, the time of day, the status of the other, and the degree of acquaintance with him or her.

Binary Features

Following Saussure (1959), Jakobson and Halle (1971), and others, structuralists also hold that language is basically binary. The development of the concept of binarism is an extension of Saussure's observation that, "In language there are only differences" (1959, p. 120). When Lévi-Strauss (1966) said that the principle was transposable to other domains, he was speaking specifically of the principle of binarism. Its clearest manifestation is in phonology. For example, in English I know "bat" and "pat" are different words with different referents and uses by virtue of the contrasting features of their initial sounds: /b/ has the feature [+voiced], that is, the vocal cords vibrate; and /p/ has the feature [−voiced], that is, they do not vibrate. We rely on such differences in articulation and acoustic features to segment the stream of speech we hear, thus making words and sentences of it.

So it goes with human social practices, cultural artifacts, and texts, structuralists argue. They can be understood in terms of binary opposite features such as raw and cooked, earth and sky, animal and beast, near and far. In each oppositional pair, items at each pole are given their meaning by their contrast with items at the other. Moreover, one does not have to claim membership in the structuralist camp to find the principle of binarism useful. For example, Watzlawick, Weakland, and Fisch have observed that

> it quickly becomes apparent that the world of our experience (which is all we can talk about) is made up of pairs of opposites and that, strictly speaking, any aspect of reality derives its substance or concreteness from the existence of its opposite ... [and further, that] such pairs are merely the two complementary aspects of one and the same reality or frame of reference, their seemingly incompatible and mutually exclusive nature notwithstanding (1974, p. 18).

These pioneers of the Relational School of interpersonal communication cite a prime example from the Chinese Cultural Revolution of the 1970s. In order to rid the country of bourgeois influences, all public signs were replaced with revolutionary names. On the surface the opposition bourgeois-revolutionary was the guiding principle at work in the transformation of their society. However, there was no transformation at all, for the replacement simply reinforced a Confucian rule that right action follows from right names, and Chinese culture was preserved intact.

Not only are oppositions observed synchronically, as in the Chinese example, but also they are observed diachronically. Over time one historical moment is often replaced by its opposite. Writing in the early 1970s, Watzlawick, Weakland, and Fisch hazarded a prediction we have seen confirmed by the subsequent 15 years. "It is a fairly safe bet that the offspring of our contemporary hippie generation will want to become bank managers and will despise communes, leaving their well-meaning but bewildered parents with the nagging question: Where did we fail our children? (1974, p. 21).

Orthogonal Dimensions

There is a third way in which the formulation, human action is language-like, may be taken. Structuralists view language as having two orthogonal dimensions, a syntagmatic one and a paradigmatic one. The syntagmatic dimension comprises the constraints on adjacent placement of speech sounds and morphemes. The paradigmatic dimension describes the classes of elements permitted to occur at each "place" within a linguistic string. Thus, syntagmatically, in English sentences, articles precede nouns; and paradigmatically, articles and adjectives are classes of words that may occur in that position preceding nouns. Within English words, too, there are such constraints on sound combinations (I'll use letters to illustrate). For example, *stug* and *slin* are possible English words, but they are not. *Bnug* is not a possible English word, for it contains a sound combination /bn/ that is not permitted by English rules of phonology (Langacker, 1968).

Human action may be viewed in the same manner. Certain classes of actions are permitted or proscribed before or after others (syntagmatic dimension), although many times social actors have their choice among several classes of actions from which to choose specific actions (paradigmatic dimension). For example, politeness rules are powerful in many social contexts. A sales clerk may sense the necessity of a concluding remark at the end of a transaction. It may be "Thank you," or "Have a nice day," or "Come again." Doing so would fit the rules. However, a clear rule violation would be noted if he or she made that remark just as you approached the cash register for checkout, or if he or she said at the conclusion of the transaction, "Hello," or "Will that be cash or credit card?"

Semantic Transformation

I cannot leave this section without calling attention to an attribute of structuralism that many commentators consider essential, transformation. Its basis seems to be the paradigmatic dimension of language that has been transposed into other domains of human action. An example from language, however, is useful. The sentence, "Colorless green ideas sleep furiously" (Chomsky, 1957) may be transformed into another sentence, one that is both grammatically and semantically acceptable, by substituting different words in the available "spaces" of the sentence. "Beautiful red sunsets occur often" might result from such substitutions. The latter sentence is made possible by substituting another word from the same class (or paradigm) as each one used in the original sentence. Thus, the two adjectives, "beautiful" and "red" were used in place of the former two adjectives, "colorless" and "green." The noun "sunsets" took the place of "ideas"; "occur often," the places of "sleep," a verb; and "furiously," an adverb. So one sentence in English can be transformed into another by the proper substitution of members of paradigmatic classes.

So it works with certain cultural products as well, declared Lévi-Strauss, especially myths. When several items in a myth "mean" the same thing, then each version of the myth may be taken as a transformation of the others. That is, one version is transformed into another version by substituting items from among a paradigmatic class. For example, there is a cycle of myths of the Alaskan Kwakiutl tribe found in Boas's *Bella Bella Tales* (1932) and recounted by Lévi-Strauss (1985). There, clam siphons, byssuses of bivalves (mussels), eagle claws, and carved horns of wild goats all form a paradigmatic class. In the myth's several versions, all four items serve the same function, to frighten or kill the evil ogress (Lévi-Strauss, 1985).

Piaget's position is that "all known structures — from mathematical groups to kinship systems — are, without exception, systems of transformation" (1970, p. 11). Consider for example, McGuire's (1977) study of Hitler's *Mein Kampf*. It produced the same kind of rows-and-columns grid that resulted from the analysis of relationship stories in Chapter 2. The result is a distribution of episodes across four columns. Episodes are "read" left to right and top to bottom, as one reads a page. Each column is composed of separate episodes that are semantically equivalent, "commutable and, thus, together constitute a mythical paradigm" (Lévi-Strauss, 1985, p. 135). "All the events in column I are births, rebirths, or beginnings, and the events in column II are related to the births but involve growth or finding divine mission through or after the birth" (McGuire, 1977, p. 6). In a similar manner,

> The concepts, events, and conditions in column III concern decadence ... facilitated usually by lack of vigilance or fanaticism on the part of the Aryans. The conditions in column III set up the events in column IV... [that] represent death or anti-life conditions and events. Yet they also lead into the rebirths in column I (McGuire, 1977, p. 11).

Transformation is thus both cyclical and cumulative. Each time the story passes through the episode types represented by the four columns, the "hero" of the myth is transformed, from birth through development and decadence and finally to death. In McGuire's reconstruction of the myth presented in *Mein Kampf*, the sevenfold repetition of this cycle constitutes its structure.

The parallels between McGuire's analysis of *Mein Kampf* and my analysis of the cases of Helen Keller, Diane, and Howard and Judy should not be lost. All are examples of transposing structuralist analytic techniques to "other domains." McGuire's application is to a formal rhetorical text; mine is to naively told relationship stories. Furthermore, my application, like McGuire's, is also focused on transformation, what I have called relational transitions. The passage of those relationships through the typology of episodes exemplified by the grids constituted their transformation.

The accumulation of cycles through the four columns also marks a kind of transformation. In the case of *Mein Kampf,* it is an intellectual transformation. The question was how to resolve the contradiction of life and death that Hitler saw in his personal and political experience. McGuire argued,

> The events and conditions in columns III and IV of the reconstructed *Mein Kampf* myth are related to each other in the same fashion as events and conditions in columns I and II; but whereas the gods are causal in columns I and II, the anti-will of Jew-Marxism is causal in columns III and IV. Hitler's myth depicts two contradictory wills at work in the world (1977, p. 11).
>
> Hitler's ideology does mediate the contradiction it poses. At a certain stage in dialectical progress we may identify the contradiction as between nationalism, represented by Aryan, culture, strength, etc., and socialism, represented by Jew, anti-culture internationalism, the Social Democratic Party, etc. Hitler's solution is National Socialism (1977, p. 13).

The concept of transformation captures much of what is critical to a structuralist view of human action. First, it most clearly depends upon the paradigmatic attribute of language. The commutability of elements in language and in social practices makes possible the systematic alteration of one sequence into a different but equivalent sequence. Moreover, sequencing itself is a product of the syntagmatic attribute of language.

Second, the principle of binarism is also an essential part of transformation. This is so because, in the structuralist view, a class or paradigm of elements is what it is "in opposition to" another class. The class of greetings, for example, "Hello," "Hi," "What's up?" — substitutable but semantically equivalent elements in social practice — comprises a class in part because its members are differentiated from the class of farewells, for example, "Bye," "So long," "See ya," also commutable elements.

Third, the principle that language has both visible and invisible dimensions is central to the process of transformation. The visible, *parole,* speech, has meaning only by virtue of the invisible, *langue,* grammar. The event of speech is contextualized and given meaning by grammar, and it is only in this invisible dimension that transformation can be "seen."

In sum, structural analysis reconstructs the object of analysis, as Barthes says, and produces "a *simulacrum* of the object, but a directed, *interested* simulacrum, since the imitated object makes something appear which remained invisible, or if one prefers, unintelligible in the natural object" (1972, p. 149).

HUMANIZED STRUCTURALISM

In discussions of transformation in structural analysis, there is a frequent omission. A particularly perceptive critic of the structuralist view, Neville Dyson-Hudson (1972), has pointed out that Lévi-Strauss ignores the subject, the consciously acting individual, in his accounts of social practices. This position echoes Gellner's criticism that structuralists typically divorce their analysis from material reality. According to Deetz, in structuralist thinking the individual is accepted as "one manifestation of mankind possessing a logic independent of the human group or of a single individual" (1973, p. 150). Moreover, Lévi-Strauss has asserted that social structures are "entities independent of men's consciousness of them (although they in fact govern men's existence)" (1963, p. 121). However, Dyson-Hudson has pointed out that "for Lévi-Strauss, the phenomena that he is trying to handle have, overwhelmingly, a subjective existence, and it is in their objectification that his real problem lies" (1972, p. 233). Subjective existence was Lévi-Strauss's focus: kinship and marriage practices, mundane habits of cooking, and myths of life and death and sexuality. But his analysis all too quickly moved from consideration of real human beings, their social practices or texts, to bloodless abstractions.

For example, in his chapter, "The Dialogue between Honey and Tobacco," Lévi-Strauss (1973) summarized three myths concerning the place of honey or tobacco in the lives of certain South American Indians. Wherever there are specifics given, they are always in terms of the generalized practices of a tribe, for example, "Before setting off to gather honey, the Ashluslay of the Chaco bleed themselves above the eyes in order to increase their luck" (p. 53) and "The Nambikwara are confirmed smokers, and are hardly ever seen without a cigarette in their mouths" (p. 59). Lévi-Strauss, and structuralists in general, are not concerned with the individual members of the Chaco or Nambikwara, the diversity of their practices, and their own view of what they are doing. Individual persons seem merely to be a medium for displaying the binary oppositions that define the relationship between honey and tobacco in these tribal groups. What is needed in Lévi-Strauss's analysis, according to Dyson-Hudson (1972), is the notion of praxis. In practical terms this means including in structural study the concepts of the individual and his or her interests and roles.

By individual Dyson-Hudson means not merely a "bag of molecules, but ... a sentient being with definable *interests*" (1972, p. 238). By "interests" he means a person's settled, avowed, and attainable aspirations. And by "roles" he means the array of choices persons have for realizing themselves. To add the notion of praxis to structural analysis would bring its results in line with the changeability and uniqueness of persons that are our common experience. Dyson-Hudson's concern is with fidelity: "the demand of our science is ... to try to bring our analytical concepts to the point at which our experience is made sense of: not to lop off stretches of our experience in conformity with our limited analytical perceptions" (1972, p. 239).

Rhetoricians, too, have expressed dissatisfactions with theories of rhetoric that are not informed by practice. For example, McGee has spoken of the necessity of praxis by arguing for a materialist perspective. "The whole of rhetoric is 'material' by measure of human *experiencing* of it, not by virtue of our ability to continue touching it after it is gone. Rhetoric is 'object' because of its pragmatic *presence,* our inability safely to ignore it at the moment of its impact." (1982, p. 29). Railsback (1983) has pointed out three kinds of rootedness that tie rhetoric to material reality. They constitute anchors on the tendency of language to be wholly subjective and relativistic. The basis of her position is the simple observation that language is used by human beings.

First there is reference. One function of language is to refer. What it refers to is based on what exists "out there" to refer to. Second, language is "physically instantiated in human beings" (p. 355). Biochemical brain processes have been shown to reflect subvocal responses to arguments. Third, some conditions of human material existence are so powerful they intrude upon language structures. For example, the word "food" takes on special meaning and use in the experience of a hungry person; so does the word "freedom" to a person deprived of it.

So what is the solution? How shall we inject into structural analysis the notion of "the subject," the individual's praxis or intercourse with the material world of his or her action? To do so would humanize structural analysis by bringing to it that degree of fidelity with our actual experience of human action that Dyson-Hudson called for. Can structuralism be redeemed? It would seem that the answer is yes, at least regarding the study of relational transitions. Glucksmann has argued, "What he [Lévi-Strauss] has done for myths can now be done for other cultural products" (1974, p. 175). The solution for our purposes is to use stories, personal accounts of relationships, as data and to apply to them an adaptation of Lévi-Strauss's (1963) method of myth analysis.

Myths, to Lévi-Strauss, have the purpose of providing "a logical model capable of overcoming a contradiction" (1963, p. 229). For example, with regard to the Oedipus myth, he concluded, "The myth has to do with the inability, for a culture which holds the belief that mankind is autochthonous . . . to find a satisfactory transition between this theory and the knowledge that human beings are actually born from the union of man and woman" (p. 216).

In like manner a personal account of a relational transition may be seen as a personal myth, a vehicle for coming to terms with contradictions in one's relationship experience. Duck's (1984) formulation of relationship dissolution is a good example. The last phase of the process he characterized as "grave dressing," meaning the participants' efforts to save face in light of public knowledge that their relationship has failed. These face-saving efforts are stories told in their own friendship networks, and in the other's as well, to explain, justify, and otherwise put a pleasant face on the whole affair. Here we have personal myths, stories created for the purpose of overcoming contradictions. The contradictions might be of the type observed by a researcher who takes a dialectical approach, for example, Baxter (1990) and her oft-cited dimension of autonomy and connection. Or the contradictions might be of the kind a firsthand observer would note, for example, between one's previous and one's current opinions of the relationship, expectations for its future, or emotional attachment to the relationship.

The following analysis (Conville, 1988) uses one of the case histories in Chapter 1, detailing the analysis and showing its relationship to the humanized structuralism proposed above.

From a procedural perspective, structural analysis systematically follows three steps. Parse the narrative into a chronological list of important episodes or events. Next, categorize the episodes by arranging them, still in sequential order, into a rows-and-columns grid in which each class or type of episode constitutes a separate column. The members of each column function as semantic equivalents in the relationship story. Finally, name the columns (episode types or classes), selecting labels that summarize the significance of the episodes in the column for the narrative.

The structural analysis that follows demonstrates a "humanized structuralism," one that permits the analysis of texts that recount the ordinary life experiences of actual relational partners (partner narratives or personal accounts). Howard and Judy had quite different styles of remembering and of writing. These were reflected in the detail and length of the cases. However, the similarity of content that the narratives shared is strong evidence of the experience's validity for the couple. Judy and Howard agreed that they did go through a relational transition.

The first step in structural analysis is to create a chronological list of important episodes found in the narrative. "Important" distinguishes the pivotal episodes, those whose outcome seemed to drive the account toward its conclusion. This chronology is preserved by the numerical order of episodes in Figure 3.1. (A full text of the narrative is presented in Appendix C.)

The second step in the analysis is to arrange the episodes into a rows-and-columns grid (Claus, 1976; Conville, 1983; Lévi-Strauss, 1963; McGuire, 1977). The purpose of the grid is "to reconstruct [the narrative] in such a way as to manifest thereby [its] rules of functioning" (Barthes, 1972, p. 149). This procedure preserves the temporal order of episodes while gathering together episodes of the same type. The rows of the grid (read left to right and top to bottom, as in reading a page) present the sequential relationship among episodes, or their syntagmatic dimension. The columns, in turn, present the types of episodes that comprise the narrative, or their paradigmatic dimension. Each column is a vertical array of episodes judged to be of approximately the same type. Figure 3.1 presents the grid analysis of Howard's account.

In Howard's case, the creation of episode types or classes proceeds as follows. Note the first two episodes. Ask the question, "Are they quite similar or quite different?" Episode 1 (E 1) is "Moved to Raleigh," and episode 2 (E 2) is "Deterioration of H & J's relationship." My answer

FIGURE 3.1 — Howard's Account Analyzed

Anticipation	Separation	Discovery	Reconciliation
1. Moved to Raleigh	2. Deterioration of H & J's relationship		
	3. H left	4. At seashore: a lot of remembering & setting priorities	
		5. "Rediscovered" J	6. H returned to Raleigh
			7. H & J reconciled

Source: Conville, 1988, p. 430; used with permission.

was "quite different." E 1 involved change of location; E 2 did not. E 1, viewed in the context of the narrative, involved a pent-up desire on Howard's part to escape his home town whereas E 2 referred to his growing desire for support from Judy. E 1 and E 2 then seem to represent two different types of episodes in the narrative.

COLUMN 1   COLUMN 2
E 1   E 2

Continue the process by focusing on the next pair of episodes, E 2 and E 3. Pose the same question as before, "Are they quite similar or quite different?" E 2 is "Deterioration of H & J's relationship," and E 3 is "H left." My answer was, "Quite similar." Again, consider the text of the narrative. Their relational deterioration (E 2), to Howard, was due to Judy's failure to support the move and her continued attachment to her best girlfriend Tracy. His leaving, E 3, seemed to be a natural extension of E 2, a not unexpected outcome of their relational deterioration. Leaving was simply a more extreme version of his alienation from Judy that was already underway in his doubting her love, his blaming her for dousing his idealism, and in their frequent verbal combat. Therefore, E 3 became a second member of the second episode type (column 2).

COLUMN 1   COLUMN 2
E 1   E 2
                   E 3

If my answer to the "same-different" question regarding E 2 and E 3 had been "quite different," then I would have had to ask the same question of the E 1–E 3 pair. If they in turn had been interpreted as quite similar, then E 3 would have been a member of the first episode type along with E 1.

COLUMN 1   COLUMN 2
E 1   E 2
E 3

But if E 1 and E 3 had also been determined to be quite different, then E 3 would have become the first member of a new or third class (column) of episodes.

COLUMN 1   COLUMN 2   COLUMN 3
E 1   E 2   E 3

Thus one proceeds through the episodes creating new episode classes or distributing episodes among existing classes (columns) based on the "same-different" question. On this basis it would appear that E 4 and E 5 share greater similarity to each other than they do singly to the episodes in the first two classes established. The same judgment was made for E 6 and E 7.

COLUMN 1	COLUMN 2	COLUMN 3	COLUMN 4
E 1	E 2		
	E 3	E 4	
		E 5	E 6
			E 7

The result of structural analysis then is a recasting of narrative episodes into a typology while maintaining their temporal sequence. Analysis indicated that Howard experienced four kinds of episodes during the process of relational transition.

The third step in structural analysis is interpretation, explication of the "depth semantics" of the narrative as reconstructed in the grid. One form of interpretation is devising a label for each column or class of episodes in the grid. Howard's experience of relational transition was composed of episodes that signified Anticipation, Separation, Discovery, and Reconciliation.

Anticipation	Separation	Discovery	Reconciliation
E 1	E 2		
	E 3	E 4	
		E 5	E 6
			E 7

Refer to Chapter 2 for a detailed interpretation of Howard's relationship story. Briefly, to review, the structure of Howard's relational transition was constituted by certain syntagmatic and paradigmatic constraints, seen in the order of the episode types he experienced and by a system of relations observed in the types of binary (dialectical) oppositions latent in the accounts: affect (positive-negative), intimacy (separation-reconciliation), and time perspective (past-future).

The outcome of interpretation "is therefore actually a *simulacrum* of the object, but a directed, *interested* simulacrum, since the imitated object makes something appear which remained invisible, or if one prefers, unintelligible, in the natural object" (Barthes, 1972, p. 149). The natural objects are the unanalyzed texts of relationship accounts. The grid is the simulacrum of the natural objects, recast to reveal a deep structure or underlying pattern latent in the narratives.

CONCLUSION

Structuralism (Lévi-Strauss, 1966) has enjoyed wide currency in the human sciences, in literary studies, and more recently, in communication studies (Hopkins, 1977; McGuire, 1977; Warnick, 1987). However, in ordinary structural analysis, the individual social actor is absent.

The solution to this omission is to use personal histories as the data for structural analysis. Narrative accounts of relational transitions produced by the participants themselves comprise the data for a humanized structuralism (Conville, 1983).

Structural analysis of personal narratives necessarily takes into account the subject, the individual social actor, and makes possible theoretical formulations that reflect their ordinary experience (Dyson-Hudson, 1972). Thus the researcher is equipped to formulate theory that is rooted in social and material reality as disclosed by the actors themselves.

Such an approach prevents structural analysis from merely pointing to an inaccessible, symbolic world (Gellner, 1985). Rather, the results of humanized structural analysis have actual referents in the social-material world (Railsback, 1983).

4

From Description to Explanation in Relationship Transition:
REPETITIVE WITHOUT REPEATING

Life is not definable by situations but by mutations.

Antoine de Saint-Exupery
Flight to Arras

Descriptive modeling of the evolution of relationships proved interesting and useful in the early stages of research. Moreover, such models enabled researchers to characterize relationships with a somewhat standardized vocabulary. One could then refer to a particular relationship as being in the Integrating stage (Knapp, 1984), the Continuation phase (Levinger, 1983), or the Grave-dressing phase (Duck, 1982). Investigators could then go into the field or the laboratory and identify specimens of one relationship phase or another by observing the communication between relationship partners. Thus relationship change was viewed as a sequence of different ways in which relational partners communicated. From this perspective, however, the process nature of relationship evolution was often obscured.

RELATIONSHIP AS PROCESS

An analogy may be useful. Let us say I am a naturalist interested in measuring the salt content of water in marsh lands, rivers, and bays. One method I could use would be clumsy and inefficient. I could mix 100 beakers of salt solution, each with the same amount of distilled water but with a measured, graduated amount of salt dissolved in each one. If in my lab I set up the beakers in a row from least to most salty, I could bring in a water sample from the field, taste it, then go about tasting the water in my beakers until I found a match. If, for example, the taste of the sample water matched the taste of the water in beaker 17, I could rate the sample's salinity at 17.

Now I might have described the salinity of the sample water correctly, but I would have done it in an awfully cumbersome manner, and I would have had a difficult time keeping good tasters on the payroll. Worse, I would know nothing of the process by which water becomes more and less salty. However, if I understood salinity as a process, the dispersion of sodium chloride molecules among water molecules, and not merely a property by virtue of placement in a category, I could dispense with my 100-beaker measuring instrument. I could then estimate the salinity of a given water sample by duly noting the relevant conditions governing the process of salt dispersion in water, for example, temperature of the water, distance from a saline source, and volume of water.

In like manner, if we understood relationship evolution as a process, then we could dispense with the more cumbersome stages-and-phases descriptive models. There are several advantages that accrue from process thinking about relationships. First, we do not engage in premature generalizations about how relationships develop. Some models overgeneralize, such as those of Levinger (1983) and Knapp (1984). Both models present relationships as paths, Knapp's in the form of a double staircase and Levinger's in the form of a two-dimensional curvilinear graph. Marital and romantic relationships, by definition, are presumed to pass up and down Knapp's steps toward or away from greater intimacy or move along Levinger's line graph from Attraction to Building to Continuation (to optional, Deterioration) to Ending.

However, such sets of stages or steps fly in the face of logic as well as our experience of the uniqueness of relationships. A relationship is a merging of unique autobiographies, and it is only reasonable to expect that a pair of individuals will form a close relationship that is also unique. Research confirms that relationships develop along a variety of different paths. Baxter (1984) deduced eight different trajectories that college-aged romantic partners followed through the dissolution of their relationships. The various paths were characterized by such attributes as whether the decision to part was unilateral or bilateral and whether the terminating actions were direct or indirect. Baxter's (1984) discussion of her findings is most interesting in that she contrasts her eight-trajectory solution favorably with Kressel, Jaffee, Tuchman, Watson, and

Deutsch's (1980) four-trajectory solution and Davis's (1973) two-trajectory solution. Her interpretation exposes the inherent inadequacy of such models as those of Knapp and Levinger: "A single set of stages or steps does not generalize to all, or even most, relationship dissolutions" (Baxter, 1984, p. 43).

Construing relationship evolution as a process, by contrast, would have prompted researchers to raise questions such as, "By what process does a relationship move through the observed stages, steps, or phases?" Or more pertinent to Baxter's (1984) findings, "What processes account for the eight trajectories observed?" The intervention of this question is particularly useful here, for Baxter seems to be arguing that eight relational trajectories or paths are better than four, and four are better than two. And, of course, eight are better in that finer grained distinctions can be made, thus explaining more of the data. But who is to say that 16 or even 32 trajectories are not also possible to observe? The likelihood is that we would soon be dealing with relationship trajectories in the same way that our hypothetical naturalist dealt with salinity. And we may well be able to identify a relationship trajectory as, for example, a number 17, that is, a trajectory of a particular type, and still know very little about how a relationship moves along its trajectory, that is, about the process of being a relationship.

So a second advantage of process thinking about relationships is that it moderates a tendency toward proliferation of possible courses in the life of a relationship. Process thinking about relationships thus changes the grounds of discussion. Paths or trajectories, whether the "right" one, as with Knapp and Levinger, or whether the correct number of different ones, as with Kressel et al. and Baxter, are no longer the issue. Rather, the question becomes, "What is the process that generates the observed trajectories?"

But process thinking need not be limited to the domain of relationship evolution. Even more fundamental would be to understand relationships themselves as processes, "continuous ... with temporal energy, changing form, and a place in the history of the participants' lives" (Duck & Sants, 1983, p. 32). One clue for rethinking process and relationships is to consider the term "process" itself. Process entails repetition. An event that occurs only once is not a process. Thus we do not speak of the eruption of Vesuvius and destruction of Pompeii as a process. Rather, we speak of volcanic eruption as a class of similar events and a natural process, one that occurs many times during a year and in many places around the world. In like manner, we speak of the process of respiration, the political process, and the process of maturation.

Several extant models of relationships have implicit in them this seed of process thinking, repetition. Consider Knapp's (1978, 1984) staircase model. When a relationship moves from the Intensifying to the Integrating stage, for example, or from the Differentiating to the Circumscribing stage, a line is crossed. If a relationship moves from Initiating to Bonding (or from Differentiating to Terminating), four lines have been crossed — repetition. According to the model, qualitative changes in the relationship have occurred four times. And we speak of that multiple crossing of lines in the model as a process of relationship growth and development (or relationship dissolution). But what is the nature of that line, that narrow band of ink on the page? What does it represent?

Then consider Levinger's (1983) five-phase (A-B-C-D-E) model of marital development. Four transitions, evenly dispersed, connect five phases of Acquaintance, Buildup, Continuation, Deterioration, and Ending. There are A → B, "the transition from a superficial to a deeper relationship"; B → C, "the transition to a more enduring bond" (p. 322); C → D, "occasions when things go from good to bad, from pleasant to unpleasant, from easy to difficult" (p. 344); and D → E, the transition from dependence to independence. Four times the quality of the relationship has taken a significant turn — repetition — and the term "process" becomes appropriate. But what is the nature of those transitions? What do they represent? If we knew the process at work in those transitions, then we would move toward understanding relationships as processes.

Finally, examine Duck's (1982; 1986, p. 102) model of relationship dissolution. Between a relationship partner's Breakdown state and his or her Intrapsychic phase is a threshold labeled, "I can't stand this anymore." On either side of the threshold the relationship (at least from the point of view of one partner) is qualitatively different. Moving farther down the model, between the Intrapsychic phase and the Dyadic phase is the threshold, "I'd be justified in withdrawing." Then, between the Dyadic phase and the Social phase is the threshold, "I mean it." And finally, between the Social phase and the Grave-dressing phase is the threshold Duck entitled, "It's now inevitable." Four thresholds have been crossed — repetition — and it now becomes reasonable to speak of the process of relationship dissolution. And each crossing is significant, as is the case with the lines and transitions in the other two models, for after each one the relationship is qualitatively different from what it was before the crossing. Knowing the process that underlies the repetition of crossing thresholds would be a clue to understanding relationships as processes.

Clearly the various sorts of repetition noted above are not "mere repetition." They are not trivial. That is, the line between Knapp's Experimenting and Intensifying stages does not represent the same thing as does the line between Circumscribing and Stagnating. In like manner, the threshold between Duck's Intrapsychic and Dyadic phases is qualitatively different from (involves making different sorts of decisions) the threshold between the Dyadic and Social phases. Granted, the lines and the thresholds have in common the fact that they represent "whatever it takes" for a qualitative change to take place in the relationship. But, by the same token, each line is unique in that the stages that bound it are a unique pair. One and only one line is bounded on one side by Bonding and on the other side by Differentiating; only the B → C transition in Levinger's model is adjacent to the Beginning stage on one side and the Continuation stage on the other.

So there is an aspect of each descriptive model that simultaneously has the attributes "same" and "different." Something is repeated — the lines, transitions, and thresholds reoccur — so we are looking at a process. But each time one of them is repeated, the relationship is different from what it was before the line was crossed. Among geometrical figures the helix or spiral also holds in itself these opposing attributes of "same" and "different." With each turn about a helix, one has gone 360 degrees and thus is back, apparently, to the same place (repetition — process — and sameness). But a helix is not a circle, so with each revolution one has necessarily moved up or down in space upon a coil (difference). The result is that the several points one comes to after several 360-degree turns about a helix form a group or class of points. Their commonality can be described by their starting/ending point on the helix (sameness) while at the same time their distinctness is in their being unique points in space (difference) (Conville, 1978; Dance, 1967).

So here we have collected some tools for understanding relationships as processes: the concepts of sameness and difference and of the helix. The notions are not new but are closely kin to the principle of *différance* as espoused by Derrida and the concept of binarism encountered in structuralist thought and linguistic theory. Moreover, these understandings are implicit in much of the writing in the field of personal relationships.

THE IMPLICIT HELIX

Altman and Taylor's *Social Penetration* is an example of the implicit helix. Interpreting the therapeutic work of Polansky, Weiss, and Blum

(1961) with children, they concluded that the relationships between caseworkers and children developed, not in a simple linear fashion, "but as one in which there is cycling between integration and disturbance in a spiral-like fashion" (1973, p. 73). Later on in the book, they presaged the findings of Baxter (1984) and Kressel, Jaffee, Tuchman, Watson, and Deutsch (1980) regarding the number of developmental stages for relationships: "To speak of a set number of stages of the social penetration process is artificial. The process ebbs and flows, does not follow a linear course, and cycles and recycles through levels of exchange" (p. 135). Moreover, when addressing the role of conflict in the growth of relationships, Altman and Taylor stated their view that "conflict is viewed as an essential part of developmental phases, with relationships growing in an ebb-and-flow fashion, from periods of crisis to periods of tranquility in a cyclical fashion" (1973, p. 166). Finally, in a discussion of relationship dissolution, what they called depenetration, the research- ers spoke of habitually conflictful marriages: "Progressive conflicts move in a spiral fashion from disagreement to disagreement until they are stopped or destroy the relationship" (p. 177).

Thus we can see that the helix is latent in Altman and Taylor's (1973) conceptualization of how relationships evolve. Spirals and cycles and alternations (ebb-and-flow) are all encompassed in the helical form. Altman, Vinsel, and Brown (1981), in their recent dialectical revision of social penetration theory, adopted the same position. In this context, a word on the word "cycle" is in order. The term is used by Altman and Taylor (1973) and by others whose work is examined below. The normal usage seems to be a synonym for "repetitive": something that cycles or repeats; that is, the same event occurs over and over again, such as the movement of the piston and valves in a small engine. That usage is appropriate for machines, for they have no memory. But for people the usage is not appropriate; human beings never experience the same event twice. My lawn mower engine cannot say to itself, with each turn of the crankshaft, "I've done this before. There it is again. Now a third time." As far as the engine is concerned, each revolution is unique; it has no memory of the last turn.

But people have memories, more or less, but memories just the same. So when my son goes out on a date with the same girl, say for the third time, both he and she know in general what to expect. The event is not all new all over again. Date 3 is influenced (for example, regarding what to talk about, where to go, what time to be in) by dates 2 and 1. The memory of dates 1 and 2 influences date 3. So from this perspective, humans in relationships do not, cannot I would rather say, experience cycles. Because of their memories where people are concerned, the same event cannot occur. What then do we experience? Instead of a cycle our experience presents itself as a spiral or a helix. Because of memory, whenever we go round in a circle and seem to wind up where we started, the very fact that we recognize that we have returned proves that we have not returned to the same place. The "place" is now grown over with memories. Memory is the one thing that we bring back to the "same" place that keeps it from being the same place. Humans experience an apparently repeated event not as the same event but as an event of the same type. It is both like a previously encountered event and different (enough) from other types to be of this particular type. The reader may be experiencing some sameness in this argument, for memory will indicate that we are back to a place we have been before, to the paradox of same and different.

Murray Davis, that other early explorer of personal relationships, has also spoken of cycles:

> a second major force [has been] uncovered that transforms isolated individuals into interlocked intimates — *the routinization of their cycle of coming togethers and going aparts*. Intimates increase the binding power of this force insofar as they intersect, or even overlap, their customary routines of movement and insofar as they puncture the pellicle of privacy that causes the unacquainted and, to a lesser extent, the merely acquainted to bounce off each other whenever they run into each other by chance (1973, p. 55).

From the perspective outlined above, the "cycle of coming togethers and going aparts" is actually a helix, with each meeting of the relational partners not a mere repetition of the earlier one, but rather a full turn about the helix to a place on the coil that is simultaneously the same yet on a different plane.

Whereas Davis (1973) rather offhandedly spoke of a cycle, Wilmot (1987) has made explicit use of the spiral to describe a particular form relationships may take in their development. In contrast to my use of the helix to represent the central process in human relationships, Wilmot's use is more narrowly focused. To his way of thinking, the image of the spiral (helix) accurately describes the changes a relationship may experience at the episode level of analysis where each partner's reactions are fed by and enhanced by the other partner's reactions. When this acceleration is in a positive direction, with the relationship growing and developing, and providing mutual enjoyment or support, the spiral is a progressive one, similar to Jourard's (1964) "dyadic effect." A regressive spiral, by contrast, commences when each partner's reaction to the other's is increasingly negative, mean spirited, or aimed at trying to score a verbal hit a little harder than the one he or she just received. Bateson's (1935) "schismogenesis" is its basis: the circumstance occurring when persons' or groups' reactions sustain each other and accelerate toward aggression, violence, and destruction.

Something akin to schismogenesis was observed by Fisher and Drecksel (1983) in a data based study of informal interaction. In simulated submarine living conditions (men in pairs confined in small rooms for ten days and assigned individual, periodic tasks), conversations during free times were randomly videotaped and analyzed for five categories of relational communication: Domineering ($\uparrow$ +), Structuring ($\uparrow$ –), Equivalence ($\rightarrow$), Deferring ($\downarrow$ –), and Submitting ($\downarrow$ +). The data were analyzed in five phases or time periods and produced "a 2-stage cyclical pattern." The cycle (read "helix") was most clearly observed in the rising and falling probabilities of certain conversational sequences. The probabilities of a Domineering conversational act following another Domineering act were, in order of the five phases, .22, .58, .13, .58, .28 — low, high, low, high, low — pattern, cycle, helix. Moreover, the probabilities (more frequent or less frequent than the statistical expectation) of a Structuring conversational act following another Structuring act were, in order of the five phases, less frequent than expected, more frequent, less frequent, more frequent, less frequent — the same pattern inscribed by the occurrence of Domineering acts.

Strangers who were confined and apparently obliged under the circumstances to establish some kind of relationship so managed their talk as to create a helical pattern. In phase one there was little probability of conflict. The probability of competing for dominance was low as was the frequency of making suggestions about how to proceed (Structuring acts). By phase two, however, subjects had begun to try to exercise influence over the relationship as evidenced by the high probability of pairs of domineering and structuring acts. But then in phase three, subjects retreated and demonstrated less competition for influence. Phase four saw them resume their competitive mode whereas in phase five the subjects again became more cooperative.

Fisher and Drecksel (1983) concluded: "the changes in interaction patterns . . . of [the] dyads almost exclusively result[ed] from the rising and falling levels of competitive symmetry in both the domineering ($\uparrow$+$\uparrow$+) and structuring ($\uparrow$–$\uparrow$–) modes" (p. 73). Moreover, in an observation more pertinent to our present task of arguing that helical movement is the central process in relationships, the investigators surmised: "The two-stage cycle . . . may allow the interpersonal system/culture to ward off the disintegrative forces of schismogenesis (i.e., too much symmetry or complementarity)" (p. 72). Thus helical movement (the two-stage cycle) in relationships is called upon to account for relationship continuation. The relationship moved from a period of low competition (around) through a period of high competition then (back around) to a "repeat" of the period of low competition. The authors seem to be suggesting that relationships endure as long as they do mainly because the partners are willing to alternate periods of competitive interaction with periods of cooperative interaction.

Other investigators have introduced concepts that are also subject to periodic fluctuation and, consequently, may be conceived of as helical in nature. They include, for example, mutuality of relationship definition (Morton, Alexander, & Altman, 1976), perceptual congruity (Sillars & Scott, 1983), and interpersonal solidarity (Wheeless, Wheeless, & Baus, 1984). Each of these concepts represents a way to think about the degree of partners' closeness in a relationship. But relationships do not remain unchanged. There is no more widely held proposition about relationships than that they are dynamic in nature. Moreover, because relationships join unique autobiographical trajectories, closeness can never be an enduring state.

Rather, nonmutuality of relationship definition is a normal and periodic occurrence in both new and established relationships. It is a crisis brought about by ordinary processes of social exchange: "expanding domains of interaction and diversification of exchange modes" (Morton, Alexander, & Altman, 1976, p. 110). As a relationship develops, the topics of conversation may be expected to increase in number, and the participants may find it necessary to employ a wider range of communication skills. This done, relational partners may discover topics, even important ones, on which they disagree and occasions for talk for which they are unprepared. For example, a close friend may decide to return to school full time for a graduate degree in public health. Consequently, your frequent conversation may turn to AIDS and its treatment as well as public policies guiding research. And you may find that you do not agree on issues such as reallocating federal research dollars and speeding FDA testing of new drugs. You argue heatedly. Moreover, your friend wants to talk at length about his experiences each day in school. "Listening to him tell about school" is new for you, requiring skills you have not practiced. Your frustration builds. Soon you begin to see your relationship as changed from what it was and different from how your friend sees it. Mutuality of relationship definition has been lost for the time being. But that was not planned. The crisis came about as a result of ordinary processes of social exchange, and the crisis will pass for the same reason, if the friends are committed to preserving the relationship (see Fisher and Drecksel, 1983).

Perceptual incongruity (Sillars & Scott, 1983) has similar crisis-producing potential for relationships. Its focus, however, is not upon the degree of consensus relationship partners have regarding the definition of their relationship, but rather upon the degree of similarity in perception that relationship partners have of things outside the relationship. Sillars and Scott's evidence suggested that there is a positive relationship between perceptual congruity and adjustment on the part of married couples.

Two of their interpretations are pertinent to the argument that certain interpersonal processes are subject to periodic fluctuation, or helical movement. First, there is the assumption that perceptual congruity entails self-disclosure and information seeking. Second, greater perceptual congruity (that is, resulting from greater self-disclosure and information seeking) can increase conflict and dissatisfaction in a relationship — can actually bring about greater perceptual incongruity. A perceptually congruent relational partner may discover or tell things that precipitate an occasion for disagreement based on a (newly discovered) perceptual incongruity. For example, with enough talk about politics, we may discover that I revere former President Jimmy Carter whereas you revere former President Richard Nixon. But, if we soon tire of the argument and change the subject, that is, if we keep the conversation going long enough, as in enduring relationships such as marriage or close friendships, we could expect to experience periods of perceptual congruity punctuated by periods of perceptual incongruity. Thus a helix is inscribed.

There is, of course, an important affective dimension to relationships as well, and it is addressed by the concept of interpersonal solidarity (Wheeless, 1978; Wheeless, Wheeless, & Baus, 1984). "High solidarity relationships refer to those in which 'closeness' derived from 'similarity' finds expression in sentiments, behaviors, and symbols of that closeness" (Wheeless, 1976, p. 48). Measurements of interpersonal solidarity successfully distinguished among seven developmental stages of relationships (Just Beginning, Moderately Developed, Well Developed, Highly Developed, Disengaging, Terminating, and Final Termination). Scores of overall solidarity were significantly higher for stage 4 (Highly Developed) than for the other stages, and scores for stages 1–3 did not differ significantly from each other; nor did scores for stages 5–7. The seven developmental stages accounted for 45 percent of the variance in interpersonal solidarity ($n = .67$) (Wheeless, Wheeless, & Baus, 1984). Wheeless's conjecture was confirmed by these results: "Adequate measurement of solidarity can serve as a criterion for assessing . . . the development, maintenance, or deterioration of the interpersonal relationship" (1978, p. 145).

Just as mutuality of relationship definition and perceptual congruity are not constants in relationships, due to the ordinary processes of social exchange, neither is interpersonal solidarity a constant. Rather, the affective closeness one feels toward the other in a relationship is also subject to fluctuation. This may be due to a variety of factors. One's feelings of closeness to another may be interrupted by boredom with the routine, by tasks that are a part of one's work, by social upheaval or natural disaster, by other relationships that may need one's attention, or by biological and health needs. Whatever the case, if the relationship is an enduring one, the likelihood is that, if the partners are close now, they can be quite sure that a period of feeling at some distance will follow and vice versa. If they are experiencing some distant feelings toward each other, they can be quite sure that a period of closeness will follow. Thus the evolution of the relationship inscribes a helix, for each period of feeling close to the other is not entirely new but, rather, is one of a class of earlier similar times one remembers.

Loss of definitional consensus, slippage out of congruity, and softening of solidarity, while precipitating relationship crisis, may, nevertheless, be expected as a normal result of the development of close relationships: the range of conversational topics expands, and communication skill repertoires need to grow. As more personal subjects are addressed in the close relationship, and as partners' message exchanges become more complex, periods of disagreement as to the nature of the relationship are bound to ensue as are periods of disagreement about issues, persons, or events and feelings of distance. Morton, Alexander, and Altman conclude, "Relationship crisis, then, is a *transitional* process associated with dynamic changes involved in the formation, expansion, and dissolution of social bonding" (1976, p. 110).

DIALECTICS

This natural, periodic fluctuation common in relationships has been clearly depicted in dialectical analyses of interpersonal communication. Dialectical interaction is marked by "oppositional patterning . . . so that the two opposed items (parties, people, social classes, etc.) would take meaningful definition, *one from the other*" (Rychlak, 1984, p. 370). Moreover, dialectical relationships are marked by the dual characteristics of process and contradiction (Baxter, 1988). Wilmot speaks of the "dynamic *interplay*" between dialectical opposites (1987, p. 167): a *process* brought about by the associated characteristic of *contradiction*. Baxter asserts that the upshot of dynamic interplay is change: "Change . . . is caused by the struggle and tension of contradiction" (1988, p. 258).

Rawlins's (1983a) use of a dialectical perspective echoes the concepts of contradiction and change (as does Altman, Vinsel, and Brown's [1981]) but with the added notion of interconnectedness or the unity of opposites. That dialectical opposites provide each other their definitional basis exhibits the interdependence of the polar concepts and, according to Rawlins, suggests a certain "wholeness of a given social domain" (p. 256).

One might argue, however, that a social domain, rather than being the given grounds for enacting a relationship, is itself the space or locale created by the dialectical oppositions at work in a relationship. To imagine how that might be the case will illustrate the dynamics of contradiction, change, and interdependence. In a recent textbook treatment of the dialectical perspective by Trenholm and Jensen (1988) the authors proposed that two dialectical dimensions are at work in close relationships: expressiveness-protectiveness and togetherness-autonomy. Their choice of nomenclature accurately reflects, in summary fashion, the dialectical oppositions proposed in a number of studies, for example, Masheter and Harris's (1986) detachment-intimacy, Altman, Vinsel, and Brown's (1981) openness-closedness, Wilmot's (1987) separateness-connectedness, Conville's (1988) separation-reconciliation, Baxter's (1988) autonomy-connection, and Rawlins's (1983a) expressiveness-protectiveness.

The social domain of the close relationship is marked out by each member's oscillating between the poles of the two dialectical dimensions. The dialectical poles provide a way to describe the partners' preferences for conducting the relationship at a given time. The social domain of the relationship is the sum of the dialectical dimensions plus the relational partners' preferences for enacting the relationship within those dimensions. For example, at Expressiveness, Partner A wants to share feelings and experiences; and at Togetherness, A wants to enjoy B's company. At the same time, however, Partner B may desire much less self-disclosure than A in order to guard his or her privacy (Protectiveness), and B also may want to engage in projects of his or her own creation (Autonomy). Consider this hypothetical example. At a given time Partner A may be at Expressiveness and Togetherness, and Partner B may be at Protectiveness and Autonomy. This state of affairs with regard to the dimension of Togetherness and Autonomy is depicted at Time 1 in Figure 4.1

Time 1 would clearly demonstrate a period of tension brought on by the contradictory desires of A and B regarding Togetherness. Dialectical theory asserts that this tension will precipitate change in the relationship. Four options obtain. The first two represent redefinitions of the relationship toward a more intimate one. At Time 2 Partner A might change preferences for relational enactment from Togetherness to Autonomy, thus temporarily defusing the tension; or at Time 2' Partner B might change preferences for relational enactment from Autonomy to Togetherness, with the same effect. The next two options represent redefinitions of the relationship toward a less intimate one. At Time 2'' both A and B might change, thus swapping places and continuing the tension; or at Time 2''' both A and B might persist in their Time 1 preferences.

The dynamics of contradiction and change are apparent in the example, but where is interdependence or wholeness? It is in two places it would seem. Interdependence is evident in that the dialectical poles are definitional reciprocals: Expressiveness is what Protectiveness is not and vice versa; Togetherness is the inverse of Autonomy. But beyond the level of definition, wholeness is evident at the level of communicative action: the two pairs of dialectical poles mark out the boundaries of the field on which the relationship is played out. What Rawlins (1983a)

FIGURE 4.1 — Dialectics and the Creation of a Social Domain

TOGETHERNESS		AUTONOMY
Partner A	Time 1	Partner B
	Time 2	Partner B
		Partner A
Partner A	Time 2'	
Partner B		
Partner B	Time 2''	Partner A
Partner A	Time 2'''	Partner B

called a social domain is thus created: the actors and the issues are assembled. The relationship is thus a process: Partners A and B move within the space provided by the dialectical poles. And the relationship transcends the contradictions of the poles by virtue of its enactment by the partners.

TOWARDS A HELICAL MODEL

The helix seems to be a most useful visual image for conceiving of the process nature of relationships, for capturing the paradox of same and different, and for illustrating the dynamics of contradiction, change, and interdependence. The helix permits one to illustrate the dialectical nature of personal relationships.

Here again the focus is on the process nature of relationships, in particular, the process of a relationship moving through qualitative changes. The helix is useful in this regard, for it allows the investigator to focus on change without having to deal with a predetermined set of relationship stages. For example, one can raise the question of the process of getting from Duck's (1982) Dyadic phase to his Social phase without having to place the relationship in the context of dissolution. For example, after a couple has discussed marriage (rather than divorce) privately and decided that that is their choice, they naturally share their news with others or even devise an occasion for public announcement.

Or again, one can examine the process of moving from what looks like Knapp's (1984) Intensifying to Integrating without being limited to those two alternatives. One may, for example, get to know the friends of one's romantic partner without becoming more intimate with him or her.

Put another way, at the relationship level instead of the individual level, a helical model permits one to raise the question of what actually happens between two persons in the space of that line of ink on the page between any two relationship "stages" — the question of what actually happens during the crossing of a "threshold." Examining relationship development as a process and relationships themselves as processes requires the assumption that what a relationship is, is most clearly seen, not in the stages or phases of development, but in the transitions between them. To picture relationships as processes, one must turn the stage models inside out and give prominence to the boundaries (transitions, thresholds) and the spaces-between that they represent.

What is needed at this point is a means of structuring our thinking. The focal concepts of our inquiry are relationship (as opposed to individual), process, boundary, and change. The kind of change at issue is qualitative change, change in the interpersonal system that the relational partners have created. Raush has referred to this kind of change as "generic restructurization of a matrix, creating new constitutive and regulative rules and constructing new social realities" (1981, p. 111). First-order change in a relationship would be change within the context of the given grounds for interaction; second-order change would be change that itself creates new grounds for interaction (Conville, 1983).

Boundaries are what we are magnifying, holding up for scrutiny, for they are the fingerprints of a relationship and the clues to their change. Process is another matter, and here we return to the helix. Visualize that spiral cone with one significant dimension drawn across it as in Figure 4.2. The poles of the dimension are Security and Alienation. Consider this the archetypal pole. Security marks the place where (time when) a partner is comfortable with the roles that come with the relationship and the resulting coordinated action. Alienation is the time when (place where) a partner has rejected his or her former roles and the actions they entail. Think of them as dialectical poles. That is, they are definitional

FIGURE 4.2 — Structural Helical Model of Human Action

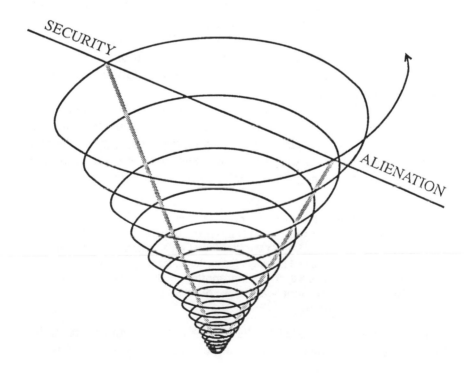

reciprocals. Their contradiction creates stresses that precipitate change. They are, nevertheless, one whole, for these two poles delineate a part of the space in which the partners act out their relationship by virtue of their moving round the helix from Security to Alienation and on round to Security again, over and over. In fact, every time their relationship experiences a qualitative change, it moves from Security around to Alienation and on around to coalesce at Security again. Only the next Security is not the same as the first; memory is there. The relationship has been redefined, and a new interpersonal system has been created. Second-order development has been accomplished (Conville, 1983; Watzlawick, Beavin, & Jackson, 1967; Watzlawick, Weakland, & Fisch, 1974).

The dimension of Security-Alienation illustrates a consistent finding in the literature (Guntrip, 1973; Hampden-Turner, 1973; Lifton, 1976; Novak, 1970; Schein & Bennis, 1965; and Sheehy, 1974): the kind of perspectival changes we are concerned with in second-order development entails passage through turbulent psychological straits (Alienation) between successive Security positions. However, I must conclude from the cases analyzed in Chapter 1 that the movement of a relationship from one Security position to the next on the helix is more complicated than is indicated by this single dimension. Intervening processes need to be added to the model to better fit the data. Useful in this regard is the work of Anthony F. C. Wallace (1956a, 1956b, 1957) on cultural regeneration that presents the concepts of mazeway disintegration and mazeway resynthesis. They provide the basis for adding an additional dialectical dimension to the model.

Central to Wallace's thinking is the notion of mazeway. The laboratory rat running a maze is his analogy for what a human being faces when obliged to live in society. There may be many ways to run the maze in order to get to the cheese at the other end, yet the maze is the hard reality the rodent must negotiate in order to get there. Explains Wallace:

> The mazeway may be compared to a map of a gigantic maze. On this map are represented 3 types of assemblage: (1) goals and pitfalls (values, or desirable and undesirable end states), (2) the "self" and other objects (people, other organisms, and things), and (3) ways (procedures, techniques, and relations) that may be circumvented or used, according to their characteristics, to facilitate the self's attainment or avoidance of values (1956a, pp. 631–32).

Thus the mazeway "is used by its holder as a true and more or less complete representation of the operating characteristics of a 'real' world"

(1956a, p. 631). Its basic function "is to give meaning to messages, to relate incoming sensory data to the whole complex of objects, values, and techniques that is the mazeway" (p. 632).

But, of course, a severe problem develops if a person begins to get messages that his or her mazeway cannot adequately explain. He or she may conclude "that the sociocultural system no longer does, or perhaps never did, operate according to the principles which his mazeway assigned to it" (1956a, pp. 633–34). Such a person begins to experience "mazeway disintegration" (Wallace, 1957).

Typically what follows, but by no means automatically or simply, is "mazeway resynthesis," a process that has "the function of restoring an internal biopsychic equilibrium" (Wallace, 1956a, p. 635). For mazeway resynthesis to take place, the individual must have reconstituted his world representation or mazeway to the extent that he can have confidence in it as a reliable picture of how things operate.

Return now to the structural helical model for relationships in Figure 4.2. The processes of mazeway disintegration and resynthesis may be depicted on the model by drawing another dimension perpendicular to the Security-Alienation dimension, one labeled Disintegration-Resynthesis. It is placed so that the movement of a relationship around the curved line of the spiral, starting at Security, would first encounter Disintegration, then Alienation, then Resynthesis, then return, having come "full circle" back to a new Security. The completed model is seen in Figure 4.3. Like its companion, the Disintegration-Resynthesis dimension inscribes a dialectic. The poles represent contradictions, the one being the reciprocal of the other; and being inherently unstable relationship states, they entail tension toward change as well. Interdependence is theirs as well, for, again, a relationship's oscillation between both poles as it revolves around the helix marks out a portion of the significant locale of the relationship.

Consistent with process thinking about relationships, an additional revision of the model is in order. Rather than let the dimensions remain perpendicular lines set within the helix, they are more accurately portrayed as regions on the helix. As depicted in Figure 4.4, the structural helical model displays four kinds of social domains, a region of Security, a region of Disintegration, a region of Alienation, and a region of Resynthesis. Thus a relationship is never "nowhere." It always can be identified as being "somewhere," that is, in one of the regions in its processual life. Perhaps an analogy would be useful. Imagine a young married couple whose conflict style you are investigating. Perhaps they argue from time to time about money or whose parents to visit on

FIGURE 4.3 — Structural Helical Model of Human Action

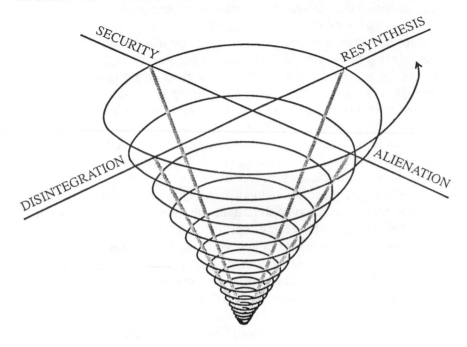

holidays. When their discussions reach a certain level of tension, the husband goes outside, literally out the front door. Moreover, certain topics are broached outside that are never mentioned inside; and whether she follows him outside depends upon who introduced the subject. The structure of their relationship is based in part upon the dialectical opposition, Inside-Outside. You discover through further questioning that there is a pattern to the inside spouse's location within the house: sometimes she follows him out the door, sometimes she follows him to the door that he has slammed and leans against it while he is outside, but sometimes she simply remains where she was when he took his leave. Thus it seems that wife-location in the house is an important marker of the seriousness of the argument. Sometimes she is outside, sometimes inside, but sometimes she is much closer to being (that is, closer to going) outside than merely remaining inside. She is inside and he outside — the dialectic holds — but knowing her proximity to the door (boundary) is important. So it is with the Regions version of the model. The two dialectical dimensions remain intact while the relationship may be more or less near the boundary of a neighboring dialectical region.

FIGURE 4.4 — Structural Helical Model of Human Action

RESYNTHESIS

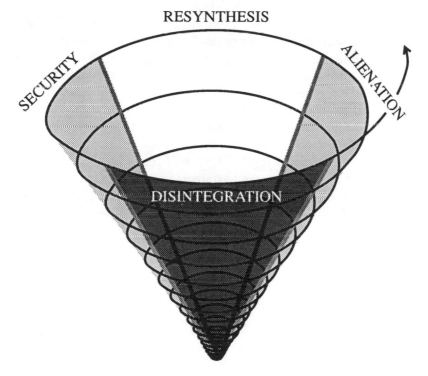

CONCLUSION

In the program to conceive of personal relationships as processes, repetition is the focal issue. In the literature, repetition is implied by the crossing boundaries (lines, transitions, and thresholds) as in the work of Knapp (1984), Levinger (1983), and Duck (1986).

But mere repetition will not do. Rather, the figure of the helix allows a relational partner to "come full circle" without returning to one's starting point. Helical patterns of relationship development are implicit, for example, in the work of Bateson (1935), Altman and Taylor (1973), Davis (1973), Fisher and Drecksel (1983), and Wilmot (1987). The helix portrays change in relationships, which may be conceived as relationship redefinition, movement between perceptual congruity and incongruity, and alterations in relationship solidarity.

Dialectical theory (Baxter, 1988) assists our thinking about personal relationships as processes, for it provides concepts of contradiction, change, and interdependence. Movement of a relationship along dialectical dimensions creates the social domain of the relationship, the field of play in which it occurs (Rawlins, 1983a).

The structural helical model employs two dialectical dimensions, Security-Alienation and Disintegration-Resynthesis. They are drawn from the case studies examined in Chapter 2 and supported by the literature reviewed in subsequent chapters. The four phases proposed in the model comprise the indigenous, evolutionary, and recursive process that is the context of all personal relationships.

The next four chapters are organized around the four regions of the structural helical model. One will focus on the relational condition of pleasant fit, the Security region. One will focus on the noticing and questioning of relationships, the Disintegration region. One will focus on the rejection of earlier relationship roles, the Alienation region. The last will focus on the reconstitution of relationships, the Resynthesis region.

5

Relationship Security:
FITTING RELATIONS

The plausibility and stability of the world, as
socially defined, is dependent upon the strength and
continuity of significant relationships in which
conversation about this world can be continually
carried on. Or, to put it a little differently: — The
reality of the world is sustained through conversation with significant others.

Peter Berger and Hansfried Kellner
"Marriage and the Construction of Reality"
Diogenes

The next four chapters flesh out the structural model proposed at the
end of Chapter 2 and revised in Chapter 4 as a structural helical model.
An assumption of the model is that personal relationships have their own
natural history: not a natural history in the sense of a museum of natural
history in which is depicted a succession of ages (Stone, Iron, Bronze) or
a succession of living arrangements (nomads, hunter-gatherers, village
dwellers) but a natural history in the sense of a recursive process that
enables the succession of epochs. The structural helical model is intended
to represent just such a process on the level of personal relationships.
That indigenous, evolutionary, recursive process is the context of all
interpersonal communication.

That context is, moreover, a period of time in which certain events
transpire. Personal relationships may stabilize at whatever level of
intimacy members agree upon. A condition of security results, and the

relationship operates "in kilter" as opposed to "out of kilter." But then, with the passage of time, which brings with it personal, interpersonal, and societal changes, the relationship-as-defined may be interrupted by one or both participants' calling into question its adequacy. Duck has attributed "changes in the form of the relationship" to "natural reformulations" that "take the two partners out of kilter" (1984, p. 168). Here disintegration commences, and sooner or later, the earlier definition of the relationship is judged unacceptable. The participants become alienated from the roles entailed by the relationship as they had formed it. The relationship is out of kilter.

A turning point has thus arrived, and the partners now begin to build a new relationship. This redefinition or resynthesis could be so radical as to exclude the other, or a new mutuality might only fine tune the rules while retaining the players. Either way, a new vision has been forged regarding the relationship and how it shall be conducted. The relationship has come full circle, but the turn has been helical not circular. This new resting place of security is not the same "place" the partners were in when they first agreed they had a relationship. Hence, the natural history of the relationship inscribes the coil of a helix. Moreover, the force moving the relationship about the helix is Difference, specifically, the tensions inherent in the dialectical oppositions of Time, Intimacy, and Affect (see Chapter 2).

However, at this place of temporary stability and consensus, Security, the relationship operates in kilter as opposed to out of kilter. My object in this chapter is to show that the literature in interpersonal communication supports the claim that there is such a place of security, comfort, and alignment in personal relationships. In the process I hope also to offer an accurate and reliable description of that unique type of circumstance in the life of a relationship. The three subsequent chapters complete the picture of relational evolution I am proposing.

But first we need to examine "kilter," sometimes "kelter," usually used in the phrase "out of kilter." Accordingly, the phrase, "in kilter," is an appropriate designation for this first phase of Security: it denotes a state of affairs in which the persons involved feel comfortable, share complementary roles, and act in coordinated fashion. Examples in the *Oxford English Dictionary* (Simpson & Weiner, 1989, p. 382) show the term "out of kilter" applies to humans and indicates confusion or disorientation. A nineteenth-century usage reads, "I must rest awhile. My brain is out of kilter"; and a twentieth-century example is similar, "Jack's death sort of knocked you out of kilter." Under such conditions of cognitive fatigue or emotional upheaval, a person hardly feels confident dealing with even ordinary events. They no longer seem predictable or familiar, and the outcome of such dealings is uncertain — hardly a comfortable circumstance to be in.

"Complementary" usages include much earlier citations such as (1643) "a little out of frame or kelter" (perhaps a door frame that was not square or was warped) and (1677) "out of kelter or out of tune" (perhaps the pipes of an organ were not pitched with the proper intervals between them). In both cases, the parts of some whole do not fit together as they should, and, consequently, the whole that is created from the parts (the doorway or melody) is distorted or is not completed as it should be. The human analogy to "fit" is best exemplified by fitting or complementary roles.

Finally, a sermon by William Bradford of Massachusetts in 1628 exemplifies the sense of "coordinated": "Ye very sight of one [a gun] (though out of kilter) was a terror unto them." The parts of some complex entity do not work together properly. Modern usages often refer to machines, as in, "Some of the government machines are out of kilter." The human analogy to properly working parts is best exemplified by coordinated actions.

A relationship that is in the Security phase of evolution is one that is in kilter, in good working condition in the sense of order, adjustment, balance, and alignment. Moreover, "in kilter" denotes three desirable attributes of personal relationships: comfortable (relational partners feel good about being in the relationship); complementary (relational partners' roles fit together in an interdependent fashion); and coordinated (relational partners' actions with each other proceed smoothly and gracefully). As we see below, current theorizing about personal relationships confirms this tripartite characterization.

IN KILTER: THE COMFORT MODEL

Writers in interpersonal communication fall into two camps on the basic nature of stability in personal relationships. Some argue that, in that state, relational partners are comfortable, relaxed, and satisfied. Others, however, suggest that relational partners must expend energy and work against countervailing forces to maintain a personal relationship at a given level of intimacy.

A scene in Arthur C. Clarke's (1968) novel, *2001: A Space Odyssey,* furnishes an archetype of the comfort model. David Bowman is the lone surviving crew member of the spaceship *Discovery* that has reached its destination, Japetus, the largest moon of Saturn. With *Discovery* securely locked into orbit, Bowman descends in the small space pod to inspect a strange object on the surface of Japetus, a gigantic obelisk some 2,000 feet high. To his surprise the top of the great column opens and draws the tiny vehicle at light speed through a warp in time and space. Spit out into an unimaginable kaleidoscope of stars in a far corner of the universe, the pod soon comes to rest on a hard surface.

Bowman has come to a place that stands in stark contrast to his just ended tour of arcane star types and extinct, advanced civilizations. He peers out onto a finely appointed, metropolitan hotel suite. There are chairs and tables, bookcases, a sofa, lamps, a Van Gogh on one wall, a Wyeth on another, and a television set. Familiar, to be sure. As soon as his curiosity outweighs his suspicion, he ventures out into the room, only to discover that there are four rooms, not one — a bedroom, an adjoining bath, and a kitchenette, in addition to the living room.

The fixtures in the bath work, and he soon discovers that those in the kitchen provide distilled water. "His unknown hosts were obviously taking no chances with his health" (Clarke, 1968, p. 213). Clothes are hanging in the closet, the air is hospitable, the gravity normal. The books and magazines are familiar (but only the titles are discernible), as is the food in the refrigerator (recognizable by its packaging only, for all the containers hold the same blue "food" of Play-doh consistency and smell). The telephone directory reads Washington, D.C., on the front, although the pages are not readable, and there is no dial tone on the phone.

The TV is no replica, however, and the fare is recognizable from about two years before. His attention is arrested when on one channel he sees a melodrama set in what seems to be a replica of the living room in which he landed. But he understands that it is actually the other way round. "So that was how this reception area had been prepared for him; his hosts had based their ideas of terrestrial living upon TV programs. His feeling that he was inside a movie set was almost literally true" (Clarke, 1968, p. 214).

As an archetype of the comfort model of Security, the most striking attributes of Bowman's landing site are these: it appears real, permanent, and benign — but its "reality" is uncertain; its permanence can be nothing but temporary considering his journey there; and its benevolence is, well, a gift. Richardson (1969) has argued that *2001* is a myth of transcendence in which Bowman's journey constituted his personal transformation. He "came full circle," it seemed, but the pod's resting place was clearly not back on Earth. A helix is thus the appropriate figure to represent such movement: repetition without repeating (Conville, 1978). So it is with the evolution of personal relationships.

In its Security phase, a relationship is, for a time, in kilter. First, it is comfortable. Bowman feels "at home." He takes note of all the familiar, if stereotyped, accoutrements of a late twentieth-century, Western, upper-class, urban, living space and responds with recognition. He understands that OTHERS have prepared the place and appreciates THEIR intentions for his comfort and safety. Moreover, Bowman believes that THOSE who have taken him on this odyssey are benign. THEY have taken pains. He feels safe.

Second, the scene depicts interaction that is complementary. "Whatever is going on" (not a little teleology is suggested here) depends upon both Bowman and THEY occupying roles that fit. THOSE who have conveyed Bowman across galaxies were dependent upon someone to search the solar system for the obelisk and then to inspect it closely enough to be gulped down through the Star Gate. THEY needed an explorer. And once he entered the time tunnel of the obelisk, Bowman clearly needed THEM. He was completely under THEIR control and protection; and finally THEY prepared a familiar place for his landing and refreshment. The great experiment (if that is what it is) succeeds when their complementary roles guide the participants' actions.

Third, the interaction presented in the scene is coordinated. Here the emphasis is on organized, graceful action. From the time the space pod was swallowed down the obelisk, Bowman has been flung through unimaginable galaxies and shot across unexplored sectors of the universe. Now he has been placed in a movie set replica of a Washington hotel suite, and through it all Bowman has acted to facilitate his movement; he has meshed his actions with THEIRS. He has not fought back nor tried to hinder THEM from doing what THEY would. His appropriate role was clearly a passive one, and he acted accordingly. The players worked together in an organized manner to move the relationship along.

Being in a personal relationship that is comfortable, in which the roles are clearly delineated and in which actions are completed smoothly, is a pleasant place to be. That is the state of relationship that we shall call Security. It occurs when a relationship is in kilter, when it is working well and comfortable to be in. On the structural helical model, this is the space that represents a kind of home port in which the relationship rests at anchor before another voyage about the helical curve, and this is a stretch of time in which a relationship experiences temporary stability. It is temporary because of the ubiquity of Difference, that elusive ingredient that is both problematic and necessary for personal relationships. Indeed, we have no choice but to confront Difference; both biology and biography thrust it upon us. As Morton, Alexander, and Altman have observed, "Because both new and established relationships are characterized by expanding domains of interaction and diversification of exchange modes, frequent relationship redefinition may occur resulting in temporary or longer periods of nonmutuality, of relationship crisis" (1976, p. 110).

A number of the classic works in personal relationships confirm this description. Levinger contrasted the Beginnings of an intimate relationship that are "marked by the partners' experience of novelty, ambiguity, and arousal" with the Middles (the stages of Continuation and Deterioration), which are "accompanied by familiarity, predictability, and the reduction of cognitive and emotional tension" (1983, p. 336). In similar fashion, Altman and Taylor (1973) have characterized Stable Exchange as the place where a relationship operates at the positive poles of their eight "generic dimensions" of social penetration: richness, that is, breadth of interaction, uniqueness of interaction, efficiency of exchange, nonsubstitutability (of the other), synchronization of actions, openness, spontaneity, and willingness to evaluate. Research reported by Knapp, Ellis, and Williams (1980) indicated that these eight dimensions may collapse to only three yet demonstrate the same power to discriminate among relationships as well as describe the same comfortable, in kilter relationship site. Specifically, as the relationships they examined approached greater intimacy, communication between partners became more personalized, more synchronized, and less difficult. Clearly this is a comfortable state of affairs.

Others too have observed that a condition of comfort reigns in personal relationships from time to time. Wilmot has presented four factors that facilitate the maintenance of a close relationship. Three, when they obtain, would make for a comfortable arrangement. The first is that the relationship "serves its functions well" by providing support and friendship that yield happiness. The second is equally practical. Relationships may provide security in the form of emotional support, recognition in the form of being remembered, and a general sense of meaningfulness in one's life. Third, we may infer that the members are comfortable if they gain satisfaction from "expending the effort to make a relationship work" (1987, pp. 194–95). In a similar vein, McCall and Simmons have proposed five interpersonal ties. The first, reward dependability, seems unambiguously to lead to a comfortable personal relationship. They argue that we "seek one another out repeatedly in order to 'use' one another as dependable sources for role-support for prominent identities and for other exchange rewards" (1978, p. 168). In contrast, the other "ties" presented by McCall and Simmons (1978) could easily become nooses, for example, ascription, the relationships that are handed to us, such as blood kin and bosses, relationships that are not easily shed, and investment, expenditure of time and energy on a relationship that inevitably has a downside risk of having been unwise but that cannot be cashed in without sustaining unacceptable losses — both manifestly uncomfortable situations.

Not only do personal relationships provide for comfort at the level of the dyad, but also the same provision may obtain at the macrolevel. Berger and Kellner have conceived of personal relationships as havens from the often alien, powerful, and incomprehensible institutions of society. We seek refuge from them in the private sphere, they argue, in the realm of relationships with significant others. "As a rule, only in the private sphere [can] the individual . . . take a slice of reality and fashion it into his [sic] world" (1964, pp. 7–8). There, with significant others, relational partners establish power, intelligibility, and recognition (literally, a "name"). So it is vis-à-vis the larger institutions of society that personal relationships are often constructed. And it is beyond the dyad as well that those personal relationships often exercise their influence. Berger and Kellner have observed, "The plausibility and stability of the world, as socially defined, is dependent upon the strength and continuity of significant relationships in which conversation about this world can be continually carried on" (1964, p. 4). When those personal relationships are intact, relational partners are comfortable, and the relationship is in kilter.

Heavily influenced by Berger and Kellner's (1964) seminal essay, Wood extended their thinking by delineating the concept of relational culture. Relational culture is the ground of understandings that members of a personal relationship walk upon. It provides a basis for the kind of alignment and mutuality introduced above as a temporary site for enacting the relationship. Not simply inert, relational culture also acts as both anchor and compass for relational partners. Explained by Wood,

> Relational culture refers to a privately transacted system of definitions, values and meanings that establish for partners in a relationship a consensual order of interpretation and action. Relational culture is highly dynamic and dialectical; through discourse partners create their relational culture and amend it and, then, they become constrained by their own creation as it acts back upon them, legitimizing certain codes of conduct and precluding others (1982, p. 77).

Having a relational culture in common takes much of the guesswork out of a personal relationship. Greater predictability and familiarity and self-confidence make the partners more comfortable with each other.

Raush, writing out of a clinical tradition, has developed a concept similar to relational culture. He refers to shared schemata or myths as central to our understanding of personal relationships. I would argue that they are also central to our understanding of the recurring occasions of apparent stability and seeming permanence in personal relationships.

> Myths create and are composed of shared constitutive and regulative rules, but by virtue of their central salience and affective loading they are more than simple rules for meanings and action. Myths become in a sense "third parties" monitoring the communicational patterns between individuals. Thus, couples may speak of their "relationship," and they may evaluate consequences not in terms of individual reinforcement values (or practical force) but in terms of the myth of relationship (1981, p. 110).

Judgment and decision making are thus simplified. That spells comfort for relationship members. They now have a standard to rely upon. The myth of their relationship oversees its life course. "Meanings and actions are chosen to be *conjunctive* with the myth" (Raush, 1981, p. 110). The task of relationship management then is to fit the conduct of their relationship with the myth of their relationship. Moreover, the partners' relationship myth is a coding device for interpreting phenomena around them, and it is a monitoring device as well for evaluating the state of the relationship (Raush, 1977b).

The shared outlook of a relationship's myth, as long as it is maintained by a relational pair, should provide an organizing principle for deciding upon appropriate roles and actions. It should further provide for perceptual congruity (Sillars & Scott, 1983) and interpersonal solidarity (Wheeless, Wheeless, & Baus, 1984) and the numerous other pleasant attributes of "in kilter" relationships that researchers have attested to.

The story is not always a pleasant one, however. Security as a relationship state may lull to sleep the unsuspecting. Baxter and Wilmot (1983) have suggested that participants in a stable relationship (as compared to those in a growth trajectory) may switch to an "auto pilot" mode in which they monitor the relationship less carefully than they did earlier in the relationship. Having reached consensus on the definition of the relationship, the members may become less vigilant than before as well as tend to engage in less disclosure than they did in their growth trajectory. Therefore, feeling comfortable with the relationship may work against its long-term prospects when neglect is the outcome.

Neglect may also result from diverted attention. McCall and Simmons have referred to a flagging awareness of the relationship as a unique unit on the part of its members "when dealing with matters more internal to the relationship than external" (1978, p. 174). For example, in the middle of a disagreement over money matters, a married couple may be totally focused on that issue, their attention diverted temporarily from the uniqueness of their marriage bond. However, when their son is confronted with problems in junior high math, the same couple may rally together as a team to get him the tutoring he needs, to meet with the teacher, and to consult with the principal. Being a part of a team that is taking coordinated action based on clearly delineated roles may then be a source of pleasure for the couple.

The pleasure that relationship members derive from this period of alignment and mutuality may come from taking a break from working to maintain the relationship; contrariwise, the pleasure derived from this period of respite from relationship issues may come from activating and using those previously decided upon roles in coordinated action. The risk in the former case is in neglect of the relationship; the risk in the latter case is the chance absence of circumstances that would galvanize them into a team.

IN KILTER: THE CONFLICT MODEL

Consensus is virtually complete among writers in interpersonal relationships that times of Security occur in personal relationships. To some, that time is easy and comfortable, but to others, hard work is necessary to maintain the alignment and uphold the mutuality. Davis (1973), for example, has asserted that "relationships require energy to operate, and will waste away unless their energy supply is constantly renewed" (p. 236). He did not see all relationships in the same light in this regard either, for he believed that "it takes more energy to sustain an intimate relation than an acquaintance one" (p. 211). To Davis the achievement of a personal relationship did not mark a discontinuity in the relationship (a time of relaxation and enjoyment) but, rather, was merely a continuation of the effort needed to build the relationship: "Once intimates manage to attain their communion ["merger between selves of individuals" (p. 171)], they discover they have to struggle to sustain it" (p. 200).

Barnlund (1982) agrees, but for reasons lodged in the nature of human existence, not because of the nature of personal relationships themselves. "Even under the best of conditions," he argues, "we confront not merely an ambiguous world, but a restless, mutable one which, while it is being perceived, changes before our eyes" (p. 115). The implications are profound. "Thrust into a world of endless sensation we are forced to make it intelligible, to make the amorphous recognizable, the uncertain predictable, the mysterious fathomable" (p. 116). A personal relationship that is in a place of alignment and mutuality is intelligible, recognizable, predictable, and fathomable. Consequently, Barnlund would argue that personal relationships are monumental achievements, accomplished as they are, against this background of potential chaos. From this perspective, the members of a personal relationship that is in kilter are not enjoying a period of pastoral ease. Although the relationship may bring pleasure and be appreciated, it takes work, even struggle, to maintain the relationship's Security position.

Barnlund (1982) further argues that struggle is the hallmark of the stable personal relationship because humans display the characteristics of open systems. Not only must humans make sense of otherwise chaotic phenomena around them, but also they are capable of receiving information from their environment and learning from it, that is, using the feedback as a basis for modifying their intercourse with that environment. We are capable of maintaining our well-being as humans by being responsive to exigencies about us. Think of the analogy of steering a small sailing vessel. I may spot a landmark miles across the sound. Between my departure and my destination lie water currents, wind, and other vessels. The only way I can keep my course is to be constantly changing courses, that is, constantly working the tiller and adjusting the sail. The maintenance of my relationship with my destination is due to my ability to correctly change the boat's steering mechanism in response to changes in the wind, the currents, and the courses of other vessels. Out of change comes permanence. I stay on course by constantly appearing to change courses. Again, although there may be much pleasure in maintaining alignment and mutuality (back to personal relationships again), that is accomplished only by considerable effort.

Barnlund's (1982) open systems analogy suggests a homeostatic state. Consider an analogy from the balance in body chemistry necessary for maintaining health. A sudden increase in blood sugar is brought about by eating a Snicker's bar. In response, under normal conditions, the pancreas dispenses an extra amount of insulin into the blood stream, the blood sugar level is quickly lowered to a normal level, and the ill effects of a high sugar level are avoided. Homeostasis, a kind of steady state, is maintained in such thermostatic fashion.

Raush agrees with this formulation.

> Change is fundamental. Stabilities derive from and are constructed from change. Our most mundane activities — the simple satisfactions of our daily physical needs, as well as our long-term imaginative ones — imply changes. Even if only to maintain homeostatic stabilities, as living organisms we must continually change. As with all living organisms, we as humans must keep moving just to stand still (1981, p. 107).

His emphasis is on the necessity of change, as it is rooted in our biological nature; and terms such as "constructed," "maintain," and "must" point to the effort needed to accomplish it.

The expenditure of effort in relationships is not limited to the biological realm or even to biological analogies. Humans seem to exert considerable effort to achieve an acceptable level of predictability regarding the other and oneself in relationships to satisfy a communicative need as well. This seems to be true whether on the level of government and business or on the dyadic level: "To interact in a relatively smooth, coordinated, and understandable manner, one must be able both to predict how one's interaction partner is likely to behave and, based on these predictions, to select from one's repertoire those responses that will optimize outcomes in the encounter. Uncertainty is not reduced for its own sake" (Berger, 1987, p. 41). Not a bad description of the in kilter relationship — smooth, coordinated, understandable — a state of affairs that takes considerable effort to maintain, that is, to sustain the flow of useful information coming to partners. So it seems that there is some urgency to take actions that will facilitate the reduction of uncertainty and maintain it. Berger and Bradac (1982) cite interrogation and self-disclosure as two interactive strategies in particular that lend themselves to this process. Both suggest effort put forth in order to maintain a relationship in kilter.

Raush has further called attention to the monitoring power of myth with its ability to evoke maintenance effort from relational partners: "It is as though 'the relationship' achieves a status that is quasi-independent from the individual participants" (1977b, p. 302). As such the relationship myth acts as a standard against which to judge the participants' actions. For example, relational partners may develop a relationship myth in which a central tenet is honesty with each other. Violation of the rule of honesty may then trigger actions to rectify the situation and to maintain the state of the relationship in kilter.

A final kind of evidence that there is a specifiable period of time in a personal relationship in which partners work at maintaining a comfortable level of Security lies in those studies that focus upon strategies for maintaining relationships. They indicate that often effort is consciously expended by at least one partner to hold the relationship steady. Further, we must also presume that at least one partner desires the relationship to be in that state, that is, that the relationship for him or her is working in a comfortable, complementary, and coordinated manner.

CASES IN SECURITY

In the analysis of cases in Chapter 2, I suggested that relational transitions operate within three dialectical dimensions: time, intimacy, and affect. In the case of Helen Keller, the dimensions of intimacy and affect, in particular, define a period of Security. The times Helen felt in kilter with Anne Sullivan were during their early, simple learning games (episode 2) and at the end of the narrative (episode 14) where Helen was eagerly anticipating the next day (Figure 2.2). During these times Helen felt close to Anne Sullivan (intimacy), and her feelings (affect) about their relationship were positive. However, in between E 2 and E 14, their relationship disintegrated, and circumstances intervened that prompted Helen to redefine their relationship.

That space between the initial and final periods of Security was marked by Helen's distancing herself from Miss Sullivan (intimacy) and actively disliking her (affect). Moreover, the structural helical model I am proposing predicts that the "space between" also consists of a period of Disintegration at the end of which lies a period of rejection of the relationship-as-previously-defined (Alienation), which in turn leads to a period of redefining the relationship (Resynthesis) with an eye toward achieving a renewed period of relationship security.

The case of Diane is quite different. John and Diane experienced Security when they went together while she was still in high school and on through episode 1 in her narrative (Figure 2.4). Diane considered them close (intimacy) and liked it that way (affect). However, when John began pushing marriage, to Diane their relationship began to Disintegrate. Her uncertainty about their future (in contrast to his certainty: time) had crystallized when she told him she would not marry him (Alienation). Diane's friend's probing question started a rebuilding process on Diane's part (Resynthesis). In the end, however, only she came round to a new Security phase. John disappeared, despondent and unwilling to redefine their relationship as "just friends." Diane clearly did redefine her relationship with John, and it did not include him as a romantic partner. The structural helical model accurately predicts the form of John and Diane's relational transition and, it should be noted, from the particular point of view of the narrating partner, Diane.

Howard and Judy's relational transition also involved all three of the central dialectical dimensions of time, intimacy, and affect. Things had been fine in their relationship before they moved, before the start of their narratives per se. Howard and Judy had apparently been happy newlyweds, in kilter as it were, enjoying mutuality and alignment in a Security phase. In Howard's account, (episodes 1 and 2) and in Judy's (episodes 1, 2, and 3), they were out of kilter on the time dimension (Figure 2.5). Howard was looking to the future with its new venture of professional school while Judy was looking over her shoulder to the past, to the special friend and her family she was leaving. Moreover, their intimacy and affect were marked by distance and negativity. But they reached consensus and mutuality by the ends of their accounts, at Reconciliation: Howard's E 5–7 and Judy's E 7–9.

Their strong negative feelings (affect) toward each other drove them to a trial separation; and during separation they both admitted to themselves a desire for renewed closeness (intimacy). The structural helical model of relational transition predicts that, between the two periods of relational security, there will occur a deterioration of the relationship (Disintegration), which will lead a relational partner to distance himself or herself from the relationship-as-previously-defined (Alienation) and eventually to reconceive of the relationship (Resynthesis) in order to come to terms with it. This is the course taken by Howard and Judy's relational transition.

CONCLUSION

A long-standing consensus among students of personal relationships holds that an identifiable period exists in which Security reigns (Altman & Taylor, 1973; Levinger, 1983). There, relational partners feel comfortable, occupy complementary roles, and coordinate their actions. The relationship operates in kilter and may even appear to be stable. Clarke's (1968) *2001: A Space Odyssey* furnishes an archetype of this phase of relational transition.

Scholars part company, however, over the nature of this period, some arguing that it is smooth, easy, and effortless whereas others aver that it is a balancing act members struggle to maintain (Barnlund, 1982; Wilmot, 1987). Regardless of its dynamics, they hypothesize such a period, an observation that is corroborated by the structural analysis of ordinary cases of relationship transition.

Moreover, that idyllic period of time is further hypothesized to be the first phase of an indigenous, evolutionary, and recursive process that is the context of all personal relationships. The process is driven by Difference, encountered by relational partners as the dialectical oppositions of time, affect, and intimacy.

6

Relationship Disintegration:
TAKING NOTICE

"They have begun to discern certain unfortunate
patterns."
"What patterns? There are no patterns."
John LeCarré
A Perfect Spy

Personal relationships create as well as dwell within a recursive, indigenous, and evolutionary process called relational transition. Before entering this vortex of change, relationship members enjoy an apparently stable but clearly temporary period of Security. The entry point for beginning to turn about the helix of relationship transition is the phase of Disintegration.

Members have entered Disintegration when they begin noticing their relationship, noticing it instead of simply being in it. Something is askew, out of kilter. What they notice is Difference; Difference is becoming problematic. The problematic differences they encounter include the dialectical oppositions of time, affect, and intimacy. Encountering such Difference shoves a relational partner out of ordinary routines so that the relationship is observed as if from the outside. Thus partners experience ecstasy, in its simplest etymological sense: "Greek *ekstasis,* from *existanai* to put out of place, derange, from *ex* out of + *histanai* to cause to stand" (*Webster's Third New International Dictionary,* 1986, p. 720). They are beside themselves, peering in at their relationship, as it were, from the outside. The routine becomes momentarily strange, and they see what they had looked through before.

A GATHERING OF FORCES

One reason personal relationships are noticed is that they are plagued by simultaneous and competing forces, some centrifugal and some centripetal. This state of affairs engenders uncertainty, the central attribute of the Disintegration phase.

The vision of persons as sense makers is securely established in communication studies. From Heider (1958) and Kelly (1963) to contemporary attribution theorists (Derlega, Winstead, Wong, & Greenspan, 1987), constructivists (Delia, 1977), and uncertainty theorists (Berger, 1988), the human subject is seen as actively formulating rationales and plans. It follows, therefore, that the uncertainty and ambiguity that come with Disintegration are not long tolerated. Just as nature abhors a vacuum, personal relationships flee Disintegration. Whereas Security (comfort, complementarity, and coordination) is actively sought in relationships, forces for Disintegration, centrifugal forces, also abound. They arise from "confrontation with an ambiguous world that offers no meanings yet insists upon them . . . [and from] our dialogical relations with other persons" (Barnlund, 1982, p. 116).

Both "confrontation with an ambiguous world" and "dialogical relations with other persons" come together in a peculiar way as events that increase uncertainty in personal relationships. Such events are the essential ingredient in the Disintegration phase of relationship evolution. Two recent studies shed light on the nature of the phenomenon. Both study 1 (Planalp & Honeycutt, 1985) and study 2 (Planalp, Rutherford, & Honeycutt, 1988), a replication, indicated that the experience is not uncommon. Of the subjects who volunteered to participate in the studies, 80 percent to 90 percent had experienced an event that increased their uncertainty in a personal relationship. Moreover, the types of events reported in both studies fell into rather predictable categories that included competing relationship, loss of contact or closeness, sexual behavior, deception, change of personality or values, and betraying confidence.

These events may appropriately be called powerful because of their extensive effects upon the relationships involved. Both studies' subjects reported very strong emotional reactions to the events (8.03 in study 1 and 7.51 in study 2 on 1 to 9 scales), very strong effects on their beliefs about the other person (7.21 and 7.13), and strong to very strong effects on their beliefs about the relationship. The two studies also shared similar factor structures regarding effects of the events on subjects' beliefs about the relationship. Those beliefs sorted into the three factors of trust, involvement, and rules.

Relationship partners' communicative behavior was also extensively affected by the events. Much talk was prompted. Some was with the relationship partner, for example, talking over the event or talking around it, explaining or negotiating, or avoiding talk about the event. In response to questions unique to study 2, subjects reported that 75 percent of them talked to someone else about the event. Some asked for advice, but most talked to gather information, to understand, or to complain about their partners' behavior.

The findings that most directly affect understanding of the Disintegration phase of relationship evolution are those concerned with relational outcomes. In study 1, 67 percent of the relationships analyzed (66/98) changed; in study 2, 75 percent (57/76) changed. That is, in both studies substantially more relational partners became closer as a result of the event, became less close, or terminated the relationship, as opposed to the number who remained at their same level of closeness. These are extremely powerful effects and account for my arguing that the distinctive characteristic of the Disintegration phase is the occurrence of events that increase uncertainty in personal relationships. Once a relational partner's confidence in the relationship is broken by such an event, mindfulness increases — he or she notices the relationship and is likely to question its viability.

Perhaps one explanation for the powerful effects of these uncertainty increasing events is that they were generally unanticipated. In study 2 subjects were questioned about their awareness that such an event was about to occur. Over 75 percent were either unaware of conditions that might have led up to it or were only aware of those conditions after the fact. As Planalp, Rutherford, and Honeycutt reflected, "for most respondents events that increased uncertainty came as bolts from the blue; they were not anticipated and in many cases could not have been anticipated" (1988, p. 541).

At the same time, however, forces against Disintegration, centripetal forces, are also at work. Entropy is the fate of all systems, but open systems also work to preserve their integrity. "This rage for order, for the comprehensibility of phenomena, is . . . prerequisite for any action, routine or revolutionary" (Barnlund, 1982, p. 117). Thus "our dialogical relations with other persons" play a dual role. On the one hand, they may throw a personal relationship out of kilter (Barnlund, 1982, p. 116); but, on the other hand, as Krippendorf has argued, they may act as an antidote to entropy, *"Communication is that observer-created relational construction which explains what makes a system defy its decomposition"* (1984, p. 29). Additionally, Levinger has observed that "relationships are systems amenable to regeneration" (1983, p. 344). Thus dialogue within a personal relationship may work on two levels. To the members it may threaten the quality of their relationship; but to observers it may be the "myth" that explains the continuation of the relationship (Raush, 1981; see also Krippendorf, 1984; Levinger, 1983).

Personal relationships are inevitably caught in the tug-of-war between forces of fragmentation and forces of consolidation. When the struggle escalates to a level that draws the attention of relational partners, their relationship has entered the Disintegration phase of evolution in personal relationships. The additional business of this chapter is to document and characterize this phase of relational transition by demonstrating the consensus of relationship theorists that Disintegration is a normal process in personal relationships and to consider certain ancillary issues: relational partners' mindfulness of the process, the social context of the process, and the degree of determinism in the process.

THE UBIQUITY OF DISINTEGRATION

Like Difference, Disintegration is everywhere. Unlike Difference, which is a state of affairs, Disintegration is a process that is triggered when the relationship is out of kilter. Participants take notice of the loss of Security and question the relationship's legitimacy. However, what may be overlooked is that all relationship theorists discuss the disintegration of personal relationships. So strong is this consensus that one could argue that impermanence is an inherent characteristic of personal relationships. The present form of a personal relationship is ever passing away, in the process of evolving into another.

Wilmot called attention to this phenomenon when he observed, "Our dyadic relationships with others progress through initiation, maintenance, and dissolution" (1987, p. 179). He elaborated:

> One of the realities of life is that every significant relationship we have with another person will dissolve, either through the drifting apart of the participants, through a decision to part, or through death. . . . We act toward our most intimate friends and lovers as if they will be with us always, yet there is a good chance they will not (p. 176).

But it would be a mistake to assume that entering the Disintegration phase of relationship evolution sounds the death knell of the relationship. More times than not, personal relationships do not simply end, stopping dead in their tracks. Rather, dissolved relationships are more usefully seen as redefined relationships; and the termination of a relationship is more reasonably seen as a transition phase (see Wilmot, 1987, pp. 211–12). Memory is the culprit. Although I do forget some persons I meet casually, I do not soon forget close, personal relationships. And ordinarily I cannot, by act of will, erase sectors of my memory; nor can I prevent those relationships from drifting into consciousness by chance or rushing into consciousness, thrust there by circumstance. Entering the Disintegration phase is the first step toward reformulating or rebuilding the relationship; and doing so seems endemic to personal relationships.

In the same tradition of relational stages as Wilmot (1987) is the more elaborated model by Knapp (1984). The first five steps he labeled "coming together," and the last five steps, "coming apart" (p. 33). Thus a relationship that goes through all ten stages of Knapp's model will experience the characteristic cycle of initiation, maintenance, and dissolution that Wilmot observed. The ten stages are based on changes in how relationship partners communicate under conditions of greater and lesser intimacy (see Knapp, 1984, pp. 14, ff.; see also Altman & Taylor, 1973). Knapp elaborated:

> we would expect the Initiating [#1] and Terminating [#10] Stages to be characterized by communication that is more narrow, stylized, difficult, rigid, awkward, public, hesitant, and with overt judgments suspended; the stages of Integrating [#4], Bonding [#5], and Differentiating [#6] should show more breadth, uniqueness, efficiency, flexibility, smoothness, personalness, spontaneity, and overt judgments given. In short, it is proposed that we communicate within a prescribed range of content, style, and language at different levels of intimacy (1984, pp. 34–35).

The Disintegration phase of relational transition would be most evident at Knapp's Differentiating and Circumscribing stages. Here one or both relationship partners notice and begin to emphasize ways in which they differ and identify certain topics of conversation as taboo and certain objects or relationships as "mine" versus "yours." The previously presumed mutuality of relationship definition has been called into question. Partners have gone off auto pilot, they are on notice, and the future is uncertain.

However, not all relationships run the gamut of Knapp's ten stages. As he asserts, relationships may stabilize at any level of intimacy. And so they do. For most persons, few relationships move beyond the lower levels of Knapp's (1984) stages of intimacy (Initiating, Experimenting). But that does not change the transitory nature of even those relationships, as Wilmot put it, "through the drifting apart of the participants, through a decision to part, or through death" (1987, p. 176).

Because relationships may stabilize at any level of intimacy, we may presume that, at whatever level it is, the partners got there somehow, through some process. That is, mutuality of relationship definition was not instantaneous. It developed by moving from some other mutually agreed upon level of intimacy, even if that was only the minimal Initiating stage that marked their meeting as strangers. Even in this case, the partners had to redefine the relationship. And even here Disintegration is entailed: for a relationship to cross a boundary, that is, one of Knapp's lines separating one stage from another, the relationship-as-it-existed was noticed and called into question; uncertainty about that earlier mutuality surfaced. As Baxter and Wilmot have observed, "the significant feature to note about relationships is that they experience change and its shadow companion, uncertainty" (1984, p. 174).

Hence, one way to conceive of the structural helical model of relationship evolution that is being presented here is to imagine the line of ink that separates any two stages in Knapp's (1984) model and ask what occurs during the time a relationship passes through that line. Picture one of those lines magnified so that it covers about half a page. Within that line-as-magnified, picture a helix that describes the fundamental process of relationship evolution. The first phase of that process is what one encounters as a relationship enters the line and begins to cross it, Disintegration.

Thus Disintegration can be thought of in macro terms, over the life of a relationship, as well as in micro terms, as part of a relationship's move from one relationship stage to another. Either way, Disintegration is preparatory to reformulating the relationship.

Levinger's (1983) model of the evolution of marriage relationships is subject to the same macro-micro distinction as Knapp's (1984) model. Levinger's "modest aim is to examine heterosexual relationships between similar-age adults, which may progress from a casual acquaintance to courtship and marriage and may later face issues of conflict and deterioration or ending" (1983, p. 320). That aim has issued in a five-phase model of Awareness, Buildup, Continuation, Deterioration, and Ending. So there at the macro level is an equivalent of Wilmot's (1987) Initiation, Maintenance, and Dissolution. However, Levinger also noted the micro level: "Particularly important . . . are the *transitions* between adjacent phases or periods" (1983, p. 321) — equivalent to the lines that separate Knapp's stages. Levinger phrased his interests in these transitions between phases as questions:

What will lead a pair to move from phase A to phase B, from a casual acquaintance to a significant buildup of their bond (A → B)? After a bond has been formed, what factors impel partners to commit themselves to a more enduring continuation of their pairing (B → C)? Later, during phase C, what conditions lead to decline or deterioration (C → D)? Finally, given that a relationship has indeed deteriorated, what conditions lead to its ending (D → E)? (1983, pp. 321–22).

His observation on the transitions between phases remains accurate today. "Knowledge about phase-to-phase transitions or change processes has remained fragmentary" (p. 322).

Levinger's treatment of the transition from Continuation to Deterioration is concerned with the same kind of relationship change as is the present treatment of Disintegration. In seeking causes of relational downturns, Levinger (1983) turned to social exchange theory (Thibaut & Kelley, 1959), as Knapp (1984) had done, cited an ensuing "negative cycle of actions and reactions" [read downward spiral or helix] (p. 345), and observed, "How such a change actually occurs has not yet been well documented in the literature on close relationships" (p. 345). Levinger also suggested a reliable warning signal of relational downturns — "either partner's worry about mutual equity or the fairness of the marital exchange" (p. 345) — and cited cases of relational downturn, or Disintegration, characterized by partners' noticing the relationship, thus moving out of the auto pilot mode into one of vigilance.

Finally, in what seemed to be a largely methodological comment, Levinger reminded us and clearly illustrated that "the same objective action can elicit very different reactions" (1983, p. 346). Such differences he accounts for by recourse to relational partners' differing personalities, social environments, and relationship histories and the combination and interplay of these three elements. In other words, each relationship is unique. Thus he inadvertently noted the difficulty of making useful generalizations using conventional, quantitative, variable analysis and, by implication, he called our attention to the usefulness of qualitative case studies for understanding relational transition.

In the earlier work of Altman and Taylor (1973) there is less emphasis upon the seeming inevitability of Disintegration than in other theorists' work. However, relationship deterioration is still seen as an integral part of the process of relationship development. For example, Altman, Vinsel, and Brown's reassessment referred to social penetration theory as "a process-oriented theory of the development, management, and deterioration of social relationships" (1981, p. 109). Moreover, Altman and Taylor's pair of concepts, social penetration and social depenetration, form the same kind of symmetry as Knapp's (1984, Chap. 2) coming together and coming apart and Wilmot's (1987, Chap. 6) initiation, stabilized definitions, and dissolution.

There are three points at which the near inevitability of Disintegration in personal relationships is pertinent to social penetration theory. One is where Altman and Taylor (1973) discuss long-standing marriages. They noted research suggesting that, over time (up to 20 years), marriage relationships begin to "decay" due to such normal developmental changes as a decrease in interdependence and a decline in certain forms of interaction.

Further, they contrasted relationships that gradually decay to those that deteriorate more quickly because of conflict. Relationships that merely decay may be marked by less interaction, less explicit conflict, and perhaps a diminution of rewards whereas relationships that deteriorate more quickly may be characterized by more interaction, more explicit conflict, and perhaps an increase in costs. Altman and Taylor observed that "conflict is . . . an essential part of developmental phases" (1973, p. 166). To the extent that relational partners do not handle conflict effectively and their costs exceed their rewards, the relationship deteriorates and Disintegration has occurred. However, even when relational partners are successful in managing conflict, Altman, Vinsel, and Brown (1981) argue that this entails cycling in dialectical fashion between poles of openness and closedness. This process amounts to nothing less than successive redefinition of the relationship. And each new, although temporary, definition requires the previous one to have been noticed, called into question, and rejected — a process of Disintegration.

The third point at which social penetration theory is relevant to Disintegration is in the social penetration process itself. Altman and Taylor (1973) proposed four stages of development — Orientation, Exploratory Affective Exchange, Affective Exchange, and Stable Exchange. As a relationship moves forward through the four stages, interaction becomes less stereotyped, topics move from peripheral to central issues, there is increased length of association, partners become more relaxed around each other, code switching increases, positive and negative evaluation are more frequent, nonverbal closeness increases, interpretation of messages becomes more accurate and efficient, and relational partners improve in predicting each other's actions.

Whether the focus is on the four stages of social penetration or on the dimensions of interaction that describe them, for relational movement to take place at all, a previous stage (or, for example, a previous level of self-disclosure) must have been noticed and questioned as to its appropriateness, usefulness, or desirability. That is, an earlier place of Security must disintegrate in the process of giving way to a new one. Any passage through stages entails Disintegration in this sense.

Davis's (1973) seminal treatise on intimate relations was based on the biological metaphor of the life cycle and thus emphasized the near inevitability of that cycle for relationships. "I have attempted," he reflected, "to enumerate the essential characteristics of an intimate relation throughout all phases of its existence: from birth, through maturity, to sickness and death" (p. 284). Earlier he had observed: "There seems to be no necessary reason an intimate relation should not continue until one of the participants dies. . . . However, there are several contingent reasons most intimate relations do not live out their theoretically maximum life spans" (p. 245). So on two counts, Disintegration cannot be avoided in personal relationships. Either a relationship rides out the course of the life cycle and ends naturally, or a relationship terminates "under a combination of internal weaknesses and external pressures" (p. 245).

In Davis's (1973) scheme intimate relations may end either by "passing away" or by "sudden death." Intimate relations may pass away because of the introduction of a new and competing intimate into a social network, because of greater distance between relational partners, and because of aging. A good example of Disintegration appears in his discussion of the effects of the introduction of a new and successfully competing intimate upon information sharing among former primary intimates. First, the quantity of information is affected. The person who imported the new intimate now shares less information about her life activities with her old intimates. Because the new intimate gets this news first, there is also less interest in sharing stale news with the former primary intimates. Second, Davis continued,

> The quality of his information output to his old intimates declines even more drastically than its quantity. He need no longer confide any private information about himself to his old intimates, for his new one now provides him with a single storehouse for all his secrets. Conversely, his input of confidential information from his old intimates lessens once they come to realize that (1973, p. 249).

Under such conditions of information deprivation, one can only expect increased feelings of uncertainty and ambiguity on the part of the former primary intimates about their relationship with the brash importer of the competing relationship. They begin to notice the relationship (it may seem strange now instead of comfortable) and question its viability. That means Disintegration.

Duck has spoken of relationships as having "mental maps" and as "mental creations" (1986, pp. 92, 93). Thus in his analysis of relationship deterioration he starts at a period before any changes in the quantity or quality of information that is shared between intimates; that is, he starts at each partner's private interpretations of and thoughts about the relationship. Duck's guiding premise in the project is that "Discrepancies of interpretation — even between close partners — are an inevitable part of everyday social life" (1986, p. 92). Of necessity relational partners will from time to time disagree on the nature of their relationship and their desires for its future. Disintegration is thus an inevitable phase in personal relationships.

The model of relationship deterioration proposed by Duck (1982, 1986) commences with the first stirrings of dissatisfaction on the part of one partner and describes a route that arrives finally at the termination of that relationship, including its being appropriately laid to rest. In contrast to Duck, I believe that a more economical and elegant solution to the problem of change in personal relationships is to view relationship termination, "the permanent dismemberment of an existing relationship" (Duck, 1982, p. 2), as one of many forms of transition that a personal relationship may experience.

Thus the first two phases in Duck's model are comparable to what I am here calling Disintegration. In the first or intrapsychic phase, the relational partner becomes aware that the relationship is out of kilter, noticing, for example, negative aspects of the partner's actions and wondering what it would be like to be out of the relationship and into another. Clearly the future is uncertain, and one's own place in the present relationship is in question.

These feelings are amplified when the relational partner decides to share these feelings with the other in the dyadic phase. As Duck (1986) notes in the later version of the model, research shows that often this sharing or confrontation does not happen, but rather the dissatisfied relational partner simply drops out of sight, taking an indirect, innocuous exit from the relationship (Baxter, 1984). Furthermore, this occasion of sharing one's belief that the relationship is not working may open the door to negotiations and eventual redefinition of the relationship. In any case, "The *dyadic phase* is the phase when partners try to confront and talk through their feelings about the relationship and decide how to sort out the future" (Duck, 1986, pp. 101–2). Thus dissatisfaction and uncertainty dominate the relationship, at least in the mind of one partner, and may prompt forms of metacommunication between the partners. From the perspective of relationship transitions, relational partners who have experienced the intrapsychic and dyadic phases are in Disintegration.

Raush's (1977a) concept of disjunction is similar to Duck's "discrepancies in interpretation." Disjunction is clearly understood in contrast to its antonym, conjunction. In a condition of conjunction, Raush observes, there is alignment among personal, interpersonal, and societal perspectives; there is congruence among these three perspectives due to commitment to common goals, purposes, and ideals. Disjunction, however, seems to be the norm. According to Raush, "Most often the congruence fades rapidly: individual rights are reasserted [personal], intimacy forms coalitions [interpersonal], and the social unit becomes fragmented [societal]" (1977a, p. 173). In a personal relationship, the elevation of individual desires over the continuation of the relationship would move a relationship into Disintegration. In dialectical language this move on the part of a relational partner would involve choosing autonomy over connection or distance over intimacy.

In personal relationships one partner may decide that the relationship is not working, begin to notice it, and question its viability. When this happens, the partner has stepped outside the web of shared schemata on which the relationship was based. However, a willingness to be governed by the myth of the relationship had sustained it. Removing one's support from the myth, one partner may reassert personal goals over goals of the relationship; or one partner may ally with a movement on the societal level against the other partner. In any case the earlier fit between personal and interpersonal perspectives is thrown out of kilter. The relationship-as-previously-defined is called into question. As Raush summarized, "What kills myths or creates them is, I would suggest, not so much their practical consequences but rather their fit as conjunctive elements bridging between societal and personal or interpersonal structures" (1981, p. 111). The Disintegration phase has been entered when a relational partner begins to rebel against the myth of the relationship.

Disjunction is also understood in contrast to isomorphism — isomorphism between person and situation. Starting with this fundamental differentiation of person and situation, Raush's premise is that "*each person is situation for the other*" (1977b, p. 298). Here the issue is a match of capacities between person and situation. Consider one example Raush used: the mismatch between the extensive ability of a mother to perceive a range of emotional expressions and the very limited ability of her infant to signal a range of emotions. Thus in a personal relationship the ability of one partner to perceive a broad array of emotions in the other and, in the other partner, a very limited capability of expressing emotions would be a case of disjunction. In adult relationships, such a mismatch would surely cause the partners to notice the relationship and question its viability. If the condition persisted, they would probably be uncertain about the future of the relationship and would see their places in it as ambiguous. Disjunction as loss of isomorphism between person and situation places a relationship in the Disintegration phase of relational transition.

Not only are losses of (or lapses in) isomorphism commonly encountered in humans, Raush has further suggested that we humans have a "capacity for disjunctiveness" (1981, p. 106). This would imply that disjunction is seen as natural. Indeed, examples abound, whether on the international scene or in your and my ordinary social interaction. For good or ill, individual persons often choose to set themselves against the situation and act contrary to its expectations. Indeed, looters materialize after hurricanes, and terrorists terrorize, and there are also the likes of Ghandi and King.

The life cycle metaphor is so strong among students of personal relationships that it approaches the status of a myth in Raush's sense above. Davis (1973) and Levinger (1983) and Wilmot (1987) affirmed it, as did McCall and Simmons (1978). The presumption that personal relationships have a beginning, middle, and end — that they grow and develop into maturity and eventually wither and die — seems to serve a monitoring function in their thinking, just as the myth of a personal relationship may shepherd it and help maintain it, rather like a benign third party. Early in a chapter entitled, not surprisingly, "The Career of a Relationship," McCall and Simmons laid out a plan: "We shall examine, first, the processes by means of which relationships are created, maintained, and cultivated and, then, the more taxing processes by means of which they may come to be destroyed" (1978, p. 177).

Such destruction is not necessary, as the authors point out, but a look at the circumstances that can prompt the end of a personal relationship suggests that the probability may be quite high. First, changes in the contents of one partner's role-identity or in the relative priorities within it may diminish the rewards gained from continuing the relationship. Further, an increase in the costs required for continued interaction with the other may be more than the relational partner is willing to sustain. Finally, if the ties of ascription, commitment, and investment are not strong enough to override a gradually less rewarding relationship, the partners will probably let the relationship slip away.

Examination of the kinds of circumstances that can initiate the weakening of a personal relationship suggests that occasions for uncertainty and ambiguity about the relationship are not uncommon. Thus, from McCall and Simmons's perspective of role-identity, one would expect a high probability of personal relationships' experiencing Disintegration. In some cases the Disintegration would be a precursor to redefining the relationship as terminated, the partner as "former" or "ex." However, in the case of enduring relationships, Disintegration would be a precursor to relational regeneration.

> A lasting interpersonal relationship of any degree of intimacy must change apace with the changing of its members. The contents of the interrelated personas change many times over as the couple progresses. . . . The relationship must undergo metamorphosis at each major turning point in the personal career of each participant. If it does not or cannot, it will fade away or be destroyed (1978, p. 198).

As has been pointed out before, changes in the qualitative levels of personal relationships (for example, stage to stage transitions) entail a rejection of the former level as inadequate or somehow dissatisfying. That means Disintegration, the temporary dominance of uncertainty and ambiguity regarding the relationship, one's place in it and its future. Thus metamorphosis entails Disintegration.

A similar view has been espoused by Hinde (1979). Like McCall and Simmons (1978), he does not subscribe to a set of stages through which relationships progress. However, Hinde does describe personal relationships as proceeding through repeated cycles of redefinition: "progress towards greater involvement in a relationship is seldom smooth. Progress may occur, there may be a pause, perhaps for consolidation, or the relationship may regress. . . . each change in the relationship must involve a change in the definition of the relationship" (1979, pp. 303–4). To alter one's definition of a relationship requires that the former definition be abandoned and a new one adopted. The partners' former ways of seeing and being in the relationship were determined to be out of kilter. One experienced uncertainty and ambiguity. So a new way to characterize the relationship was sought, one that would accurately reflect the desired, new ways of seeing and being in the relationship. Abandoning the former definition of the relationship amounts to Disintegration. Disintegration is the entry into the wilderness relational partners must traverse as they move from one relationship definition to another.

ANCILLARY CONSIDERATIONS

Three issues accompany a consideration of Disintegration. First, there is the degree of mindfulness of relational partners who are experiencing Disintegration; second, there is the context in which Disintegration occurs; and, finally, there is the issue of determinism, the degree to which a relationship's Disintegration predisposes it to a particular developmental route.

Mindfulness

On a theoretical level, relational partners' becoming more mindful of their circumstances may be conceived as "movement from rules as lived to a consciousness about rules" (Raush, 1981, p. 100). A variety of circumstances may bring about such movement. Raush has spoken of a loss of isomorphism among personal, interpersonal, and societal orientations held by relational partners. Such disjunctions, he has observed, may come about in a personal relationship through ordinary interaction. "A continuing close relationship involves differences in viewpoints, and through these differences partners may come to question what was formerly taken for granted. In this process that which was internalized as characterizing 'us' may come to be seen as no longer valid" (1977a, p. 186). Or such changes in awareness may be more conscious, according to Levinger: "People assess their relationships primarily when they are trying to decide about making transitions from one to another phase of relationship" (1983, p. 330). Moreover, data gathered by Baxter and Wilmot (1983) indicated that relationship partners who are on "growth trajectories" may monitor their interactions more carefully (to prevent misunderstandings) than do relationship partners whose interaction patterns are considered stable.

Finally, Berger and Douglas have espoused a typology of conditions expected to increase relationship partners' awareness of their interactions:

> (1) in novel situations where, by definition, no appropriate script exists, (2) where external factors prevent completion of a script, (3) when scripted behavior becomes effortful because substantially more of the behavior is required than is usual, (4) when a discrepant outcome is experienced, or (5) where multiple scripts come into conflict so that involvement in any one script is suspended (1982, p. 46).

It is not difficult to imagine any of these conditions prevailing when a personal relationship is in a phase of Disintegration, the process of noticing, questioning, and rejecting the relationship-as-it-has-been. In particular would these conflictful circumstances cause relational partners to take notice of their relationship in a unique way.

Context

Disintegration clearly does not occur in a social void, as these conditions for mindfulness suggest. The social context as well as the partners' own mindfulness play a part. Parks and Adelman's (1983) study of romantic relationships indicated that the best predictor of uncertainty in a relationship is one partner's communication with the other's social network of friends and family. With less communication, uncertainty increased, and there was greater likelihood of relationship instability. Moreover, relationship stability was found to be positively associated with lower uncertainty, more communication with the partner's network, and receiving more support for the relationship from the partner's network.

Not everyone, however, has access to the other's social network in a personal relationship. Indeed, certain common kinds of social context seem to facilitate Disintegration in personal relationships. Raush has argued that the move from "rules as lived" to "consciousness about rules" has been necessitated by contemporary social life, marked as it is by "increased heterogeneity of inputs from others into our lives along with massively increased heterogeneity of rules, patterns, and styles for interaction" (1981, p. 100). One result is that relationship rules are now more "obscure, ambiguous, and confusing" than in pre-industrial society. Moreover, rules proliferate for given relationships, even rules for breaking rules. A second result of contemporary social life is that personal relationships are now "on their own" in a way they were not in times past. Without the undergirding role of consensual rules, "Each relationship bears the burden — or opportunity, if you will — of exploring, defining, and ever redefining its own rules" (Raush, 1981, p. 100).

When personal relationships are forced to survive alone without a supporting community, they are uniquely vulnerable to the onset of Disintegration (Berger & Kellner, 1964; Davis, 1973). In the complex society that Raush describes, the influence of kinship, for example, is often diluted (McCall & Simmons, 1978). Apart from a community that supports the continuation of the relationship, its survival rests exclusively on the shoulders of the relational partners; and whether to dissolve the relationship rests, finally, on the choice of each single partner in the relationship (Simmel, 1950).

Determinism

Disintegration, however, is not the beginning of the end, even though that may appear to be the case. Relationships do have the potential for entering regressive spirals (Wilmot, 1987) in which one destructive comment elicits a matching one in cyclical, accelerating fashion. Bateson (1935) had observed the phenomenon of "schismogenesis" in his field work as the tendency of assertive responses between groups to feed off one another, each one trying to best the other. Leary's (1955) "interpersonal reflex" and Jourard's (1964) "dyadic effect" are confirmations of Bateson's observations, but on the level of personal relationships.

Sillars and Parry have argued that there is a cognitive basis for this phenomenon, basing their position on findings that one's "ability to engage in complex, integrated thought" is impaired under stressful conditions, circumstances one might be expected to experience in the Disintegration phase of relationship evolution. Under these conditions of reduced conceptual complexity, one would expect, they reason, reduced information search, failure to discriminate between items of information and points of view, adoption of stereotyped attitudes and responses, perception of only one side of an issue, and lessened ability to interpret others' thoughts, motives, and intentions. Communicative behavior during high stress periods (for example, Disintegration), they predicted, would manifest lessened communicative complexity, or "conceptual complexity of spontaneous verbal communications" (1982, p. 206). The potential disintegrating effects of such circumstances on personal relationships are evident.

Sillars and Parry operationalized relational adjustment as satisfaction, closeness, and frequency and importance of conflict, the very kinds of conditions indicative of the Disintegration phase. Relational adjustment was found to correlate positively with communicative complexity. That is, when relational partners felt less satisfied with their relationship, felt less close, and experienced more conflict, they were also less able to "differentiate multiple perspectives and provide integrative explanations for differences in perspectives" (1982, p. 206). Moreover, the investigators found that relational adjustment was positively correlated with self-blame and negatively correlated with other blame. So the less "well adjusted" a relationship was, that is, the more into a Disintegration phase, the more partners blamed each other during arguments, but, the more well adjusted a relationship was, the more partners blamed themselves during arguments.

Caught in such a regressive spiral, one might expect that once a relationship entered the Disintegration phase of relationship evolution, dissolution would be inevitable. However, this is not the case. As Wilmot (1987) has argued, even stable personal relationships normally experience both downward and upward spirals as they fluctuate within limits. Fisher and Drecksel's (1983) analysis of partner talk in isolated work situations indicated that periods of competitive symmetry alternated with periods of complementary exchanges. Clearly personal relationships are systems that are able to override the force of a regressive spiral; that are capable of regeneration. For many relationships, Disintegration is a necessary precursor of renewal.

However, another kind of determinism does seem to be at work in the evolution of personal relationships. Once relationship partners take notice of their relationship and question its viability, even if they do not wholly reject the relationship-as-it-was, they necessarily see it in a different light. The genie is out of the bottle. The process of shifting from auto pilot to manual control in a relationship and back again changes a relationship. Disintegration necessarily leads to some form of redefinition or resynthesis of the relationship.

CASES IN DISINTEGRATION

The relationships depicted in the cases are seen as operating within a social domain marked by three dialectical dimensions, time, intimacy, and affect. The question at this point is whether, and to what extent, the dialectical characteristics of the cases illustrate a movement from the Security phase of the structural helical model into the Disintegration phase.

Between episode 2 and episode 14 (Figure 2.2), at which times Helen was in a Security phase, her relationship experienced two periods of Disintegration. The first encompassed the period between E 3 and E 6. Helen's learning came to a halt when she became impatient with her teacher (actually E 3, 4, 5, 3, 4, 6). Here she clearly noticed their relationship. Difference became salient. Intimacy diminished, and affect turned negative. The relationship was not working as she wished. Then again in E 11 and E 12, Helen remembered breaking the doll, Anne Sullivan's gift to her, and regretted her action. Concern for their relationship was in the forefront of Helen's consciousness. The dialectic of time intruded into Helen's awareness; Helen brought a past episode into the present. Likewise, she desired to be close to her teacher (intimacy) and became aware of how much she cared for her (affect).

Diane's attention was drawn to John and her relationship (as opposed to simply being in it) when he first began discussing marriage in episode 2 (Figure 2.4). Her intimacy with John diminished steadily to E 10. As time passed in this interval, her questioning of the relationship increased as did her negative disposition toward immediate marriage (affect). By E 12 she realized that, while they had been going together before college, marriage to her lay in the distant and ill-defined future (time). Her relationship with John was clarified (for herself at least) as she imported past into present in narrative form. In so doing she was prompted to question the viability of their relationship.

Disintegration, for Howard and Judy, began with their move to Raleigh (Figure 2.5). For Judy the move itself called attention to the relationship, rife with Difference. She immediately focused on her regret at leaving her best friend. For Howard, the deterioration of their relationship came to the fore after the move. He began to wonder whether they could last, under the circumstances. Their intimacy diminished (Howard: E 2; Judy: E 2–4). The constant verbal battles reflected their negative feelings for being together (affect), and their temporal orientations (time) were out of kilter (Judy: regretting moving; Howard: looking forward to a new school adventure).

So it appears that the three cases can be reinterpreted in terms of the structural helical model. Further, the dialectical dimensions of time, intimacy, and affect are useful in doing so. Moreover, the structural analyses of the relationship narratives assist the reinterpretation by locating significant episodes and highlighting relations among them.

CONCLUSION

In the phase of relationship disintegration, a relational partner feels as though he or she is on the outside looking in. The relationship is now noticed and questioned instead of simply enacted. The noticing and questioning are prompted by certain events that increase uncertainty about the relationship (Planalp, Rutherford, & Honeycutt, 1988). Such ambiguity acts as a centrifugal force tending to pull apart the relationship and is balanced by a countervailing need for order and predictability in the relationship.

The literature in personal relationships confirms that such a period of relationship disintegration is a common occurrence. For example, Knapp (1984) speaks of relationships coming apart; Duck (1986) sees discrepancies of interpretation by relational partners as normal; and Raush's (1977a) focus is upon disjunction among personal, interpersonal, and societal domains.

A corollary to relationship disintegration is the movement of a relationship from a condition of rules-as-lived to consciousness-of-rules (Raush, 1981). Various forms of interruption seem to increase partners' mindfulness of their relationship (Berger & Douglas, 1982).

The social context of a relationship is important to its continuation. Such dependence on others underlines the fragility of personal relationships. Moreover, personal relationships display both a tendency toward regressive spirals and a potential for rejuvenation.

7

Relationship Alienation:
STILL LIFE

The tranquil waterway leading to the uttermost
ends of the earth flowed somber under an overcast
sky — seemed to lead into the heart of an
immense darkness.

Joseph Conrad
Heart of Darkness

The phase of relationship Alienation is like a field in autumn. It
contains both the lifeless stalks of last summer's growth and the seeds of
next spring's blooming. In this phase, at the same time desolate and
resolute, customary role-taking ceases to be possible, and possible new
roles are crafted. Here the relationship behaves like a child's ball when it
is tossed into the air. When the sphere reaches its apogee, its rising flight
stops ever so briefly before it begins to descend. The phase of
relationship Alienation is like those last few moments of deceleration
before apogee and those first few moments of acceleration. It is a cul-de-
sac of transformation.

The third phase of that indigenous, evolutionary, recursive process
that is the context of all interpersonal communication is relationship
Alienation. From the beginning, I have taken it as a given that all personal
relationships change, that is, that they move from one stage or state or
definition to another. Moreover, I have argued that the best way to
understand the evolution of personal relationships is to grasp the process
whereby their partners make those transitions from one kind of
relationship to another and that scrutiny should be focused on the space

between the stages. Raush's evocative statement echoes the position: "There are no systematic transformational 'equations' between individual as individual and his/her relations with intimates. . . . if we are to understand communication fully, it is this discontinuity which must become a major focus for study" (1981, p. 102). From this perspective, Difference is the central concept in personal relationships, in relational transitions, and in the interpersonal communication that constitutes them.

A META-DIALECTIC

From being in kilter and comfortable at first, relationship partners can, second, begin to notice their relationship. Events can cause an increase in one or both partners' uncertainty about the relationship and prompt them to question the viability of the association. In the third phase, relationship Alienation, one or both partners reject the relationship-as-presently-constituted, become alienated from it. Thus, at Alienation, we have the dialectical opposite of the starting phase of Security. This oppositional pair, Security-Alienation, is the first of two meta-dialectics we can use to understand the period of relationship transition. As such, it has much in common with the routinely observed dialectic of independence and separation versus interdependence and connectedness (Baxter, 1990; Bochner & Eisenberg, 1987; Conville, 1988; Rawlins, 1983b; Trenholm & Jensen, 1988).

Accordingly, the pair shares the qualities of contradiction, change, and interdependence that characterize dialectical relationships. Security and Alienation are opposites; they contradict each other. In a circumstance of Security, relational partners share a sense of comfortable fit, and their complementary roles result in coordinated action. However, a circumstance of Alienation is unstable. One or both relational partners reject the relationship-as-defined. Reciprocity malfunctions, commitments move elsewhere, and roles no longer fit. In this unstable circumstance, change is inevitable. New mutualities, commitments, and roles are sought. Unsuccessful experiments may draw partners back together temporarily only to find themselves repelled again. Finally, partners, as they embody the dialectical poles of Security-Alienation, may, nevertheless, depend upon each other for definition of what attracts and repels and, in addition, for definition of the social domain in which they play out the relationship.

THE DEFORMATION OF SOCIALITY

A personal relationship can be conceived as a unique configuration of roles one takes vis-à-vis the other. From this perspective the life of the relationship depends upon partners' role-taking, but at a deeper level, upon what Natanson has called the "primordial activity" of role-action, "the intentionality of role-taking" (1966, p. 375). Role-action, he argues, is "a grounding condition of social order"; and alienation, "a structural deformation of sociality" (1966, p. 376). This is the sense in which I am using the term alienation. The social order instanced by a particular personal relationship ceases when role-action, and, hence, its customary role-taking, are curtailed. Current researchers Baxter and Dindia agree: the maintenance issue for relationship partners is "to sustain the essential features of their relationship's identity" in terms of roles and rules (1990, p. 188).

When the a priori conditions of role-action are not in place, role-taking cannot take place, and, consequently, the particular relationship in question cannot continue to function as it had. Relationship partners become alienated from their relationship when the conditions that had permitted them to conduct their relationship are absent. Thus the social order as manifested in their relationship is deformed.

The five conditions of role-action can be illustrated by reference to role-taking. An underlying assumption of Natanson's and of mine is, as he put it, "social action has a periodic cast" (1966, p. 380). Because social action occurs within relationships, the unavoidable and equally obvious assumption is that relationships change. From their pragmatic stance, Altman, Vinsel, and Brown concur: "external and internal events eventually press the relationship toward change" (1981, p. 141). The cardinal application of Natanson's a prioris of role-action is to account for change in role-taking and, hence, in relationships.

First, there is The Assumption of Power. Here the social actor is permitted, that is, experiences, the possibility of taking up a role. He or she is able to set aside time and dedicate a part of his or her field of action to a different activity or role. Second, there is The Assumption of Recourse. Natanson refers to this grounding condition of role-taking as its "essential repeatability" (1966, p. 378). Roles we enact do not typically come to us as one-time events. Rather, having once assumed a role, we may take it up again.

The Assumption of Uniformity is Natanson's third a priori of role-taking. Not only can the social actor take up a role (The Assumption of Power) and, having put it down, take it up again (The Assumption of

Recourse), but also, when he or she does take up the role again, it is recognizable. Reperformance of the role is seen as just that — familiar, so familiar that it is deemed to be the same kind of social action as before. A given performance of the role has continuity with both earlier and successive instances of the role's enactment.

Openness, Againness, and Sameness in role-taking are followed by Mineness, The Assumption of Recognition. When the social actor takes up a role again, it is recognizable to the actor as his or her own, as reflecting his or her own peculiar style. Here, "the idiosyncratic texture of his [sic] action" becomes "a constitutive feature of role-action" (Natanson, 1966, p. 379). The final grounding condition of role-taking presented by Natanson is The Assumption of Release. Here we come full circle, to the first assumption, the possibility of taking up a role at all. To wit, a role, once taken up is at some time in the future, laid down. He seems to be saying a role that is never relinquished is not a role, but something else. Part of what constitutes a role is its having a termination, a conclusion.

With the violation of any one of these grounding conditions of role-action, social action that depends on role-taking is fundamentally altered. That is the condition of alienation. In our terms, the conduct of a personal relationship-as-it-had-been-defined cannot be continued, for the roles in terms of which the relationship had been played out are no longer available to the relational partners. They have become alienated from that relationship, literally unable to continue as before. This is the phase in the structural helical model of relationship transition that is the focus of this chapter, relationship Alienation.

Relationship theorists have spoken of the relationship as a third party to a dyad. Relational partners begin to see their relationship as a separate entity from themselves. They refer to it, reifying it; and it serves a monitoring function in the maintenance of the relationship. Such references are typically benign. But in the phase of Alienation the ordinarily friendly third party (our relationship) becomes unfriendly, even malignant. Relational partners decide that they dislike the entity they had grown accustomed to calling "our relationship," for it now has come to represent a place to which they cannot or do not wish to return. When it was otherwise, earlier in the relationship, their relationship resided in the first phase on the structural helical model, that place of Security, even comfort, where the relationship had come to rest for a time.

Consider an example of role-action and the maintenance and deformation of relationships. Imagine a potentially amorous relationship that is presently in Knapp's (1984) Experimenting stage. The level of self- disclosure is increasing, and after a time, one says, "I love you" to the other, and the other accepts that declaration as authentic and intimates the same. They find themselves in the Intensifying stage, and their roles have changed. They cannot continue to act toward each other as they had before their mutual declaration of affection. Yet the social order is maintained insofar as their personal relationship is concerned because of the functioning of those five a priori conditions of role-taking. The relational partners both laid down the earlier role of close-acquaintance-with-strong-attraction (Assumption of Release) and took up the role of girlfriend-boyfriend (Assumption of Power). If this was not their first such relationship, they were reclaiming a role (Assumption of Recourse). Moreover, the new roles they took up vis-à-vis each other were recognizable as to the kind of roles they were (Assumption of Uniformity). And finally, the relational partners enacted their newly adopted roles in their own unique manners (Assumption of Recognition). Thus role-action provides for relational evolution. When role-action malfunctions, however, relational transitions are blocked.

In the context of their newly adopted roles and those grounding conditions of role-taking, Alienation was not the outcome. The grounds of social action were in place, and the social order (their relationship) was preserved. However, in the context of their earlier roles as friends, Alienation is an accurate description of their relationship's condition. Because of their newly disclosed commitments, they cannot or will not resume the role-taking characteristic of their earlier relationship as friends. Having once declared their amorous affections closed the door on acting as merely good friends again (Assumption of Recourse). With the fall of the Assumption of Recourse also went the Assumptions of Uniformity and Recognition. With the option of taking up their former roles denied, whether the resumed friend-role was recognizable as the same kind of role or as bearing the unique style of the actor became irrelevant.

Other writers have spoken of relationship change that relied on notions similar to Natanson's theory of role-action. For example, a relationship may become stale, as McCall and Simmons have observed: one is required to continue it and so goes through the motions as "an empty round of duties" (1978, p. 196). Family relations, business obligations, and other social arrangements may be peopled by actors nevertheless alienated from those relationships. One wants to put down a role to take up another, but cannot; one wants to customize the role with his or her own style, but the dictates of the situation say no. Further, McCall and Simmons have rooted the change of relationships in the concept of roles. "All relationships begin and end," they concluded, "with unfulfilled needs for enactment and support of role-identities" (1978, p. 197).

Role-taking may depend upon the location of relational partners. In the private sphere, in contrast to public institutions (often powerful, alien, incomprehensible, anonymous), Berger and Kellner have argued, the modern person will "seek power, intelligibility and, quite literally, a name" (1964, p. 7), a place where he or she is "somebody." In the public sphere of work, one's role-action may be curtailed. For example, one may be prevented from putting down one role and taking up another or prohibited from stamping a work role with one's own personal style. In the private sphere, however, role-action is loosed in an atmosphere of choice and autonomy.

Role-action, moreover, manifests itself as having both internal and external sources. Role-action is attenuated not only by [internal] individual decisions we make (for example, to disclose one's amorous affections), but also by the practical force of [external] social circumstances that are more or less thrust upon us (for example, bureaucratic or family necessity). Regardless of the locus, however, relational partners become alienated from the relationship-as-it-has-been-defined. They conclude "that the sociocultural system no longer does, or perhaps never did, operate according to the principles" they presumed (Wallace, 1956a, p. 633). The roles by which they played out their relationship are no longer possible or desirable.

A means of melding the internal and external aspects of role-action is Wallace's (1956a, 1957) analogy of the mazeway. The mazeway "is used by its holder as a true and more or less complete representation of the operating characteristics of a 'real' world" (Wallace, 1956a, p. 631). Here again we confront the discontinuity Raush (1981) spoke of between the individual as individual and the individual's relations with intimates. That discontinuity comes into focus in relational transitions, in the space between stages of a relationship. In that space the mazeway is disassembled and rebuilt. The maze is all the elements out there, including other persons, that I must confront as a human being, and the way is my unique manner of dealing with them. One's mazeway is characterized by Wallace as having three kinds of content:

> (1) goals and pitfalls (values, or desirable and undesirable end states); (2) the "self" and other objects (people, other organisms, and things); and (3) ways (processes, techniques, and relations) that may be circumvented or used, according to their characteristics, to facilitate the self's attainment or avoidance of values (1956a, pp. 631–32).

Wallace interprets: "the individual's way is a system of behavior which articulates very neatly ... with the cues presented by the maze about him. His *way* and the maze itself, in other words, are complementary functions" (1957, p. 25).

When these internal and external dimensions (way and maze) lose their complementary nature, their fit, the result is relationship alienation. When there exists a disjunction between the facts of a relational partner's circumstances (the maze: "goals and pitfalls ... the 'self' and other objects") and his or her resources for dealing with them, (ways: "processes, techniques, and relations"), then that primordial activity of role-action is attenuated, and customary role-taking ceases. New roles begin to emerge, and the relationship is irrevocably changed. Those are the conditions and results of relationship Alienation.

RE-FORMING RELATIONSHIPS

The phase of relationship Alienation is a juncture, a cul-de-sac of transformation. There two events occur. Relational partners reject the relationship-as-previously-defined, and they commence to craft new roles that will issue in a relationship-to-be-defined. The dual nature of the phase is captured in Lifton's conclusion that *"every significant step in human existence involves some inner sense of death"* (1976, p. 149). In relationship Alienation, partners' old-ways-of-relating die, only to be replaced by their new-ways-of-relating. The relationship itself continues, but the peculiar configuration of role-taking that had marked the relationship as theirs-in-particular is re-formed.

That relationships end or terminate or dissolve is taken for granted in the relationship literature. And some relationships do end. On the one hand, I may cease to have contact with a person I knew. I may never think of the person; I may completely forget knowing him or her. That relationship has ended. But on the other hand, if I have only infrequent contact with the person, or if I have no contact but occasionally remember him or her, then it would seem that the relationship is alive in some manner. Rather than being considered dead, a more useful view is that the relationship has changed. I (or we) have redefined the relationship. After all, when we (for example, in that almost forgotten relationship, above) had occasion to interact face-to-face in the past, even then, what I was responding to was my construction of the other person, not to him or her directly. So now, even with no face-to-face contact, I am still responding to my construction of the other. I may truly forget superficial acquaintances or brief conversational partners, but I remember most close relationships, even in the absence of contact. In remembrance, the relationship lives on, changed or redefined, but hardly ended.

Thus the recent work on relationship turning points is particularly useful in elucidating the phase of Alienation. Bolton's (1961) pioneering work on "mate selection" focused attention of researchers on the evolution of romantic relationships, from acquaintance to decision to marry. He employed the term "turning points" to stand for the personal and interpersonal changes experienced by relational partners during that evolution. Specifically, the phrase stood for "transformations in actors' definition of themselves and their relations to others" (pp. 236–37). And "transformation" was no insignificant term to Bolton. It referred to "a reformulation, an employing of a new vocabulary, a shift from one perspective to another" (p. 237).

The nature of that reformulation process has been elucidated in Baxter and Bullis's (1986) study of turning points in the relationships of 40 college-aged romantic couples. Their analysis revealed that turning points were relatively infrequent in the experience of their subjects. The 80 relational partners recalled a total of 759 turning points in their relationships, or only 9.5 per respondent. The mean length of the relationships under study was 22.1 months, so each subject, on the average, reported turning points occurring a little over two months apart. Moreover, the most influential turning point types reported occurred even less frequently. For example, Disengagement, the most influential turning point type, comprised only 6.1 percent of all reported turning points. In descending order, the next four most intense turning point types were Serious Commitment (comprising only 3.2 percent of all reported turning points), Making Up (3.3 percent), Get-to-Know-Time (19 percent), and Passion (6.3 percent). So a tentative conclusion we may draw is that the phenomenon of a personal relationship entering the Alienation phase of relational transition is not an ordinary, everyday occurrence.

When turning points did occur, regardless of their intensity, over half (55.1 percent) of them were reported to involve relationship talk or direct metacommunication. They ranged from the turning point types Get-to-Know-Time (19.8 percent; get acquainted small talk) to Exclusivity (90.9 percent; decision to date only each other). Turning points also varied in intensity, that is, the extent of their influence on the relationship at the time. Baxter and Bullis (1986) measured intensity of turning points by the mean change in commitment to the relationship that respondents reported at each turning point. When those data on frequency of relationship talk are compared with the intensity data, considerable light is cast on the nature of relational turning points and hence on the Alienation phase of relational transition. Of the five turning point types reported to be associated with the greatest changes in relational partners' commitment to each other, four also had the highest involvement with metacommunication. Figure 7.1 demonstrates this relationship. Thus another tentative conclusion we may venture is that when their relationship is in the Alienation phase, relational partners are likely to talk explicitly about their relationship, and their talk is likely to be about certain kinds of important topics.

Recall that Alienation was described in terms of an attenuation of role-action, the inability or unwillingness of relational partners to resume certain roles that had marked the relationship before its redefinition. The question arises, "What kinds of events might be associated with the Alienation phase?" Here is a beginning answer. The researchers reported 14 types of turning points. Five (listed above) were associated with 20 percent or greater changes in a relational partner's commitment to the relationship. Thus, in summary, occasions when relationships enter upon the kind of serious transformation entailed by the Alienation phase are rather infrequent; they tend to involve metacommunication around certain relationship events and topics; and they vary considerably in intensity.

In contrast to this consensus within the aggregate data, agreement between relational partners was not so easy to find, Baxter and Bullis (1986) reported. Only 54.5 percent of the reported turning points were agreed upon by relational partners. There was rather high agreement on some (Serious Commitment, 75 percent; Get-to-Know-Time,

FIGURE 7.1 — The Relationship between Turning Point Types, Their Involvement with Relationship Talk, and the Intensity of Their Effects

Top Five Turning Point Types: Percentage of Subjects Reporting Involvement with Relationship Talk		Top Five Turning Point Types: Percent Change in Subjects' Intensity of Commitment to the Relationship	
Exclusivity	90.0	Disengagement	−23.28
Making Up	86.4	Serious Commitment	23.26
Disengagement	79.1	Making Up	21.60
Serious Commitment	77.3	Get-to-Know-Time	21.13
Passion	76.7	Passion	20.35

Source: Adapted from Baxter and Bullis, 1986, pp. 483, 485.

68.8 percent; Exclusivity, 67.6 percent; Reunion, 63.2 percent; Disengagement, 56.5 percent; and Making Up, 56 percent), and they tended to be events about which external verification would be easy. Others, with low agreement, tended to be those of an internal nature, for example, Sacrifice (30.4 percent) and Positive Psychic Change (38.1 percent).

The romantic couples seemed to live in phenomenologically separate worlds, but that did not seem to negatively affect their relationships. For example, Baxter and Bullis (1986) did not find a significant correlation between respondents' current satisfaction with the relationship and the proportion of identified turning points the partner agreed with. This finding held even with positive and negative turning points analyzed separately. Likewise, nonsignificant findings resulted from an analysis of the association of current satisfaction and the proportion of turning points that involved relationship talk. This finding also held when positive and negative turning points were analyzed separately.

What was associated with relationship satisfaction was the proportion of negative turning points respondents reported. A significant negative correlation was reported between current satisfaction with the relationship and the proportion of turning points that respondents judged as negative. In addition, two turning point types in particular were associated with relational satisfaction. Those respondents who identified an Exclusivity turning point in their relationship history reported a significantly higher current satisfaction level with the relationship than those who did not; and those who identified a Disengagement event in their relationship history reported a significantly lower current satisfaction level than those who did not.

What can we surmise at this point about the Alienation phase of the structural helical model of relationship transition? With regard to frequency of occurrence, the Alienation phase may not occur very often in a given romantic relationship. However, when it does occur, those turning point types that make the most difference at the time also tend to be the ones that relational partners agree have occurred and the ones that involve relational partners in talking explicitly about their relationships.

Further, recall Baxter and Bullis's (1986) findings regarding the correlation between proportion of negative turning points and partners' satisfaction with the relationship. This may indicate that the efficacy of turning points in relational transition is in their accumulation, not in their occurrence singly. If so, this is consistent with the structural helical model. The phase of Disintegration is a period of time that allows for the accumulation of turning point-precipitating events, positive or negative.

Such events may serve to increase the uncertainty of relational partners about the viability of the relationship-as-currently-defined. If that is the case, then the relationship is moving toward the Alienation phase of relational transition. Moreover, because the research data of Baxter and Bullis (1986) were subjects' recollections, "accumulation" of turning points does not refer merely to a growing number of events but, rather, to those events gradually working their way into the consciousness and memory of one or both relational partners.

Finally, Baxter and Bullis (1986) seemed concerned with the discontinuous nature of their conceptualization of relational turning points. They admitted worrying that an explicit search for turning points might obscure a "creeping incrementalism" in relationship development, a perspective that might better capture the process. My position is that these two approaches are not mutually exclusive choices. Here again, the structural helical model of relational transition is useful. Recall that it includes the Disintegration phase, a period of time for gradual change, a time in which one or both relational partners notice the relationship (instead of mindlessly participating in it) and begin to question its viability. If this process continues, one or both partners will eventually reject the relationship-as-currently-defined, thus casting the relationship into the Alienation phase. The structural helical model provides for both a gradual decline in the relationship as well as a discontinuity with the past.

A more recent study of turning points in relationships turned attention to organizational settings instead of dyadic relationships and monitored "new recruits'" development of identification with the organization. The new recruits were graduate students, and the organizations were communication departments. Bullis and Bach (1989) gathered data from 28 new graduate students in three programs using the same kind of Retrospective Interview Technique that Baxter and Bullis (1986) had used, one patterned after the work of Huston, Surra, Fitzgerald, and Cate (1981). Respondents were led through a process of plotting a graph depicting their degree of identification with their department from the time they entered the program through eight months of work. The horizontal axis was time marked in months, and the vertical axis was degree of identification with the department, from 0 percent to 100 percent. Turning point events were marked by the respondents month by month along with descriptions of the events that were associated with changes in identification.

Several of their findings are useful in shedding further light on the Alienation phase of relational transition. The 28 respondents reported a total of 283 turning points, approximately 10 each. On the average, respondents experienced just over one turning point each month. That is over twice the average frequency Baxter and Bullis (1986) found in their study of romantic relationships. So there may be considerable range in the frequency with which relationships move into the Alienation phase.

Like the previous study, however, turning points reported by Bullis and Bach (1989) were both positive and negative. The two strongest in their immediate negative effects on organizational identification were Getting Away (devoting time and emotional energy to relationships outside the department) and Alienation ("a perceived lack of community or . . . feeling of difference between self and others in the department" [p. 284]). The strongest turning points in their immediate positive effects on organizational identification were Receiving Informal Recognition (positive feedback from peers or professors; the feeling of being treated as an equal), Gaining Formal Recognition (for example, getting a good grade, being asked to work with a professor on a project), and Representing the Organization (to undergraduates as a teaching assistant or to peers in other departments when taking courses there).

These findings confirm the dual nature of the Alienation phase alluded to above. There, the relationship-as-it-has-been-defined is finally rejected, and relational partners begin to redefine the relationship in a new configuration of role-taking. In the Alienation phase a relational partner moves away from what the relationship has been. Turning points labeled Alienation or Getting Away might mark the students' flight from undesirable roles. But also in the Alienation phase a relational partner moves toward the relationship as it could be. He or she might find potential new roles confirmed in such experiences as Receiving Informal or Formal Recognition or Representing the Organization. Relational partners thus experience a push-pull dynamic in the Alienation phase of relational transition.

Bullis and Bach are correct, I believe, to interpret their results in terms of confirmation and disconfirmation. All three of those most influential positive turning points (Receiving Informal or Formal Recognition and Representing the Organization), and others they reported as well, involved confirmation or responses that "acknowledge the agency of the human being" (1989, pp. 286–87). To receive a confirming response is to be acknowledged, recognized, and endorsed by another. Communication that is confirming is "growthful, productive, effective, functional, or 'therapeutic'" (Cissna & Sieburg, 1982, p. 256).

Here then is the magnet at work in the Alienation phase of relational transition. Confirmation, or the hope for it, pulls the relational partner toward the re-formation of role-taking in the relationship. Who does not seek confirmation in personal and organizational relationships? And who does not flee disconfirmation? In parallel manner, both of those most influential negative turning points reported by Bullis and Bach's respondents involved disconfirmation. Alienation was associated with "a loss of organizational identification" (1989, p. 284). Getting Away was occasioned by strong desires to be somewhere else than the department and with someone else than those in the department. My interpretation is that the graduate students wanted to get away because they were not receiving the kind of "acknowledgment, recognition, and endorsement" they desired.

Although the five kinds of turning points analyzed above were the most intense in the short term, none of them was associated with organizational identification at the end of the eight-month period. Long-term effects were found to reside with two other turning point types. Those respondents who reported Socializing with members of the department on at least one occasion during the time period reported higher levels of organizational identification after eight months than those who did not; conversely, those who reported at least one instance of Disappointment during the period reported lower levels of organizational identification after eight months than those who did not.

Socializing clearly entailed confirmation. Graduate students who felt more closely identified with the department by the end of the academic year were the ones who had engaged in informal conversation with other graduate students or faculty members outside class, had shared jokes, stories, or gossip, and had gone to the department picnic. Disappointment, contrariwise, entailed disconfirmation and took the form of such conflicts as disagreement on a departmental emphasis (for example, on presenting convention papers) or disagreement with a professor's research philosophy or frustration with faculty inaccessibility. All these circumstances denied students the opportunity to enact the roles they desired. For example, he or she may have wanted to be one who does not present convention papers or one who agrees with the professor or one who has easy access to the faculty — all impossible. Under the circumstances, recognition, acknowledgment, and endorsement for the graduate student's desired role-identity would be difficult, if not impossible, to obtain. Disconfirmation would result. So here again, this time in the long term, the two sides of confirmation and disconfirmation give form to the Alienation phase of the structural helical model of relational transition.

The operation of the role-taking that issues from role-action in the Alienation phase plus the dual nature of the phase are concretized in

FIGURE 7.2 — Turning Point Types, as Confirming or Disconfirming: Their Long-Term and Short-Term Effects, in Romantic and Organizational Relationships

	Long-Term Effects		Short Term-Effects	
Confirming Responses	Romantic Exclusivity	Organizational Socializing	Romantic Serious Commitment Making-Up Get-to-Know Passion	Organizational Recognition, Informal and Formal Representing the Organization
Disconfirming Responses	Disengagement	Disappointing	Disengagement	Alienation Getting Away

Source: Adapted from Baxter and Bullis, 1986; Bullis and Bach, 1990.

turning point analysis. Figure 7.2 summarizes the results of these two important studies of turning points. The interpretation is in terms of the confirming and disconfirming effects of certain kinds of turning points, their occurrence in romantic or organizational relationships, and their long- versus short-term effects. Further, I would argue that confirming responses facilitate the a priori conditions of role-action.

BENIGN ALIENATION

The Alienation phase of relational transition is a cul-de-sac of transformation. When a relational partner enters this phase, he or she is fleeing one-form-of-the-relationship and pursuing another-form-of-the-relationship, as yet undefined. The basis of the Alienation phase is the primordial activity of role-action. When role-action is interrupted, Alienation results; that is, the configuration of role-taking that had in the past defined the relationship becomes impossible for the members to perform in the present. The Assumption of Release, when in place, allows one to abandon a role that had once been assumed. That is the case as a relationship enters the Alienation phase. A relational partner is laying aside a role that has been central to the relationship-as-it-has-been-defined. Further, the Assumption of Recourse, when operative, permits one to take up a role again, having once put it aside. But here is the chief marker of the Alienation phase, the relational partner's unwillingness or inability to reassume that role he or she is now rejecting, that role that had been necessary to the earlier-form-of-the-relationship. With the attenuation of role-action, Alienation results. The earlier relationship, as defined by the past configuration of roles, ceases to be possible.

The Alienation phase of relational transition is characterized by a dual nature. First, it has an internal source and an external source. Internally, a relational partner may decide he or she cannot or will not take up again an earlier role. Role-action is thus rendered nonfunctional by attenuating the Assumption of Recourse. Externally, the practical force of the social situation may require a relational partner to continue in an unwanted role. Here, role-action is made inoperative by interrupting the Assumption of Release. Whether the emphasis is on the internal or the external, Alienation from one's relationship is occasioned by a discontinuity between one's role and one's desired role.

Second, the relationship that is entering the Alienation phase exerts a push-pull force upon the relational partner. The pull is toward more, or the prospect of more, confirming responses; and the push is away from disconfirming responses. Confirming responses acknowledge, recognize, endorse, and, thus, permit the relational partner to fulfill his or her desired role-identity; disconfirming responses deny the relational partner this opportunity, blocking role-action.

CASES IN ALIENATION

With episode 7 Helen's role-action has been effectively thwarted (Figure 2.2). She is stuck in the undesirable role of unsuccessful pupil (Assumption of Release), and she is prevented from occupying the role of successful pupil, which she desires (Assumption of Recourse). Perhaps Anne Sullivan sensed this, for she took Helen to the well house ostensibly for a change of scenery. Affect had turned extremely negative, as evidenced by Helen breaking the doll in anger; Helen seemed to desire only distance from her teacher (intimacy); and time, it seemed, was standing still. Helen had clearly had her fill of disconfirming messages. Anne Sullivan seemed to be trying to position Helen for some confirming messages by the change of venue to the well house.

The Alienation phase commenced for Diane with episode 8, when she told John she did not want to marry him, and lasted through episode 11 (Figure 2.4). Although she had felt increasingly trapped once John "announced" they would be married, his threatening and arguing in E 9 and E 10 were explicit efforts to coerce her into marriage. Thus her role-action was interrupted: she was prevented for a time from laying aside an undesirable role (fiancee: Assumption of Release) as well as prevented from taking up a desired role (girlfriend with no marriage plans, or, later, just a friend: Assumption of Power).

During the Alienation phase Diane's desire for intimacy dropped to near zero. Her feelings toward John and marriage soured (affect), and she realized that she and John shared conflicting time orientations, she thinking of marriage in a distant and ill-defined future and he thinking of marriage as imminent. Time was a central issue in Alienation for Diane. In addition, Diane had her fill of disconfirming messages during Alienation. In E 11 and E 12 she began to reassess her past actions and understand how she was in part responsible for those disconfirming messages, and she began to develop a vision of the future that would provide her with confirming messages.

Alienation was simpler for Howard and Judy. They jointly decided on a trial separation (Figure 2.5). Alienation was a culmination of their movement through Disintegration. Judy would not be happy with or for Howard in their new venture in Raleigh, thus shutting off for him a role he wanted to take up (supported husband: Assumption of Power).

Likewise, Howard could or would not empathize with Judy in her sadness over moving, thus thwarting her desired role (affirmed wife: Assumption of Power). In the Alienation phase their intimacy was at its lowest ebb, and their dislike for each other at its peak (affect). The attention of both was riveted to the present (rather than she to the past and he to the future), and the present had ground to a halt in the oppressive sameness of daily verbal battles.

CONCLUSION

The structural helical model is governed by two meta-dialectics. The first is Alienation-Security. Movement between these dialectical poles marks out a part of the social domain of personal relationships.

Alienation is conceived as a condition in which role-action is attenuated, that is, a condition in which one is prevented from taking up a role one desires or from laying aside a role one dislikes (Natanson, 1966). The external and internal aspects of role-action are conceived in terms of Wallace's (1956a) "maze" (situation) and "way" (skill).

During the Alienation phase of the structural helical model, relationships begin to be re-formed. Relational partners experience turning points (Baxter & Bullis, 1986). In general, a turning point directs relational partners toward confirming responses, and the strength of a turning point depends upon the partners' agreement on its type and their amount of talk about it.

The Alienation phase is a cul-de-sac of transformation with benign effects: the internal and external aspects of role-action are sorted, and relational partners pursue confirming responses and flee disconfirming responses.

8

Relationship Resynthesis:
HOMO RELATIO

> Man is a knot, a web, a mesh into which relationships are tied. Only those relationships matter.
>
> Antoine de Saint-Exupery
> *Flight to Arras*

Despite their wide use, the words "relate," "relation," and "relationship" are difficult to define. We speak in personal terms. One is said to be "in a relationship," we hear someone say, "I just can't relate to her [or him or that]," or someone inquires into the state of your relationship with your spouse or parent or client. We also use the term in the most impersonal of contexts. It may be asked, "How do you see the budget deficit in relation to the tax code?" or "How do international oil supplies relate to economic development in the third world?" In ordinary conversation, the word often substitutes for cause or effect, correlation or antecedent conditions, quality of association, or degree of understanding.

The study of communication in personal relationships, however, calls for a rather more focused view of the terms. For "relation," *The Oxford English Dictionary* gives, "The position which one person holds with respect to another on account of some social or other connexion between them; the particular mode in which persons are mutually connected by circumstances." For the plural, "relations," it records, "The aggregate of the connexions or modes of connexion, by which one person is brought into touch with another or with society in general" (Simpson & Weiner, 1989, p. 551). *The Oxford Dictionary of English Etymology* adds, for "relate," the verb form, "bring into connexion or comparison" (Onions, 1966, p. 753). *The Barnhart Dictionary of Etymology* reports that "relate" is borrowed, through Middle French, from the Latin *"relatus,* a form serving as the past participle of *referre* to tell of, to refer . . . [hence, as "relation"] a bringing back, restoring, a report, narration, association, reference" (Barnhart, 1988, p. 906).

Here is a remarkable congruence between usage and etymology, on the one hand, and scholarship, on the other. The literature of personal relations indicates that the concern of most current work is with "connexion." How persons come to be connected in relationships, how those connections are maintained and changed, how society at large affects those connections, how relational partners understand their connections, and how talk enters into these processes at all points are questions that occupy investigators.

Moreover, the implications of these definitions also square with the new territory of relationship study opened by an emphasis on the concept of relational transition and the structural helical model supporting it. First, someone, a relational partner or an observer, compares the members of the relationship. Second, a difference between the members is observed (implied by the phrase, "position . . . [of] one . . . with respect to another.") Third, the connection can come in various modes (for example, in various degrees of closeness); and, fourth, the connection has its origin in the individuals or in circumstances (in the need to associate or in events that increase uncertainty). Finally, the etymological roots found in *relatus* and *referre* suggest that a relationship is instantiated by an act of declaring connection to one's partner or reporting the same to a third party. From this perspective, talk is at the center of personal relationships: with talk one participates in human connections by retrieving them from memory and restoring them to the present. As Berger and Kellner observed, "It is proper to view the individual's relationship with his significant others as an ongoing conversation" (1964, p. 4).

In the Resynthesis phase, a relationship is what is being remade. Hence, what we mean by the word "relationship" is of central import to this inquiry. The desire for a relationship that works right is what prompts a relational partner to move out of Alienation through Resynthesis and back to Security. In Resynthesis, a unique amalgam of connecting-talk-across-difference is being reformulated.

Resynthesis, moreover, forms one pole of a second meta-dialectic along with Disintegration. It, along with the meta-dialectic Security-Alienation, marks out the field of play of personal relationships. The social domain of personal relationships is defined by their helical movement among these four archetypal relational positions. In Disintegration accumulating uncertainties yield disassociation of relational partners. In Resynthesis a relational partner forms a view of what kind of association he or she wants (in view of the malfunction of the former version of association) and takes actions to secure it. In this way Disintegration and Resynthesis are contradictory or oppositional poles. Tension created by these opposing processes pushes and pulls relationships around the helix, thus changing them. Moreover, the polarities are interdependent in that the one is defined in terms of what the other is not, and relational partners depend upon experience of the one to understand their experience of the other.

ORIGINS OF RESYNTHESIS

In the Resynthesis phase of relational transition, relationship is central. In particular, the building of a (new) relationship is uppermost in the mind of one or both relationship partners. "In its most vital, impassioned phase, the interpersonal orientation transmutes individual experience. . . . It not only constructs a new reality, but it rewrites memory. . . . A new self is discovered or liberated through the relationship, and the world too may bear a different visage" (Raush, 1977a, p. 172). The urgency that characterizes this phase has a rather negative source. One cannot remain for long in the barrenness of the Alienation phase. Recall that in that phase, one has become alienated from the relationship-as-it-had-been-defined. Role-action has been attenuated. One can neither put down an unsatisfactory role nor take up a more satisfactory one, at least not within the relationship-as-it-currently-exists. Thus uncertainty about the relationship-as-it-might-exist is the chief concern of a relational partner. A "new reality" and a "new self" are what he or she most wants.

Berger (1988) is correct, I believe, to reinterpret various social psychological theories in terms of uncertainty reduction. As he reminds us, uncertainty reduction (Berger & Calabrese, 1975) includes the ability to explain as well as to predict the actions of the other. Thus, whether one thinks in terms of social comparison, cognitive consistency, personal constructs, or attribution theory, each perspective is an effort to understand how persons explain the actions of others and, therefore, reduce their uncertainty about them. Festinger (1954), noting his experimental evidence that persons want to know how their abilities and opinions compare with those of others, hypothesized a human drive to seek comparison with others. Berger's (1988) interpretation is that engaging in such comparisons brings about a desired reduction in uncertainty. Heider concluded that "An analysis of the phenomenal properties of balance and imbalance . . . supports the generalization that states of balance tend to be preferred over disharmony" (1958, p. 204). An unbalanced relationship with another (for example, when my enemy's friend is also my friend) raises uncertainties about the other's predispositions and actions. Seeking balance would redress uncertainty. Kelly rejected traditional views of humanity (man-the-biological-organism and man-the-lucky-guy [sic]) in favor of man-the-scientist [sic]. Thus he viewed ordinary persons as making hypotheses about the actions of others, gathering data to test them, and evaluating the results. Kelly's ordinary person does not merely react to the environment but also, like the scientist, wants to know: "he can represent his environment, he can place alternative constructions upon it and, indeed, do something about it if it doesn't suit him" (1963, p. 8).

Berger highlighted the centrality of uncertainty reduction to relationships when he surmised, "it is possible to view relationships as information exchange systems that can survive only if their subsystems can maintain requisite coordination through uncertainty reduction" (1988, p. 240). But reasons other than the discomfort of uncertainty make one urgently struggle out of the slough of relationship alienation. To form personal relationships is both normal and natural to humans. Yet, as Bochner has observed, "The inclination to form amiable bonds with members of the same species is one of the most mysterious characteristics of human life" (1984, pp. 544–45).

Conventionally, he observed, there are four perspectives on this puzzle. First, some assert that bonding is instinctual. Lorenz (1966) has argued that aggression against our own species is an innate characteristic that is more fundamental than bonding. Although causal links are inconclusive, instinctivists have further observed that *homo sapiens* would have died out long ago without personalized bonds to thwart our innate aggressiveness. In addition, Freud saw "interpersonal bonding as counterpart and opponent of aggression" (Bochner, 1984, p. 545).

Second, there is the safety and security argument for human association. Persons who are socially integrated live longer than those who are socially isolated. Even if people do not consciously establish social relations in order to lengthen their lives, the effects are the same: mortality rates are consistently higher among the unmarried than among the married (Bochner, 1984). Moreover, in numerous studies, the unmarried and more socially isolated have shown higher rates of tuberculosis, accidents, and psychiatric disorders than more socially integrated persons (House, Landis, & Umberson, 1988).

Third, there is the infant-practice argument. As Eibl-Eibesfeldt (1970) has observed, "The human child first acquires the capacity to love another through love for its mother" (quoted in Bochner, 1984, p. 546). Children deprived of such mother-contact or deprived of some form of mothering have been found to have difficulty managing personal relationships later in life.

Finally, there is the transcendence argument. Proponents of this position hold that one finds confirmation for the self and meaningfulness for existence in relationships with other persons. Thus one is able to go beyond the finiteness of human existence. Reflecting Buber's (1955) thinking, Bochner concludes, "a dialogue between I and Thou . . . validates inner conviction and heightens human meaning" (1984, p. 546). Becker (1973), however, has called our attention to the fact that escape into freedom is impossible, for even personal relationships, to which one may gravitate for their liberating and affirming nature, have their own rules of conduct and ties of commitment.

Recall that Natanson (1966) referred to the attenuation of role-action as the deformation of sociality. In contrast, relationship Resynthesis may be seen as the reformation (re-formation) of sociality. The project of building or rebuilding a relationship during the phase of Resynthesis restores the possibility of genuine role-action and, thereby, the possibility of unfettered social action. The origins of Resynthesis are found in a flight from uncertainty, in a playing out of instinctive proclivities, in a search for security, in an imitation of nurturing actions, or in a desire for existential meaningfulness.

THE PROCESS OF RESYNTHESIS

Resynthesis may take either of two forms. On the one hand, it may entail redefinition of a relationship in order to maintain it in the face of change. Relying upon conceptualizations of Altman, Vinsel, and Brown (1981), Baxter and Dindia observed that, when events push a satisfying relationship toward change, "The issue for relationship parties . . . is how to sustain the essential features of their relationship's identity" (1990, p. 188), including agreement and understanding on roles and rules. On the other hand, Resynthesis may involve transformation of a relationship in which its essential or identifying features are altered. McCall and Simmons offer this description.

A lasting interpersonal relationship of any degree of intimacy must change apace with the changing of its members. The contents of the interrelated personas change many times over as the couple progresses, for example, from young lovers, to fiancees, to young marrieds, to young parents, to grandparents, and to life companions. The relationship must undergo *metamorphosis* at each major turning point in the personal career of each participant. If it does not or cannot, it will fade away or be destroyed (1978, p. 198).

These two forms of Resynthesis, redefinition and transformation, differ by degree more than by kind. The former is a strategic adaptation intended to preserve the relationship, and the latter is accepted, if not welcomed, as a natural part of relationship evolution.

Agreement on relationship definition plays an important role in the process of relationship Resynthesis. Kingsbury and Minda (1988) had a student population of romantically involved couples classify their personal relationships as either expected commitment state (ECS), expected maintenance state (EMS), or expected termination state (ETS), depending on how they saw the future of their relationships. In addition, participants indicated their desired versus their perceived kind of relationship they were involved in: casual acquaintance, good friends, very close friends, or seriously considering marriage. ECS couples on the average produced a discrepancy of only 0.2 between their expected and their desired relationship definitions; EMS couples had a discrepancy of −0.2; and ETS couples, −2.2. The chance probability of these differences was less than 0.01. Relational partners disagreed on the definitions of their relationships depending upon the predictions they posed for the outcomes of their relationships. Those who expected more commitment to the relationship in the near future showed the most agreement between their relational definitions; those who expected merely to maintain their relationship in the near future showed less agreement; and those relational partners who expected their romantic relationships to soon end reported the least agreement about the definition of their relationship.

Thus agreement on relational definitions may be expected to play a role in the process of relationship Resynthesis. Moreover, Kingsbury and Minda's (1988) relational partners did not report difficulty thinking of their relationships in terms of relational definitions (for example, ECS or EMS) or in terms of relational redefinitions (that is, expectations for the future of their relationships).

Relationship Resynthesis also involves adaptive responses to the disjunction between the individual and his or her personal relationships that Raush (1981) cited as central to understanding communication. Baxter (1988, 1990) has proposed four alternative strategies available to relational partners for dealing with fundamental dialectical contradictions (autonomy and connection; predictability and novelty; and openness and closedness). Each dialectic captures a portion of the individual-relationship disjunction, referred to above. So focusing on how we deal with dialectical oppositions positions this inquiry at the central issue of interpersonal communication.

One strategy is Reframing, a cognitive process "characterized by a perceptual transformation of the elements [of a dialectical opposition] along different dimensions of meaning such that the two contrasts are no longer regarded as opposites" (Baxter, 1990, p. 73). A member of a couple is using the strategy of Reframing if, for example, his "saying off-the-wall-things" (novelty) comes to be taken by her as normal or ordinary (predictable). Thus his novel verbal behavior is reinterpreted as, for example, falling on an openness-closedness dialectic, with the off-the-wall-sayings seen as a form of closedness.

But Reframing is not a frequently chosen means of coping with dialectical oppositions. In Baxter's (1990) sample of 471 occasions in which relational partners made such strategy selections, only 4.7 percent were Reframing. Each of her subjects reported confronting an average of 12.2 contradiction types that they were obliged to resolve during their relationships. Thus only one incident of Reframing occurred in about every two relationships (4.7 percent of 12.2 = .57) during the period of the study. In contrast, the most frequently chosen strategy for resolving contradictions, across all three kinds of dialectical oppositions, was Separation. When a relational partner practices Separation, he or she denies the interdependence of the two opposite poles. For example, autonomy and connection can be dealt with by "taking turns." Rather than arguing over whether to take separate or joint vacations, a couple could decide to do both: you get your turn to take a together trip; then I get my turn to take a separate trip.

The next most frequently chosen strategy was Selection. Here relational partners simply choose one pole of the dialectic over the other, thus denying the other pole its influence. In confronting the openness-closedness contradiction, the partner who favors a relatively lower level of self-disclosure than the other may decide to change and adopt the style of the other, choosing openness over closedness. Thus the contradiction is defused. Neutralization is the fourth strategy Baxter (1990) has proposed that persons use for dealing with dialectical oppositions. A couple is using this approach when they choose neither pole of the opposition (in contrast to Selection) but, rather, try to compromise and have it both ways — somewhat. Partners may deny that the pull between the opposing sides of the contradiction is very strong, or they may be less than candid with each other or with others regarding the strength of the contradiction.

Here then is a better way to conceive of relationship Resynthesis, better than redefinition and better than transformation. It is this: when one or both relational partners make a choice that resolves a dialectical opposition, through Separation, Selection, Neutralization, or Reframing, they are said to be in the Resynthesis phase of relational transition. It is better in that oppositional resolution can be clearly depicted and, as Baxter (1990) has shown, can be operationalized and tested in rather straightforward fashion.

Not just Reframing, as asserted by Baxter, but, I would argue, all four of the strategies for dealing with dialectical contradictions involve "perceptual transformation of the elements along different dimensions of meaning such that the two contrasts are no longer regarded as opposites" (1990, p. 73). Relational Resynthesis is just this process of transformation. Selection of one pole of a contradiction over the other eliminates the available alternative on a given topic, and the dialectic disappears. So, too, for Separation. Denying the interdependence of the poles causes them, by definition, to cease functioning dialectically in the relevant domain. The Neutralization strategy disassociates the opposing poles by leaving them in place (unlike Selection and Separation) while relational partners deny their efficacy. Dynamism disappears. Relationship Resynthesis is the choice making relational partners engage in to resolve dialectical oppositions thrust upon them in the Alienation phase. The accumulation of such choice making inevitably changes the relationship. A different relationship is created or synthesized.

THE PROMPTINGS OF RESYNTHESIS

In the phase of relationship Alienation, role-action is interrupted. One's intentionality of role-taking is constricted such that less desired roles cannot be put aside and more desired roles cannot be taken up. Therefore one would expect this to be a period when dialectical contradictions accumulate, accompanied by a growing demand for decisions to resolve them.

From a dialectical perspective, even in the Security phase of relational transition, relational partners are faced with the dilemma of autonomy and connection with its accompanying attributes of contradiction, interdependence, and dynamism. However, in the Alienation phase the dialectical stress would be enhanced. One may be in an undesirable role that cannot be laid down (Assumption of Release), or one is prevented from taking up a desired role (Assumption of Power). One's autonomy, therefore, is diminished in favor of a connection not of one's own choosing, and one's desired connection is prevented by a thwarted autonomy.

One would also expect relationship Alienation to be a period of increased messages of disconfirmation. If a relational partner is trapped and merely going through the motions of a relationship and, further, wishes to occupy a different role vis-à-vis the other (for example, colleague-only versus colleague-friend), then his or her behavior will likely begin to elicit disconfirming messages. Moreover, one would also be expected to seek confirming messages vis-à-vis the desired relationship.

Cissna and Sieburg (1982) have proposed four dimensions of confirming messages: they recognize the existence of the other, acknowledge affiliation with the other, affirm the worth of the other, and endorse the validity of the other's experience. For research purposes, these dimensions have been operationalized as certain types of communication behaviors, and they have been shown to correlate with feelings of being confirmed. Cissna and Keating (1979) have shown that ratings of empathy, respect, and genuineness, combined into a single measure of "facilitative communication," correlated significantly with subjects' feelings of being confirmed ($r = .38$, $p < .001$). Moreover, female subjects' feelings of being confirmed were significantly correlated with males' display of facilitative communication ($r = .56$, $p < .001$) and males' level of self-disclosure ($r = .31$, $p < .05$). No significant correlations were found regarding male feelings of being confirmed in conversation with female subjects. Presumably this was a novelty response. The facilitative communication of usually more affiliative females was not noticed by male subjects, but the facilitative communication of usually less affiliative males was noticed by female subjects. The latter, thus, had more information value than the former.

A person in the phase of Alienation, where role-action has been crippled, is in a position to receive a steady diet of disconfirming messages, for example, lower empathy, respect, and genuineness than in a circumstance where role-action is intact. By the same token, he or she is expected also to produce more than normal disconfirming messages — in response to the messages being received. In the phase of Alienation, a relational partner is likely to be ignored (existence), left alone (affiliation), disregarded (worth), and routinely corrected (endorsement). A guiding presumption of this section is that one will seek confirming messages and avoid disconfirming messages. One is prompted to build a relationship in which his or her own actions will elicit from the other attention, appreciation of one's worth, the value of one's opinions, and careful attention to their relationship.

A desire, even need, for confirmation pulls the relational partner out of Alienation through Resynthesis and into the Security phase of relational transition. Resynthesis is the phase of reconstructing connections with the other that have been altered by passing through the Disintegration and Alienation phases. As noted above, persons' tendencies to associate with others may be instinctual or for security or due to modeling or to achieve meaningful existence. In any case, the result of such human association is an increase in the likelihood of receiving confirming messages from others. Watzlawick, Beavin, and Jackson have noted the centrality of confirmation to human communication:

> without this self-confirming effect human communication would hardly have evolved beyond the very limited boundaries of the interchanges indispensable for protection and survival; there would be no reason for communication for the mere sake of communication. . . . man has to communicate with others for the sake of his own awareness of self (1967, pp. 84–85).

Cissna and Sieburg (1982) point to Buber (1957) and Laing (1961) as progenitors of our concern for confirmation in personal relationships. However, the Palo Alto Group and the Symbolic Interactionist School have provided the bulk of the theoretical underpinnings. Watzlawick, Beavin, and Jackson (1967) made the distinction between the content and relationship levels of communication. Their contention that every communicative exchange contains messages on both these levels has focused attention of researchers on the means by which persons indicate the kind of relationship they have or want to have with others and the effects of these messages. Apart from the semantic meaning of the words uttered, a relational partner, with his or her tone of voice, facial expression, and gesture may demand or propose a certain kind of relationship with the other. Depending on their specific manifestation, these nonverbal messages could be seen as disconfirming or confirming. But relational messages are not limited to the nonverbal domain. For example, a relational partner's attempt to take control of decision making in a group may be countered by a statement from the other partner who resists that attempt or asserts his or her own control. The former would probably interpret the response as a disconfirming message from the latter.

Moreover, relational messages may also reside in the patterns of interactions between relational partners. Recall the study by Fisher and Drecksel (1983) that sampled the talk between randomly assigned pairs of persons in simulated submarine living conditions. A cyclical pattern of interactions was observed in which a series of highly competitive responses between pairs was followed by a series of much less competitive responses, and so on through several cycles. This would constitute a series of relatively disconfirming messages exchanged followed by a series of relatively more confirming exchanges.

Despite the great variety of means by which relational messages may be conveyed, researchers have identified a limited number of types. Some of them may be interpreted as messages of confirmation or disconfirmation. Consider the dimensions of relational meaning espoused by Millar and Rogers (1987): control, trust, and intimacy. Based on definitions given by Cissna and Sieburg (1982), we may expect that messages of high control, low trust, and low intimacy will be interpreted as disconfirming and that messages conveying low levels of control and high levels of trust and intimacy will be taken to be confirming.

The Symbolic Interactionist School has also influenced the concern of personal relationship researchers for the issues of confirmation and disconfirmation. An early source of such thinking was the work of Dance and Larson (1972). They observed that "Speech communication plays an important part in confirming identity. Through the mechanisms of role taking and the significant symbol, speech communication is constantly involved in the individual's confirmation of self. Mead says, 'selves can only exist in definite relationship to other selves'" (1972, p. 113). More specifically, Cushman and Cahn have defined interpersonal communication as "the regulation of consensus in regard to the development, presentation, and validation of individual self-concepts" (1985, p. 19).

Not only is the self-concept formed in interaction with others, not only does it evolve as a result of that process, but also the self-concept serves as a staging area from which the individual confronts and acts upon the world. As Blumer has observed,

> With the mechanism of self-interaction [the self-concept] the human being ceases to be a responding organism whose behavior is a product of what plays upon him from the outside, the inside or both. Instead, he acts towards his world, interpreting what confronts him and organizing his action on the basis of the interpretations (1966, p. 536).

Thus in interpersonal communication we produce confirming and disconfirming messages directed toward others as well as receive such messages from others. The self-concept will develop as a result of the quality of confirming and disconfirming messages one receives; and one will dispense confirming and disconfirming messages to others based upon one's sense of self.

Dance and Larson (1972, pp. 141–43) have proposed a system of classifying messages as confirming or disconfirming that continues to be useful (Trenholm & Jensen, 1988). Based upon Sieburg's (1969) work, the scheme is summarized in Figure 8.1. It contains five kinds of confirming messages and seven types of disconfirming messages.

Confirming and disconfirming messages occur in all interpersonal contexts. Friendship and marriage are two kinds of personal relationships that have received much attention from researchers. In Wright's theory of friendship, he argued against social exchange theory as espoused by Thibaut and Kelley (1959). The economic analogy, he averred, "does not do justice to the depth, the personal involvement, or the continuity of many interpersonal relationships" (Wright, 1978, p. 198). Investing is a more accurate analogy to personal relationships than purchasing, he contended, for it entails greater personal involvement and continuity, and the return is likely to be less clear and immediate (Wright, 1989). Rather than considering relationship rewards to be like the products or services

FIGURE 8.1 — Confirming and Disconfirming Messages

Confirming Messages
1. Direct acknowledgment response — acknowledges and responds directly
2. Agreement response — agrees with the content uttered by the other
3. Supportive response — expresses understanding and reassurance of the other
4. Clarifying response — inquires of the other more information on his or her ideas or feelings
5. Disclosure response — shares positive feelings toward the other's ideas

Disconfirming Messages
1. Impervious response — fails to acknowledge the other; ignores or disregards
2. Interrupting response — cuts the other short or talks over
3. Irrelevant response — disregards topic relevance
4. Tangential response — acknowledgment of other followed by abrupt topic shift
5. Impersonal response — fails to relinquish the floor; pontificates
6. Incoherent response — rambles, repeats, rephrases
7. Incongruous response — contradicts the verbal messages with the nonverbal

Source: Adapted from Dance and Larson, 1972, pp. 141–43.

one receives in return for legal tender, they should be seen as periodic returns (dividends received) on one's investment. "The dividend takes the form of one or more of the following global, self-referent rewards: an enhanced sense of individuality, facilitated self-affirmation, facilitated self-evaluation, facilitated self-growth" (Wright, 1978, p. 199).

The role of confirming and disconfirming messages is thus assigned a central place in the development of friendship. In addition, all four of the direct rewards of friendship proposed by Wright (1978) entailed confirming messages: utility value (when one expends time and resources to help the other meet needs and goals), affirmation value (when one recognizes the other's important and valued self-attributes), support value (when one supports and encourages the other to see himself or herself as competent and worthwhile), and stimulation value (when someone elaborates on or expands upon the other's knowledge or ideas). A person who provided one with these kinds of confirming messages would be, in Wright's (1978) view, providing the kind of return on the investment that would tend to facilitate the growth and development of the friendship.

Marriage is another interpersonal context in which confirming and disconfirming messages are central. In particular this is the case with relations between former spouses. Routine and memory and network ties combine to prevent most marriages from breaking off cleanly. Divorce, therefore, is often an occasion of transition and redefinition of the relationship (Wilmot, 1987). Recent research suggests that postmarital relationships are not, as a rule, harmonious, that problems indigenous to the marriage often get extended into the postdivorce period, and that the divorce per se may produce its own relationship problems (Ambert, 1988).

Even with these caveats, examination of a harmonious postdivorce relationship will shed additional light on the role of confirming and disconfirming messages in the phase of relationship Resynthesis. According to Masheter and Harris in their case study of an amiable postdivorce relationship, there is a need for studies that "account for the ways in which interacting partners move between perceived opposites or reorganize perceived opposites" (1986, pp. 178–79). Baxter's (1990) analysis of relational partners' response strategies to dialectical oppositions is a promising start. She proposed four options for resolving these contradictions — Selection, Separation, Neutralization, and Reframing — reviewed above. However, there is another view, a concern for the effects of choosing one option over the other. Some choices, for example, may be seen by the other as confirming messages whereas other choices may be seen as disconfirming.

Nicky and Steve Randall, the subjects of Masheter and Harris's case study were first interviewed separately then were guided through jointly reconstructing "a scene, complete with lines of dialogue, which represent[ed] a recurring pattern in their relationship" (1986, p. 180). One scene was to come from the past when they were married and considering divorce, one scene from the present, representing their postdivorce relationship, and one scene from the future, representing how they would resolve a conflict. Each scene was analyzed by determining, for each speaking turn, their interpretations of their own and the other's intentions and, their judgment of each turn's effectiveness.

The individual interviews indicated that both their expectations for marriage were marked by behaviors designed to seek confirmation from others. On the one hand, Nicky looked for chances for them to do things as a couple. "Such opportunities, Nicky imagined, would demonstrate to herself and others that she and Steve had a successful marriage and that she was successful as a wife and person" (Masheter & Harris, 1986, p. 181). Steve, on the other hand, "needed [Nicky's] endorsement for his time spent in graduate studies. Such endorsement would represent to himself and others that he and Nicky had a good marriage" (Masheter & Harris, 1986, p. 182). Both sought confirmation from persons outside the marriage, and neither provided confirmation to the other.

In the dialogue of the past scene, Nicky happily reported that a couple, friends of theirs, had invited them over, to which Steve responded, "Oh, yeah?" Steve interpreted her attempt to have them go out as disconfirming of his need to get his work done (Dance & Larson's [1972] Irrelevant response [to Steve, the "topic" was "work"]; Cissna & Sieburg's [1982] Indifferent response). Nicky likewise interpreted Steve's "Oh, yeah?" as disconfirming, "Rejection of me," as she put it (Cissna & Sieburg's [1982] Disqualifying response; Dance & Larson's [1972] Impervious response), and, further, that his response was effective at doing that.

Here is an example of the debilitating effects of interrupted role-action. Nicky was in a role she disliked but which she felt compelled to sustain (Assumption of Release), and Steve desired a role he could not take up (Assumption of Power), given the existing arrangement.

> Steve came to see himself as being unable to maintain the separateness he wanted, . . . Nicky described her expression of anger as effective yet "childish and immature"; . . . being able to carry off such undesirable acts so effectively (e.g., rejecting and inducing guilt) was as demoralizing as being unable effectively to carry off desired acts (e.g., going out together or relaxing at home) (Masheter & Harris, 1986, p. 183).

Neither Steve nor Nicky would or could confirm the other's desired roles, and both extended disconfirming messages to the other regarding their present roles. Thus, both the Assumptions of Power and of Release were blocked by their effective deployment of disconfirming messages. This circumstance, occurring in the Alienation phase of relational transition, propelled the relationship into the Resynthesis phase.

In the dialogue of the present scene, Nicky excitedly tells Steve of a study of postdivorce friendships and invites him to join her. He responds, "That sounds great!" Steve interprets her invitation as a confirming message, that is, she wants to know how their relationship is faring by asking him to participate with her (Dance & Larson's [1972] direct acknowledgment and Disclosure responses; Cissna & Sieburg's [1982] Recognition of affiliation and worth). Nicky interprets his response as a strongly confirming message, an expression of his caring for her (Cissna & Sieburg's [1982] Affiliation and worth; Dance & Larson's [1972] Supportive and Disclosure responses). Both also viewed their statements as being effective in their confirming.

It would appear that Nicky and Steve, in this instance, dealt with the dialectical opposition of autonomy and connection that had plagued their marriage by Separating (Baxter, 1990) the two. Having devised a mutually satisfactory "separate togetherness" they now facilitate, rather than interrupt, role-action. They are now in a position effectively to confirm each other's desired roles. As such, the redefinition of their relationship is an archetypal example of movement through the Resynthesis phase of the structural helical model of relational transition. Whether the outcome of a relational transition is positive or negative, the route the relational partners have traveled has been around the curve of the helix from Security to Disintegration through Alienation and Resynthesis then back to (a new version of) Security.

From the perspective of the helical model of relational transition, Steve and Nicky's past scene would have taken place in the Alienation phase. There an increase of disconfirming messages served to interrupt role-action. The result is presumed to be a desire to move to redefine the relationship in such a way as to increase confirming messages and decrease disconfirming messages. The solution is movement through the Resynthesis phase, where one builds just such a relationship.

In contrast, the present scene in Nicky and Steve's case would have taken place in the Security phase. There the relational partners are receiving an optimal level of confirming messages, and role-action is unencumbered. The accomplishment of this redefined relationship was the work of the Resynthesis phase. The prospect of removing oneself from a disproportionately high level of disconfirming messages and moving into a region of optimally high confirming messages is presumed to be the force behind movement of relational partners around this last curve of the helix and into the Security phase.

CASES IN RESYNTHESIS

The Resynthesis phase of Helen Keller's relationship with Anne Sullivan occupied episodes 8–12 (Figure 2.2). With their linguistic breakthrough, suddenly the role of successful pupil reopened to her (Assumption of Recourse). Moreover, the remorse she reported in E 12 suggests that the role of cooperative pupil would also reopen to her. Role-action was unblocked, thus permitting a reshaping of her relationship with her teacher. Affect was positive, for Helen was delighted with her discovery of language, but it was also negatively directed toward herself in her regret for her angry outburst at Miss Sullivan. Intimacy was of a close nature as they eagerly identified and named objects in and around the well house. And Helen hoped it would remain so in spite of her breaking the doll. The dialectic of time was equally complicated. Both Helen and her teacher were clearly focused on the present in and around the well house. However, Helen's remorse was based on a recollection from the past that she made present in her remembering and wondering what effects it would have on her future relationship with Anne Sullivan. The dialectical dimension of intimacy that had come to a head in Alienation was resolved (in Resynthesis) by Helen's selecting connection over autonomy.

Diane's relationship with John went through Resynthesis in episodes 11–13 (Figure 2.4). Her friend's question and her confrontation of John with the truth sealed her resolve to lay down the role that she had been forced to enact, that of fiancee (Assumption of Release). In doing so, she remained negatively disposed toward John and toward immediate marriage (affect). Her resolution to free herself of John's wishes suggests a low level of intimacy; however, her request for forgiveness and her desire to be his friend suggest, conversely, a high level of intimacy. As for the time dimension, Diane was looking to the future while John seemed focused on restoring the past commitments that he had presumed. Diane resolved the problematic dimension of intimacy by selecting autonomy. When John rejected her Reframing of their relationship (just friends), Diane had little choice, in light of her decision to restore her blocked role-action.

For both Howard and Judy, Resynthesis occurred in the Discovery phase of their relational transition (Howard: E 4–5; Judy: E 6–8) (Figure 2.5). There Howard looked back in time, not forward, and rediscovered his appreciation for Judy — presumably including a willingness to affirm her sadness over their move to Raleigh. By the same token, Judy looked forward in time, not just backward, and decided that the future without Howard was bleak. Being with him in the future presumably included her willingness to furnish emotional support for his schooling in Raleigh. Role-action was unblocked, for both decided they could supply the complementary role needed by the other. Thus time perspective and role-action were intimately involved in this particular case. During Resynthesis, moreover, both Howard and Judy admitted to themselves their deep affection for the other and their desire for continued intimacy. Both Judy and Howard resolved the dialectic of intimacy by selecting connection.

CONCLUSION

The structural helical model is governed by two meta-dialectics. The first is Alienation-Security, and the second is Disintegration-Resynthesis. Movement between the poles of these two dialectical dimensions marks out the social domain of personal relationships.

In the Resynthesis phase of the structural helical model, relationship and the process of rebuilding a relationship are central. Resynthesis has its origins in relational partners' fleeing uncertainty, in their natural tendency to associate, and in their desire for unfettered role-action.

The process of relationship Resynthesis involves relational partners' responses to dialectical contradictions such as autonomy-connection, openness-closedness, and predictability-novelty (Baxter, 1990). A relationship is in the Resynthesis phase when the partners make the choices necessary for resolving those relationship dilemmas.

Relationship Resynthesis is prompted, in both friendship and marriage, by a desire for confirming messages (Cissna & Sieburg, 1982); confirming messages in turn restore role-action, blocked in Alienation and freed in Security.

9

Prospect:
VIA

And suddenly a light is thrown back, as when
your train makes a curve, showing that there has
been a mountain of meaning rising behind you on
the way you've come, is rising there still, proven
now through retrospect.

Eudora Welty
One Writer's Beginnings

Calvin Schrag has argued that understanding in the human sciences
must necessarily be an interpretive understanding. To that end he
proposed that traditional "hermeneutical theory of textual-philological
analysis" be widened to include "man's socio-historical existence," that
is, "the spoken word as well as the written," and "the sphere of
perception and its comprehension of the world" — in a word, "the texture
of everyday life" (1980, p. 98).

In an early, informal presentation of the structural helical model
to a faculty group, a colleague deftly took the wind out of my sails
with the observation, "So what you're really saying is that every
relationship has its ups and downs." The tone of the comment suggested to me that he meant something like: "So *all* you're really saying
is. . . . I knew that! Who doesn't?" And, of course, he was right, to
a point. But he had trivialized the mundane, hardly what Schrag
had in mind for a hermeneutic of everyday life. The ordinary familiarity of everyday life may be investigated as well as merely
observed.

The model and commentary presented in these pages were intended to take us beyond that point where my interlocutor was satisfied to pause, that is, beyond the point in our theorizing where we observe merely that personal relationships have a repetitive or cyclical nature about them. The point beyond is a place from which we observe that a relationship's second down is not the same as its first; a relationship's third or fourth up is not a mere repetition of its first or second up. Quite simply, "Here we go again!" although it is frequently uttered or thought by distraught relational partners, is not the truth. Experience has intervened since the last time. Neither of the partners is the same this time, nor is the quarrel the same, and that Difference demands interpretation.

The model and commentary advanced in these pages, further, may be viewed as tools for a hermeneutic of everyday life, in particular, tools for interpreting transitions in personal relationships. Not unlike the rest of our existence, the always, already interpreted world of the personal relationship often seems predictably repetitive, encapsulated, even clear. However, movement of the personal relationship through time confronts the partners with new experience that demands their interpretation (Gadamer, 1976).

Structural analysis is one such interpretive tool, a discovery procedure for locating differences at work in personal relationships. Of particular concern are dialectical differences, those that energize relational transitions with their volatile mixture of contradiction, interdependence, and dynamism. Moreover, the appropriate data for structural analysis are the personal narratives of relational partners. Collection and analysis of personal accounts maximize the researcher's proximity to the relevant events and minimize the researcher's intrusion into those events.

Whereas structural analysis is an analytical tool, the structural helical model is a thinking tool. Regardless of the dialectical dimensions that seem to be driving the communication in particular personal relationships (for example, autonomy-connection or togetherness-expressiveness), the model provides a context in which to imagine their operation. The meta-dialectics of Security-Alienation and Disintegration-Resynthesis mark out the larger field on which the relationship is played out. They indicate the social domain within which relational partners exchange messages. The structural helical model inscribes the indigenous, evolutionary, recursive process that is the context of all interpersonal communication.

A more complex tool is needed for thinking about personal relationships as processes. The three parts include the concept of Difference, the structural helical model, and a conventional relational stage model. When we conceive of one stage of a relationship and an adjacent stage, the line (or threshold or transition) between the two represents their Difference, but it is typically ignored in favor of describing the alleged stages themselves or how they relate to each other. However, the point of view advanced here is that that priority can, with profit, be inverted. Magnifying the line between stages reveals, I would argue, a helix, the path traveled by a relationship when it moves from one stage to another. And it reveals not only the path but also the nature of the partners' experience as the relationship moves about the helix: Security, Disintegration, Alienation, Resynthesis.

These tools may be used to address a number of interesting questions regarding the role of interpersonal communication in relational transitions. One question concerns time. Does it make a difference to the relationship's future how much time the relational partners take to make one turn about the helix? What about the probability of dissolution for a relationship that takes a year for one helical revolution as compared with the relationship that experiences three revolutions on the average per month? If the frequency of such helical turns seems important, are certain kinds of personal relationships more prone to frequent revolutions than infrequent ones? For example, what frequency differences occur in high school romances versus married couples, or in childless, working couples versus grandparents with their grandchildren or with their children?

Another set of questions concerns the difficulty experienced by the relational partners during their passage about the helix. To what extent do they agree on its difficulty? What if the relational partners differ in this regard, the experience being very difficult for one and taken in stride by the other? Are there some implications here for the future of the relationship: did it bring them together or drive them apart? Did the partner for whom it was difficult seek support from the other partner? Was he or she able or willing to provide that support? Did the partner needing support seek it outside the relationship? Was it sought in an informal relationship or from a professional? Moreover, what if the four phases of the structural helical model differed among themselves in the levels of difficulty experienced by the relational partners?

The same questions could be posed regarding the salience of the overall experience of relational transition to the relational partners and regarding the salience to the partners of one or another of the phases of the process: Disintegration, Alienation, Resynthesis, and (renewed) Security. It is enough, I believe, to make the point that the structural helical model is useful in generating an array of stock questions regarding transitions in personal relationships and the role of interpersonal communication in that process. Those questions can be expected to grow out of such additional important research areas as the quality of communicative interaction, attachment styles of the partners, interpersonal solidarity, intergenerational communication, communication differences across the life span, and the density and extent of the partners' social networks.

The structural helical model of relational transition contextualizes the interpersonal communication through which personal relationships are conducted. The model is not only a heuristic device for generating basic research questions about the role of interpersonal communication in relational transition, but also provides a framework for viewing existing lines of research in interpersonal communication. Consider uncertainty reduction theory as an example. Studies have shown that certain kinds of events increase relational partners' uncertainty about the other, about themselves, or about their relationship (Planalp & Honeycutt, 1985; Planalp, Rutherford, & Honeycutt, 1988). Such results, however, do not (should not, I would argue) have to be viewed apart from the histories of the relationships being examined. As Bochner has reminded us, reflecting on the significance of Bateson's work for communication studies, "Whatever has meaning for us, has meaning for us by virtue of being placed into a larger context" (1982, p. 75).

The structural helical model provides such a context. It places uncertainty increasing events into the Disintegration phase of relational transition. By doing so, resources for interpreting the events are brought to bear. For example, the researcher is prompted to ask how the events fit into a system of constraint (how do the events display syntagmatic meaning?) and how the events fit into a system of relations (how do the events display paradigmatic meaning?). In other words, the investigator asks how the events under scrutiny fulfilled or violated the normal expectations of the partners or members of their networks. And he or she further asks how the events are similar to ones that could have occurred at that time in the relationship and how they are different from those events that occurred in adjacent phases on the model.

Posing such general questions, the researcher is then positioned to ask more specific ones about the relational partners' management of those events that have increased their uncertainty. He or she may ask, for example, how the relational partners dealt with one of these periods the last time it came around; how repeated periods of uncertainty increase have accumulated and caused them to redefine their relationship; what their expectations are for the next uncertainty increasing event; what feelings of competence they have to deal with it; what kinds of talk accompanied the experience; what influence other relationships have on their experience of uncertainty; or what influence other relationships have on their ways of coping with uncertainty.

An analogy is the concept of the sentence. When we hear a few words of a conversation or glimpse a word or phrase on a page, we are unprepared to interpret them until we place them into a sentence. Until we fit the data onto a general structure (sentence as noun phrase + verb phrase, and its variants) and try out several alternatives (specific possible sentences, given the social context), those words are just noise or letters and mean nothing. They are *parole* without *langue*. But, of course, that conjunction is impossible, or at least a paradox, because, as Saussure observed, "language is necessary if speaking is to be intelligible . . . but speaking is necessary for the establishment of language" (1959, p. 18). Thus, when speech is heard (or writing is seen) and instantly interpreted its structure is typically taken for granted and ignored.

So I am arguing that personal relationships have a structure analogous to the structure of language. If I am near the mark and such a structure can be usefully conjectured then scholars should no more take it for granted than they do grammar; we surely ignore it at our own peril.

But elucidating the taken for granted is no mean task. Such an ideal is easier enunciated than accomplished. Like words we hear and read and actions we view, relationships evoke interpretations, which, despite our best efforts, remain subject to confusing reflections and problematic reversals. In sight but out of reach is their natural appearance. The erudite William of Baskerville (Eco's ersatz Sherlock Holmes) would seem to agree, because, as he explained to Adso of Melk (alias Dr. Watson): "omnis mundi creatura quasi liber et pictura nobis est in speculum" (All the world's creatures are like a book and a picture to us in a mirror) (Eco, 1980, p. 18).

APPENDIXES

Appendix A:
Helen Keller's Case

The most important day I remember in all my life is the one on which my teacher, Anne Mansfield Sullivan, came to me. I am filled with wonder when I consider the immeasurable contrasts between the two lives which it connects. It was the third of March, 1887, three months before I was seven years old.

On the afternoon of that eventful day, I stood on the porch, dumb, expectant. I guessed vaguely from my mother's signs and from the hurrying to and fro in the house that something unusual was about to happen, so I went to the door and waited on the steps. The afternoon sun penetrated the mass of honeysuckle that covered the porch, and fell on my upturned face. My fingers lingered almost unconsciously on the familiar leaves and blossoms which had just come forth to greet the sweet southern spring. I did not know what the future held of marvel or surprise for me. Anger and bitterness had preyed upon me continually for weeks, and a deep languor had succeeded this passionate struggle.

Have you ever been at sea in a dense fog, when it seemed as if a tangible white darkness shut you in, and the great ship, tense and anxious, groped her way toward the shore with plummet and sounding-line, and you waited with beating heart for something to happen? I was like that ship before my education began, only I was without compass or sounding-line, and had no way of knowing how near the harbour was.

Source: Keller, H. (1961). *The story of my life*. New York: Dell. Chap. 4 (Original work published 1902).

"Light! give me light!" was the wordless cry of my soul, and the light of love shone on me in that very hour.

I felt approaching footsteps. I stretched out my hand as I supposed to my mother. Some one took it, and I was caught up and held close in the arms of her who had come to reveal all things to me, and, more than all things else, to love me.

The morning after my teacher came she led me into her room and gave me a doll. The little blind children at the Perkins Institution had sent it and Laura Bridgman had dressed it; but I did not know this until afterward. When I had played with it a little while, Miss Sullivan slowly spelled into my hand the word "d-o-l-l." I was at once interested in this finger play and tried to imitate it. When I finally succeeded in making the letters correctly I was flushed with childish pleasure and pride. Running downstairs to my mother I held up my hand and made the letters for doll. I did not know that I was spelling a word or even that words existed; I was simply making my fingers go in monkey-like imitation. In the days that followed I learned to spell in this uncomprehending way a great many words, among them *pin, hat, cup* and a few verbs like *sit, stand* and *walk*. But my teacher had been with me several weeks before I understood that everything has a name.

One day, while I was playing with my new doll, Miss Sullivan put my big rag doll into my lap also, spelled "d-o-l-l" and tried to make me understand that "d-o-l-l" applied to both. Earlier in the day we had had a tussle over the words "m-u-g" and "w-a-t-e-r." Miss Sullivan had tried to impress it upon me that "m-u-g" is *mug* and that "w-a-t-e-r" is *water,* but I persisted in confounding the two. In despair she had dropped the subject for the time, only to renew it at the first opportunity. I became impatient at her repeated attempts and, seizing the new doll, I dashed it upon the floor. I was keenly delighted when I felt the fragments of the broken doll at my feet. Neither sorrow nor regret followed my passionate outburst. I had not loved the doll. In the still, dark world in which I lived there was no strong sentiment of tenderness. I felt my teacher sweep the fragments to one side of the hearth, and I had a sense of satisfaction that the cause of my discomfort was removed. She brought me my hat, and I knew I was going out into the warm sunshine. This thought, if a wordless sensation may be called a thought, made me hop and skip with pleasure.

We walked down the path to the well-house, attracted by the fragrance of the honeysuckle with which it was covered. Some one was drawing water and my teacher placed my hand under the spout. As the cool stream gushed over one hand she spelled into the other the word *water,* first slowly, then rapidly. I stood still, my whole attention fixed upon the motions of her fingers. Suddenly I felt a misty consciousness as of something forgotten — a thrill of returning thought; and somehow the mystery of language was revealed to me. I knew then that "w-a-t-e-r" meant the wonderful cool something that was flowing over my hand. That living word awakened my soul, gave it light, hope, joy, set it free! There were barriers still, it is true, but barriers that could in time be swept away.

I left the well-house eager to learn. Everything had a name, and each name gave birth to a new thought. As we returned to the house every object which I touched seemed to quiver with life. That was because I saw everything with the strange, new sight that had come to me. On entering the door I remembered the doll I had broken. I felt my way to the hearth and picked up the pieces. I tried vainly to put them together. Then my eyes filled with tears; for I realized what I had done, and for the first time I felt repentance and sorrow.

I learned a great many new words that day. I do not remember what they all were; but I do know that *mother, father, sister, teacher* were among them — words that were to make the world blossom for me, "like Aaron's rod, with flowers." It would have been difficult to find a happier child than I was as I lay in my crib at the close of that eventful day and lived over the joys it had brought me, and for the first time longed for a new day to come.

Appendix B:
Diane's Case

When I entered my freshman year at UT, everything was great. I had been dating a boy from my home town for two and a half years. He was a junior. We had always gotten along very well, but there were two drawbacks in our relationship: I was seventeen while he was twenty-one and we really hadn't been together very much because he had been away at school. John, being older, was beginning to get very serious, but I would not consciously admit that he was. He and I had discussed getting married, but all I visualized was the new excitement involved but none of the serious, mature ideas involved. Generally, when we had discussed marriage it was in the future after we were both out of school. I suppose at the time it was easy for me to look at marriage unrealistically because it was so far off with so much in between. Now, looking back, I cannot believe I could have ever considered it so lightly.

However, in December of that year, John's best friend Paul, also a junior in college, got married. Then John began evaluating his finances and told me that he had decided that we could get married the following September before school started. This really scared me because I felt I was too young and had too much I wanted to do before I settled down. On the other hand, I didn't want to say no and risk losing John for good; I said nothing at all.

Two months passed, and John had nearly all of the arrangements tentatively made. In those two months, I realized that I hadn't dated anyone but John in almost three years, and I knew I couldn't possibly marry him yet anyway. I was still so afraid of hurting him though that I couldn't bring myself to discuss waiting with him.

After talking to my two closest friends though, I became convinced that I had to tell him. I called him to tell him that I wanted to see him, but before he came over the lady at the desk called to tell me that I had a dozen roses in the lobby. The card said "To the future Mrs. Lowrey, Love John." Needless to say, this positively ruled out the idea of telling him that day because he wasn't usually sentimental. Once again I put off our discussion.

I began to lose sleep, and I decided I positively had to do it. I had known for over three months that I wasn't going to marry him but had let him go right on planning. Finally, I told him one night around the middle of February. We had been to a concert, and on the way home he asked me why I was being so quiet. I talked in circles really sort of hinting at what was on my mind until he finally understood. He left very upset, and called me a little later to tell me that without me, he had nothing to live for and was considering suicide. He was so hurt and angry that I believed him, and yet I had no idea how to handle it. He kept talking and I don't think I said over two sentences. As usual, when I was upset or didn't know what to say, I reverted to saying absolutely nothing. This crisis passed, but in the next two months, neither my roommates nor I got any rest because he was constantly calling or coming by to argue or beg or whatever new tactic he came up with. At the end of this terrible two months, John had ulcers and I lost twenty pounds.

Finally, one night I was nearly at my wit's end and was even considering marrying John anyway to put an end to this whole mess, when a friend asked me what I could have done earlier to change things. Then I suddenly realized that if I had only been honest with John and myself from the start, the whole ugly situation might have been avoided. I had one final conversation with John and told him how I had felt all along. I explained that I had been too immature to have ever considered marriage, and I realized that it was all my fault. I asked if he could forgive me and be my friend. He couldn't, and I haven't seen him since; however, I learned from the whole ugly mess that lying, either passively or actively, only creates problems sooner or later, and, to use an old cliché, honesty is the best policy.

Since the experience, I have tried my very best to say exactly what I feel in all situations. The results so far have proved to me that I am right.

Appendix C:
Howard's and Judy's Cases

HOWARD'S CASE

In the spring of 1976, my wife, our two dogs, all our belongings, and myself rolled into Raleigh. To attempt to accurately explain our individual moods and attitudes toward this transition is near impossible, and my exact feelings in regard to our first few months in Raleigh are dynamic in that they are constantly shifting and expanding as my perspective changes. Nevertheless, the basic realizations that kept our marriage alive and strong is firmly implanted in my memory.

When we first moved here, the thought of having left the delta flats of St. Louis and rerouting 400 miles to the east left me ecstatic. I was excited further with the symbol of Raleigh as being the "home stretch of the vet shuffle." Finally, I was headed down the last bend of a long, meandering road that often challenged my sanity. But more than that, I felt an intense sense of surging freedom. I developed a romanticist view of independence and self-sufficiency. We were no longer within a parent's domain, or a hometown domain, or within anybody's jurisdiction. What we established here in Raleigh would be completely under our control, guided by our expectations; not mine, not Judy's, but *ours*. Even though we had been happily married for nine months, Raleigh would be our first "home" to nourish our infant marriage. I suppose it was kind of an adventure, at least this was the way I saw it. I was crazy and obsessed with optimistic anticipation. But for Judy, the story takes an equally understanding but different point of view. For her, our preparing and planning to move and the actual action of moving was an energy soaking nightmare. A nightmare that left her emotionally torn apart. By leaving St. Louis, Judy left behind an impenetrable "security of home." It was this same security that I frantically shed off because it was too easy; it was too well planned out, and most importantly, we were not involved in the planning. This was not the first time that I had seen someone's world constructed with that someone peering outside the finished structure, wondering how he got there. It happened to me with my family and my community. I dreaded the stagnation of being stereotyped, taken for granted, and being unknowingly contracted out and built. I really believe that in order to grow into a meaningful and productive individual, you have to search for your own destiny, your own livelihood, and your own happiness. To say the same thing with a twist, in order to grow into a natural person, you have to experience hurt and pain along the way. You have to experience life and yourself. It is not something that someone can explain to you, boasting of authority of having already experienced it; there is no growth there, just data. The point I'm making is that I have to construct my own happiness, and by having this foundation, I will have insured security.

It was this kind of unrelenting enthusiasm about making my own future and the association of Raleigh as a big step in achieving some progress, and Judy's preoccupation with the fear of losing what I called pseudosecurity that was a part of our mounting problems. But mind you, it was only a part, and perhaps a minor one at that.

There was another factor, but this time it was a person who kept Judy's mind on St. Louis and our life there — a very unique person with whom Judy became enormously attached. Her name is Tracy, who was and still is an extremely gifted and beautiful person. What made this relationship so unique was not the nature of it because it was like most other "best friend" alliances, but that this was the first person with whom Judy, by her definition, had become best friends with. It is not that Judy lacks some sort of capacity to make lasting relationships; I know this is not true, but she is a very demanding person, and she considers friendship to be a sort of sacred engagement, something that has to be cherished, protected, and worked with. By the time we were ready to move, their friendship had reached a peak and even I was a tad-bit reluctant to chance disturbing it. But I rationalized it out, saying space does not obliterate true friends and other such soothing sayings. Unfortunately, I did not convince anybody.

So we got to Raleigh with me jubilantly singing every song I could recall and Judy pouring out tears by the bucketful. We were truly a contrasting pair. But I was still budding with optimism, believing with time Judy would be all right, convinced that the move would save her soul. I was patient at first thinking I understood Judy's feelings. But soon my patience turned into annoyance. In fact, within a month I became bitter. After all, she was stepping all over my excitement, joy and challenge of a new home. And before I knew it, the excitement turned into frustrating disappointments, the joy into despair, and the challenge into apathy. I immediately realized my change in attitudes, and with scorn I blamed Judy for every aspect, for squeezing the life out of my dreams. I began to doubt her love, accusing her of lacking compassion, denying her at times (in my rage) any reason for existence. We got into some awful fights, never physical, but verbally abusive. There were things I said and heard in times of desperation that made me want to die. This type of pathetic existence continued with exhausting intensity for two months.

With Judy on the brink of a nervous breakdown and showing no improvement, and with me hating myself for falling into these barren ruins of a fading love and not being able to stop it and turn it around, I left. I decided to take an indefinite leave of absence from life, go to the ocean, climb a bunch of mountains, drive aimlessly around the countryside, just to try to make some sense of it all. I won't even attempt to try to explain the confusion that smothered my brain. I knew there was something basically wrong, and perhaps by some chance I could find it on the ocean shore or a cliff's edge. Frankly, when I left Judy, I had no hope, and I really didn't give a solid shit if I ever saw her again. I just wanted out. I didn't care about anything but myself.

I decided to go to Canada via a route through Cape Hatteras and the Shenandoah Mountains. I never made it to Canada, but I did make it to Cape Hatteras and the mountains. It was at Cape Hatteras where I camped on the beach, built some relaxing fires, fished a little in vain, and swam a whole lot that I started to understand the missing link in our marriage. I did a lot of staring into space while on that beach, allowing the summer breeze to clean out my mind. I did a lot of reminiscing about good times, and I found myself rediscovering a lost sense of equilibrium. Every once in a while an "honest to God" clear thought would wiggle into my brain, without that distortion I was feeling so intensely a week earlier. I tell you, I felt good way down; I was regaining my self-respect. Each time that my mind indefinitely left the beach and glided across those waves with old friends, I was always slammed back into reality with thoughts of Judy. It was a continuous cycle as if I was mimicking the tide. But when I allowed my anger to precipitate out of view, to release me from feelings of guilt, I realized that the slamming back into reality was not something I wanted to hide from. It was not something that I did not want. I realized if I wanted to make something worthwhile out of this chaotic but downright interesting life, I had better make a clear distinction between what is real and what is fantasy. I had better learn to distinguish between the things I love and the things I detest. And I no longer could be a self-pathetic fool.

So I headed home via the mountains, emerged [sic] in my love for Judy, hoping she too had felt similar emotions, confidently praying that she would take me back. The rest of the trip is not worth mentioning because my thoughts were engrossed with all the elements of love, all of that raw emotion, understanding, compassion, and sex. I knew everything would be fine. About thirty miles outside of Raleigh, I bought Judy a Raggedy Ann doll and wrote something very personal on its ass, in hopes that the doll would remind us of our troubled period and the subsequent lessons. I arrived home and there was that beautiful human specimen with the biggest grin and the most joyful tears all over her face. She too saw our selfishness, our inability to dismember our pride to secure our mutual treasure, our failure to stand in the other fellow's shoes in order to understand. She too was able to forgive, and I was no longer afraid to admit that I needed her.

JUDY'S CASE

Ah-h-h, one should always start at the beginning or so they say, but I'm not at all sure where the beginning is. I've a remote idea, and because that's all I do have, I shall attempt to use that vague thought as the start of an episode which is somewhat painful to write about. I find it hard to put emotion, accurately, on paper; to be able to communicate the feelings with the same intensity at the time which they were felt will be a difficult task. But because no other episode in my life has ever created such emotional conflict as this one, I feel I have no choice. I comfort myself by trying to believe that "talking about it will make it easier to live with." The comfort I'm receiving from this rationalization is minimal. Tra-la-la.

Howard, my husband, and I moved to Raleigh almost exactly one year ago — April 10th to be precise. Howard, a preveterinarian student, found it necessary to finish school at N. C. State because Wilson, the college he attended at the time, didn't offer some courses that were necessary for vet school application. We both felt the move would be a welcome change, and in some respects, it signified a final step in the "vet school shuffle," as Howard so fondly called it. I was looking forward to getting out of the flatlands of the Delta and nearer to the mountains of the east. Yet there was some slight mixed emotion gurgling about inside of me, and as the time for us to pack our belongings drew near, this conflict grew to proportional [sic] sizes. But even then, the volcano within me didn't explode completely until nearly a month after our move. I had lived in St. Louis for seven years before moving to Raleigh. Although St. Louis isn't an ideal place to live, I did have my securities: a good job, my parents, just knowing at least one person wherever I went. Yet even those securities weren't indispensable; it was leaving my friends behind or to be more accurate, leaving one particular friend — Tracy.

Perhaps it would be helpful to explain my feelings toward friends in general. I'm not exactly sure when I developed these attitudes, but somewhere along the way, around eighth grade I suppose, I discovered friends. True friends were one of the most valuable assets one could ever have. And as I grew older, the importance of that discovery also grew. I began concentrating a lot of my energies toward strengthening old friendships, and I had visions of "sugar plums" toward establishing new friendships. Another discovery soon crept into my head: it seemed very few people were willing to give as much as I desired, and it wasn't a selfish desire because I never asked anything of anyone that I wasn't willing to do myself. Nevertheless, many people weren't eager to give even a small part of themselves. As a result, I became disillusioned with people in general, wondering the inevitable "why?" About two years later, I developed a strong friendship with two girls, Angie and Flash. It restored my faith, and I was once again happy, not asking questions that didn't have good answers. I had two friends to love, to share secrets, to simply be happy with. But all good things must come to an end or so some say, and in order to make a long story short, our friendship ended rather abruptly, leaving Judy somewhat confused and very, very hurt.

It wasn't until I met Tracy that I began realizing how badly I had let the incident with Angie and Flash affect me. I had built a wall around myself thinking, "if I don't get close, then I won't get hurt." At first, it was a conscience [sic] effort; then, unfortunately, it became so routine that I did it without thinking — at least, as I said, until I met Tracy. We were in a play together at a community theatre, and one night after rehearsal, Tracy asked me if I wanted to get high. I didn't know anything about this lady except that I just liked her and was willing to know more. "Getting high" with a stranger can do one of two things: either exaggerate the tension to an unbearable degree or completely wipe out all inhibitions. Fortunately, the latter was the case, and we ended up in a parking lot for three hours talking and giggling. The ice was broken — November, 1975.

Our friendship grew rapidly, almost too fast in a way because I was having a hard time accepting that I had finally found a person who was willing to give not just a part of herself but all she had. And to be honest, it scared me because I became aware of the wall I constructed five years ago trying to fall. I wanted it to disappear, yet at the same time, I felt very vulnerable without it. There was a part of me wanting to throw my arms around Tracy, and there was a part that insisted I keep my distance. Tracy was aware of what was going through my head because she was patient with my inconsistencies. And Tracy, like me, needed a good friend. Our relationship kept getting stronger, and neither one of us could even talk about the move to Raleigh. We knew saying goodbye was going to be difficult for several obvious reasons, but the reason that hit us hardest was one of which we never spoke. Because Tracy was to be married in the near future to a fellow with a totally different lifestyle than Howard's and mine, we knew our friendship, our relationship, would be forced to change. We knew, to use an ever dependent [sic] cliché, that our paths would rarely cross. For us to think we couldn't just pick up the phone or drive ten minutes when we needed a friend was a little more than we could handle. We played games with ourselves by believing because the move was several months away, because it was in the future, it wasn't reality. It was a childish game, and we were aware of it, but somehow it gave us a little comfort while we crammed in as much time together as possible.

I was never quite sure if Howard understood how close Tracy and I had become. He was thrilled to be leaving St. Louis, and in his excitement, I felt he couldn't see "my side" — at least not with a sympathetic eye. When we would talk about it, he would say, "Yeah, I understand. I've left close friends behind too," but I couldn't help but think that he didn't understand, not to the full extent. It hurt me that I couldn't lean on him, depend on him for the strength I so desperately needed, but I did understand his anticipation of "better things to come" and left it at that. This more or less marked the beginning of my attitude towards Howard that led to total alienation.

April ninth, the night before we left, was spent with Tracy and two other close friends. It was a strange evening: fairly tense, Tracy and I rarely looked at or spoke to each other. The move no longer could be said to be in the future; it was definitely a reality. I was staying with Tracy that night, needing those few hours to say goodbye. We left about one a.m., and on the way home, it started: buckets of those salty dogs rolling down our faces, no sounds or sobs, just tear after tear. We still didn't say anything; there didn't seem to be anything to say. We held each other, trying to find comfort in the other but only finding frustration. I fell asleep crying, and about five o'clock that same morning, my eyes popped open, and tears started falling again. I hadn't said anything or even moved when Tracy also woke up. She immediately held me as if someone had snuck in her dream and told her to wake up because Judy needed her.

Howard and I rolled into Raleigh, totally exhausted, no money, and with only one car that broke down as soon as we arrived. It would take an additional three pages to explain the hassles of the following few days but instead, just believe that anything that could go wrong — did — no exceptions whatsoever. And it wasn't easy for Howard to get much done because I was an emotional time bomb. He couldn't hardly [sic] say a thing to me that wouldn't make me cry. But after a couple of days, things did begin to work out, from a physical point of view: the car was fixed; we got some money; the utilities turned on, etc. Yet it was far from the end for emotional stabilization.

This next part is the area which is hard for me to write. I've never been able to explain it satisfactorily because it was such a crazy, crazy time and there was so much involved. Only if one could have sat in my head during this period and seen my insides and how they worked could one fully understand how screwed up I was. But because that's impossible, I'll try my damnedest to put it in words. I doubt seriously that it will be in chronological order — my mind has cleverly rolled all these events into one blob and placed them in the attic.

Because Howard wasn't starting school until the summer quarter, he got a job at a lawn mower parts place. It was an eight to five job, and though not particularly challenging, it was a nice change of pace from school days. I didn't look for a job immediately because I wanted to get the house halfway settled. That's what I told Howard anyway. Actually, I just didn't have any motivation or energy. My head was occupied solely with thoughts of Tracy. Anything and everything reminded me of her. My days consisted of sipping coffee, writing Tracy, working on the house, then getting high and writing the strawberry lady [Tracy] for the rest of the afternoon. Up until then, I had never been a good letter writer, and it freaked me out that writing her was all I wanted to do. This went on for about two weeks, and in the interim, Howard and I were constantly bickering with a real good fight thrown in about once a week. My favorite time was when Howard went to work because I could escape into my stoned world and talk to Tracy.

When living in St. Louis, I had worked as a maxillofacial prosthetic technician. I made artificial parts of the face (eyes, ears, noses, etc.) for people who had lost them because of cancer, accidents, whatever. This is a relatively new field, and I couldn't find a job even partially relating to it in Raleigh. I've always had an urge to be a waitress; somehow it fascinated me. I got a job at the Casino Royale, a bar on "the strip." As circumstance would have it, my hours were totally opposite of Howard's. By the time he got home, I was leaving, usually not returning before three a.m. Needless to say, this put quite a strain on an already weak relationship.

For several days, Howard was in an exceptionally bad mood. I remember not feeling like being very tolerant; I had my own troubles. As a matter of fact, it seemed to me that our marriage was more of a burden than an asset. I was getting ants in my pants; I wanted my freedom.

One night soon, Howard finally let me know what was bothering him — despite my disinterest. He resented me, was taking it out on me the fact that moving had freaked me out so badly that I had pulled him down from his excitement. Somehow his recognition of my frame of mind gave me some comfort, some hope. Yet I still wasn't content with him or anything else.

Not long afterwards, Tracy came to visit for a weekend. I felt incredible new energies roaring about inside, and I felt I could have handled anything. It was a short visit but definitely a good one. In that small amount of time, we became even closer, which meant saying goodbye was going to be harder. As I watched her get on the bus, I felt all those "incredible new energies" just slip away; I felt that familiar empty feeling in their place, and for some reason, I remember feeling betrayed. I drove directly to a park to be by myself, and the moment the car stopped, I had these tremendous rushes that transformed to hysteria. They only lasted for a few minutes but left me totally drained. Her visit had made me the happiest I'd been in a month, just as her departure left me feeling lower than ever before.

The first of May. My head was thinking crazy thoughts about this time. For the first time in my life, I had thought about suicide. Not really in the context of going through with it, but rather just thinking about it. If I blew my brains away, who would honestly care? It was strange for me to even think this way because I've always been down on people who had committed or tried to commit suicide. This feeling of uselessness was overwhelming me, and in one last attempt to get Howard to understand, I tried to explain how crazy I felt; I tried to tell him I was on the edge; I was telling him I needed help. I don't think he understood.

Several days later, Howard's parents came to Gatlinburg, and we were to meet them after I got off work. Howard picked me up, and within fifteen minutes we were arguing. The arguing turned to yelling and because it was raining really bad, I told him to pull over until we got it settled. We were screaming, crying, then blam — I just finally lost it altogether. I was crying hysterically, confused as hell, and all I could think to do was get away from Howard. I half ran/walked, no idea of where I was going nor did I care. Howard yelled to come back and after realizing I hadn't any such intentions, he ran after me. I was scared to death of him at that moment, and when I saw him coming towards me, I started crying or screaming or both. As a matter of fact, I don't remember a great deal except the feeling of fear: of Howard, of the darkness, of the state of mind I was in. For the first time I think Howard finally grasped, almost completely, how screwed up his wife was. Yet it seemed a little late. Though he gave me more comfort and love than I deserved, I was still fighting inside. I still wasn't content.

After the above mentioned ordeal, I went through a small transition. I was no longer a blubbering baby but a lady with a "frankly my dear, I don't give a damn" attitude. Howard was trying very hard to get along with me, but I was intolerable. We really didn't fight anymore but rather just lived together, existed in the same house.

Tracy was moving to Charleston to be with her boyfriend, and Richard, a very dear friend of ours from St. Louis, rode with her as far as Raleigh. It was good that he also came because Howard and I both needed someone to talk to; we were seriously considering splitting up. Several times before, we had threatened to leave, but when it came down to the "nit-grit," we chickened out. But we had developed a hardness; we were sick of each other, our relationship, the whole affair in general. I don't remember the "how's or when's," but shortly after Tracy and Richard left, something started clicking. I began looking at Howard with a different outlook. I started seeing myself from a different viewpoint. Apparently the reality of our situation had become visible. It was time to make a big decision; we couldn't live in this atmosphere any longer.

With fairly clear heads we decided to separate for a while, to at least get away from each other so that we could look at things rationally. This decision proved to be the only intelligent step we had made in the last two months. Howard and his cousin took off a couple of days later with Canada as their destination. As for myself, I was looking forward to just being alone. Because of this solitude, I was able to do some pretty heavy thinking. I decided I needed to find a new source of energy; not a friend or husband but something or someone who would always be there, who had an indispensable [sic] amount of patience, time, energy, and love. I've always questioned that mysterious power many people call God, and during that point in my life, my questions came more often and much more serious. I was cautious in many aspects because of past experiences with so-called Christians and because of the plastic Jesus Movement as I called it. With this in mind, I decided if I was going "to find God," I was going to do it myself, without the help of Billy Graham or Anita Bryant. In the meantime, I got a wild hair in my arse [sic] and decided to take off from work and visit the ocean, the sun, and Tracy.

My trip to Charleston accomplished two very important things: one was my grasping dependency on Tracy diminished. Our visit just didn't work out; it wasn't a comfortable atmosphere. Although it hurt, it also made me realize that I needed much more than her to be content. Secondly, I made a new friend; I'll call him God for lack of a better name. One night I was extremely upset and while sitting on some old concrete steps, I told God that if He and I were going to be friends, let's do it now. I hesitate in describing what I felt for fear of sounding like a TV testimonial, but I experienced the most incredible feeling of peacefulness, of contentment at that moment that it would seem foolish not to share it. I gradually saw things with a new perspective and I felt absolutely wonderful. Even when I told Tracy goodbye, I didn't feel the least bit of regret. I was anxious to get home to show Howard the "new me," to give him all the love he most assuredly deserved. While driving home, my thoughts were running wild. I couldn't believe how alive I felt, how aware I felt. I had a lot of catching up to do as if I had been to the moon for two months, out of touch with everybody and everything. And I suppose, in a sense, I had.

Howard wasn't supposed to be home for at least another week. The idea that he might never come back had me extremely scared. Sitting on the front porch, I began to write my honey a letter. I stopped for a second, deciding I needed to have a talk with my new friend: "Hey God, I know you've already done a lot for me, but I have one more favor to ask. I would appreciate it if you would send old Burrhead home in the next couple of days, but if you can't handle that, at least send him home safely, or even better, just send him home period."

My dogs' barking interrupted me, and I went in the backyard to see what the commotion was all about. I had a fleeting thought that perhaps Howard had driven in from the alley, but alas, it was only a squirrel. As I turned around to head back to the porch, I saw something that made my heart climb right up to my throat. Standing two feet from me was my husband, brown from sunshine, a smile stretching from ear to ear, and most importantly, his arms were open, ready for me to climb into them. Within one second, I was holding onto that man for dear life. I had so much inside of me that I needed to tell him that it all came out at once in the form of ecstatic tears. We held each other and without having to say anything, we knew the past was over; we knew everything was all right; we knew we were hopelessly in love.

References

Altman, I., & Taylor, D. A. (1973). *Social penetration: The development of interpersonal relationships*. New York: Holt, Rinehart, & Winston.

Altman, I., Vinsel, A., & Brown, B. B. (1981). Dialectic conceptions in social psychology: An application to social penetration and privacy regulation. In L. Berkowitz (Ed.), *Advances in experimental social psychology: Vol. 14* (pp. 107–60). New York: Academic Press.

Ambert, A. (1988). Relationship between ex-spouses: Individual and dyadic perspectives. *Journal of Social and Personal Relationships, 5*, 327–46.

Ayres, J. (1983). Strategies to maintain relationships: Their identification and perceived usage. *Communication Quarterly, 31*, 62–67.

Badcock, C. R. (1975). *Lévi-Strauss*. New York: Holmes & Meier.

Bannet, E. T. (1989). *Structuralism and the logic of dissent*. Urbana, IL: University of Illinois Press.

Barnhart, R. K. (1988). *The Barnhart Dictionary of Etymology*. New York: H. W. Wilson.

Barnlund, D. C. (1982). Toward an ecology of communication. In C. Wilder & J. H. Weakland (Eds.), *Rigor & imagination: Essays from the legacy of Gregory Bateson* (pp. 87–126). New York: Praeger.

Barthes, R. (1972). The structuralist activity. In R. T. De George & F. M. De George (Eds.), *The Structuralists: From Marx to Lévi-Strauss* (pp. 148–54). Garden City, NY: Doubleday.

Bateson, G. (1935). Culture, contact, and schismogenesis. *Man, 35*, 178–83.

____. (1942). Social planning and the concept of "deutero-learning" in relation to the democratic way of life. In *Science, philosophy, and religion, second symposium* (pp. 81–97). New York: Harper & Brothers.

____. (1972). *Steps to an ecology of mind*. New York: Ballantine.

Baxter, L. A. (1984). Trajectories of relationship disengagement. *Journal of Social and Personal Relationships, 1*, 29–48.

____. (1988). A dialectical perspective on communication strategies in relationship development. In S. Duck (Ed.), *Handbook of personal relationships: Theory, research, and interventions* (pp. 257–73). Chichester: John Wiley & Sons.

____. (1990). Dialectical contradictions in relationship development. *Journal of Social and Personal Relationships, 7,* 69–88.

Baxter, L. A., & Bullis, C. (1986). Turning points in developing romantic relationships. *Human Communication Research, 12,* 469–93.

Baxter, L. A., & Dindia, K. (1990). Marital partners' perceptions of marital maintenance strategies. *Journal of Social and Personal Relationships, 7,* 187–208.

Baxter, L. A., & Wilmot, W. W. (1983). Communication characteristics of relationships with differential growth rates. *Communication Monographs, 50,* 264–72.

____. (1984). "Secret tests:" social strategies for acquiring information about the state of the relationship. *Human Communication Research, 11,* 171–201.

Becker, E. (1973). *The denial of death.* New York: The Free Press.

Bellah, R. N., Madsen, R., Sullivan, W. M., Swidler, A., & Tipton, S. M. (1985). *Habits of the heart: Individualism and commitment in American life.* New York: Harper & Row.

Berger, C. R. (1986). Uncertain outcome values in predicted relationships: Uncertainty reduction theory then and now. *Human Communication Research, 13,* 34–38.

____. (1987). Communicating under uncertainty. In M. E. Roloff & G. R. Miller (Eds.), *Interpersonal processes: New directions in communication research* (pp. 39–62). Newbury Park, CA: Sage.

____. (1988). Uncertainty and information exchange in developing relationships. In S. Duck (Ed.), *Handbook of personal relationships: Theory, research, and interventions* (pp. 239–55). Chichester: John Wiley & Sons.

Berger, C. R., & Bradac, J. J. (1982). *Language and social knowledge: Uncertainty in interpersonal relations.* London: Edward Arnold.

Berger, C. R., & Calabrese, R. J. (1975). Some explorations in initial interaction and beyond: Toward a developmental theory of interpersonal communication. *Human Communication Research, 1,* 99–112.

Berger, C. R., & Douglas, W. (1982). Thought and talk: "Excuse me, but have I been talking to myself?" In F. E. X. Dance (Ed.), *Human communication theory* (pp. 42–60). New York: Harper & Row.

Berger, P., & Kellner, H. (1964). Marriage and the construction of reality. *Diogenes, 46,* 1–24.

Berlo, D. (1960). *The process of communication.* New York: Holt, Rinehart, & Winston.

Berman, A. (1988). *From the new criticism to deconstruction: The reception of structuralism and post-structuralism.* Urbana, IL: University of Illinois Press.

Bloom, A. (1987). *The closing of the American mind.* New York: Simon & Schuster.

Blumer, H. (1966). Sociological implications of the thought of George Herbert Mead. *American Journal of Sociology, 71,* 535–44.

Boas, F. (1932). *Bella bella tales* (Memoirs of the American Folklore Society, 25). New York: American Folklore Society & G. E. Stechert.

Bochner, A. P. (1976). Conceptual frontiers in the study of communication in families: An introduction to the literature. *Human Communication Research, 2,* 381–97.

____. (1982). Forming warm ideas. In C. Wilder & J. H. Weakland (Eds.), *Rigor and imagination: Essays from the legacy of Gregory Bateson* (pp. 65–81). New York: Praeger.

____. (1984). The functions of human communication in interpersonal bonding. In C. Arnold & J. Bowers (Eds.), *Handbook of rhetorical and communication theory* (pp. 544–621). Boston: Allyn & Bacon.

Bochner, A. P., & Eisenberg, E. M. (1987). Family process: System perspectives. In C. R. Berger & S. H. Chaffee (Eds.), *Handbook of communication science* (pp. 540–63). Newbury Park, CA: Sage.

Bolton, C. D. (1961). Mate selection as the development of a relationship. *Marriage and Family Living, 23*, 234–40.

Bradac, J. J., Tardy, C. H., & Hosman, L. A. (1980). Disclosure styles and a hint at their genesis. *Human Communication Research, 6*, 228–38.

Buber, M. (1955). *Between man and man.* (R. G. Smith, Trans.). Boston: Beacon Press.

____. (1957). Distance and relation. *Psychiatry, 20*, 97–104.

Bullis, C., & Bach, B. W. (1989). Socialization turning points: An examination of change in organizational identification. *Western Journal of Speech Communication, 53*, 273–93.

Burke, K. (1950). *A rhetoric of motives.* New York: Prentice-Hall.

Caputo, J. D. (1987). *Radical hermeneutics: Repetition, deconstruction, and the hermeneutic project.* Bloomington, IN: Indiana University Press.

Chomsky, N. (1957). *Syntactic structures.* The Hague: Mouton.

Cissna, K. N. L., & Keating, S. (1979). Speech communication antecedents of perceived confirmation. *Western Journal of Speech Communication, 43*, 48–60.

Cissna, K. N. L., & Sieburg, E. (1982). Patterns of interactional confirmation and disconfirmation. In C. Wilder & J. H. Weakland (Eds.), *Rigor and imagination: Essays from the legacy of Gregory Bateson* (pp. 253–82). New York: Praeger.

Clarke, A. C. (1968). *2001: A space odyssey.* New York: The New American Library.

Clarke, S. (1981). *The foundations of structuralism: A critique of Lévi-Strauss and the structuralist movement.* Totowa, NJ: Barnes & Noble.

Claus, P. J. (1976). A structuralist appreciation of "Star Trek." In W. Arens & S. P. Montague (Eds.), *The American dimension: Cultural myths and social realities* (pp. 15–32). New York: Alfred.

Conrad, J. (1926). Heart of darkness. In *Joseph Conrad, complete works* (Vol. 16). Garden City, NY: Doubleday, Page.

Conville, R. L. (1978). Change, process, and the future of communication education. *Southern Speech Communication Journal, 43*, 265–82.

____. (1983). Second-order development in interpersonal communication. *Human Communication Research, 9*, 195–207.

____. (1988). Relational transitions: An inquiry into their structure and function. *Journal of Social and Personal Relationships, 5*, 423–37.

Culler, J. (1973). Phenomenology and structuralism. *The Human Context, 5*, 35–42.

____. (1977). In pursuit of signs. *Daedalus, proceedings of the American academy of arts and sciences, 106*, 95–111.

____. (1982). *On deconstruction: Theory and criticism after structuralism.* Ithaca, NY: Cornell University Press.

Cushman, D. P., & Cahn, D. D. (1985). *Communication in interpersonal relationships*. Albany, NY: State University of New York Press.

Dance, F. E. X. (1967). Toward a theory of human communication. In F. E. X. Dance (Ed.), *Human communication theory: Original essays*. (pp. 288–309). New York: Holt, Rinehart, & Winston.

Dance, F. E. X., & Larson, C. E. (1972). *Speech communication: Concepts and behavior*. New York: Holt, Rinehart, & Winston.

Davis, M. S. (1973). *Intimate relations*. New York: The Free Press.

Deetz, S. (1973). Structuralism: A summary of its assumptive and conceptual bases. *Review of Social Theory, 1*, 138–63.

De George, R. T., & De George, F. M. (Eds.) (1972). *The structuralists: From Marx to Lévi-Strauss*. Garden City, NY: Doubleday.

Delia, J. G. (1977). Constructivism and the study of human communication. *Quarterly Journal of Speech, 63*, 66–83.

Delia, J. G., & Grossberg, L. (1977). Interpretation and evidence. *Western Journal of Speech Communication, 41*, 32–42.

Derlega, V. J., Winstead, B. A., Wong, P. T. P., & Greenspan, M. (1987). Self-disclosure and relationship development, an attributional analysis. In M. E. Roloff & G. R. Miller (Eds.), *Interpersonal processes: New directions in communication research* (pp. 172–87). Newbury Park, CA: Sage.

Derrida, J. (1972). Structure, sign, and play in the discourse of the human sciences. In R. Macksey & E. Donato (Eds.), *The structuralist controversy* (pp. 247–65). Baltimore: Johns Hopkins University Press.

_____. (1981). *Positions* (A. Bass, Trans.). Chicago: University of Chicago Press. (Original work published 1972.)

_____. (1982). Différance. In A. Bass (Trans.), *Margins of philosophy* (pp. 1–27). Chicago: University of Chicago Press.

Duck, S. W. (1982). A topography of relationship disengagement and dissolution. In S. W. Duck (Ed.), *Personal relationships 4: Dissolving personal relationships* (pp. 1–30). London: Academic Press.

_____. (1984). A perspective on the repair of personal relationships: Repair of what, when? In S. W. Duck (Ed.), *Personal relationships 5: Repairing personal relationships* (pp. 163–84). London: Academic Press.

_____. (1986). *Human relationships: An introduction to social psychology*. London: Sage.

_____. (1990). Relationships as unfinished business: Out of the frying pan and into the 1990s. *Journal of Social and Personal Relationships, 7*, 5–28.

Duck. S. W., & Perlman, D. (1985). The thousand islands of personal relationships: A perspective analysis for future explorations. In S. W. Duck & D. Perlman (Eds.), *Understanding personal relationships research: An interdisciplinary approach* (pp. 1–15). London: Sage.

Duck, S. W., & Sants, H. (1983). On the origin of the specious: Are personal relationships really interpersonal states? *Journal of Social and Clinical Psychology, 1*, 27–41.

Dyson-Hudson, N. (1972). Structure and infra-structure in primitive society: Lévi-Strauss and Radcliffe-Brown. In R. Macksey & E. Donato (Eds.), *The structuralist controversy* (pp. 218–41). Baltimore: Johns Hopkins University Press.

Eco, U. (1980). *The name of the rose.* New York: Warner.

Ehrmann, J. (Ed.) (1970). *Structuralism.* Garden City, NY: Doubleday.

Eibl-Eibesfeldt, I. (1970). *Love and hate: The natural history of behavior patterns.* New York: Schocken.

Festinger, L. (1954). A theory of social comparison process. *Human Relations, 7,* 117–40.

Fisher, B. A., & Drecksel, G. L. (1983). A cyclical model of developing relationships: A study of relational control interaction. *Communication Monographs, 50,* 66–78.

Fisher, W. R. (1989). *Human communication as narration: Toward a philosophy of reason, value, and action.* Columbia, SC: University of South Carolina Press.

Fitzpatrick, M. A., & Best, P. (1979). Dyadic adjustment in relational types: Consensus, cohesion, affectional expression, and satisfaction in enduring relationships. *Communication Monographs, 46,* 167–78.

Forster, E. M. (1968). *A room with a view.* New York: Alfred A. Knopf. (Original work published 1923.)

Gadamer, H. (1976). The universality of the hermeneutical problem. In D. E. Linge (Ed.), *Philosophical hermeneutics* (pp. 3–17). Berkeley, CA: University of California Press.

Gellner, E. (1985). *Relativism and the social sciences.* Cambridge: Cambridge University Press.

Gergen, K. J. (1982). *Toward transformation in social knowledge.* New York: Springer-Verlag.

Glucksmann, M. (1974). *Structuralist analysis in contemporary social thought.* London: Routledge & Kegan Paul.

Goss, B., & O'Hair, D. (1988). *Communicating in interpersonal relationships.* New York: Macmillan.

Gove, D. B. (Editor-in-chief) (1986). *Webster's third new international dictionary.* Springfield, MA: Merriam-Webster.

Guntrip, H. (1973). Science, psychodynamic reality, and autistic thinking. *Journal of the American Academy of Psychoanalysis, 1,* 3–22.

Hampden-Turner, C. M. (1973). An existential "learning theory" and the integration of t-group research. In R. T. Golembiewski & A. Blumberg (Eds.) (2d ed.), *Sensitivity training and the laboratory approach* (pp. 41–57). Itasca, IL: F. E. Peacock.

Hastorf, A. H., & Cantril, H. (1954). They saw a game: A case study. *Journal of Abnormal and Social Psychology, 49,* 129–34.

Hawkes, T. (1977). *Structuralism and semiotics.* Berkeley, CA: University of California Press.

Heider, F. (1958). *The psychology of interpersonal relations.* New York: John Wiley & Sons.

Hinde, R. A. (1979). *Towards understanding relationships.* London: Academic Press.

Hocker, J. L., & Wilmot, W. W. (1985). *Interpersonal conflict* (2d. ed.). Dubuque, IA: William C. Brown.

Hopkins, M. F. (1977). Structuralism: Its implications for the performance of prose fiction. *Communication Monographs, 44,* 93–105.

House, J. S., Landis, K. R., & Umberson, D. (1988). Social relationships and health. *Science, 241,* 540–45.

Huston, T. L., Surra, C. A., Fitzgerald, N. M., & Cate, R. M. (1981). From courtship to marriage: Mate selection as an interpersonal process. In S. W. Duck & R. Gilmour (Eds.), *Personal relationships 2: Developing personal relationships* (pp. 53–88). London: Academic Press.

Jakobson, R., & Halle, M. (1971). *Fundamentals of language.* The Hague: Mouton.

Johnson, B. (1980). *The critical difference: Essays in the contemporary rhetoric of reading.* Baltimore: Johns Hopkins University Press.

Jourard, S. M. (1964). *The transparent self.* New York: Van Nostrand.

Keller, H. (1961). *The story of my life.* New York: Dell. (Original work published 1902.)

Kelly, G. A. (1963). *A theory of personality: The psychology of personal constructs.* New York: W. W. Norton.

Kingsbury, N. M., & Minda, R. B. (1988). An analysis of three expected intimate relationship states: Commitment, maintenance, and termination. *Journal of Social and Personal Relationships, 5,* 405–22.

Knapp, M. L. (1978). *Social intercourse: From greeting to goodbye.* Boston: Allyn & Bacon.

____. (1984). *Interpersonal communication and human relationships.* Boston: Allyn & Bacon.

Knapp, M. L., Ellis, D. G., & Williams, B. A. (1980). Perceptions of communication behavior associated with relationship terms. *Communication Monographs, 47,* 262–78.

Kressel, K., Jaffee, N., Tuchman, B., Watson, C., & Deutsch, M. (1980). A typology of divorcing couples: Implications for mediation and the divorce process. *Family Process, 19,* 101–16.

Krippendorf, K. (1984). An epistemological foundation for communication. *Journal of Communication, 34*(3), 21–36.

Laing, R. D. (1961). *The self and others* (2d. ed.). Baltimore: Penguin.

Lane, M. (Ed.) (1970). *Introduction to structuralism.* New York: Basic Books.

Langacker, R. W. (1968). *Language and its structure: Some fundamental linguistic concepts.* New York: Harcourt, Brace, & World.

Leach, E. (1974). *Claude Lévi-Strauss* (rev. ed.). New York: Penguin.

Leary, T. (1955). The theory and measurement methodology of interpersonal communication. *Psychiatry, 18,* 147–61.

Le Carre, J. (1986). *A perfect spy.* New York: Alfred A. Knopf.

Lee, L. (1984). Sequences in separation: A framework for investigating endings of the personal (romantic) relationship. *Journal of Social and Personal Relationships, 1,* 49–73.

Lehmann, W. P. (1972). *Descriptive linguistics: An introduction.* New York: Random House.

Levinger, G. (1980). Toward the analysis of close relationships. *Journal of Experimental Social Psychology, 16,* 510–44.

____. (1983). Development and change. In H. H. Kelley et al. (Eds.), *Close relationships* (pp. 315–59). New York: W. H. Freeman.

Lévi-Strauss, C. (1963). *Structural anthropology* (C. Jacobson & B. G. Schoepf, Trans.). New York: Basic Books. (Original work published 1958.)

____. (1966). The culinary triangle. *New Society, 8,* 937–40.

____. (1973). *From honey to ashes* (J. Weightman & D. Weightman, Trans.). New York: Harper & Row.

____. (1985). *The view from afar* (J. Neugroschel & P. Hoss, Trans.). New York: Basic Books.

Leymore, V. L. (1975). *Hidden myth*. London: Heinemann.

Lifton, R. J. (1976). *The life of the self*. New York: Simon & Schuster.

Lorenz, K. (1966). *On aggression* (M. K. Wilson, Trans.). New York: Harcourt Brace Jovanovich.

Masheter, C., & Harris, L. M. (1986). From divorce to friendship: A study of dialectic relationship development. *Journal of Social and Personal Relationships, 3*, 177–89.

Macksey, R., & Donato, E. (Eds.) (1972). *The structuralist controversy*. Baltimore: Johns Hopkins University Press.

McCall, G. J., & Simmons, J. L. (1978). *Identities and interactions: An examination of human associations in everyday life* (rev. ed.). New York: The Free Press.

McGee, M. C. (1982). A materialist's conception of rhetoric. In R. E. McKerrow (Ed.), *Explorations in rhetoric: Studies in honor of Douglas Ehninger* (pp. 23–48). Dallas, TX: Scott, Foresman.

McGuire, M. (1977). Mythic rhetoric in *Mein Kampf*: A structuralist critique. *Quarterly Journal of Speech, 63*, 1–13.

____. (1982). The structural study of speech. In R. E. McKerrow (Ed.), *Explorations in rhetoric: Studies in honor of Douglas Ehninger* (pp. 1–22). Dallas, TX: Scott, Foresman.

MacIntyre, A. (1984). *After virtue: A study in moral theory* (2d. ed.). Notre Dame, IN: University of Notre Dame Press.

Metz, C. (1974). *Film language* (M. Taylor, Trans.). New York: Oxford University Press.

Michelfelder, D. P., & Palmer, R. E. (Eds.) (1989). *Dialogue & deconstruction: The Gadamer-Derrida encounter*. Albany, NY: State University of New York Press.

Millar, F. E., & Rogers, L. E. (1987). Relational dimensions of interpersonal dynamics. In M. E. Roloff & G. R. Miller (Eds.), *Interpersonal processes: New directions in communication research* (pp. 117–39). Newbury Park, CA: Sage.

Morris, G. H., & Hopper, R. (1980). Remediation and legislation in everyday talk: How communicators achieve consensus. *Quarterly Journal of Speech, 66*, 266–74.

Morton, T. L., Alexander, J. F., & Altman, I. (1976). Communication and relationship definition. In G. R. Miller (Ed.), *Explorations in interpersonal communication* (pp. 105–25). Beverly Hills, CA: Sage.

Nakanishi, M. (1986). Perceptions of self-disclosure in initial interaction: A Japanese sample. *Human Communication Research, 13*, 167–90.

Natanson, M. (1966). Alienation and social role. *Social Research, 33*, 375–88.

Nichols, M. H. (1963) *Rhetoric and criticism*. Baton Rouge, LA: Louisiana State University Press.

Novak, M. (1970). *The experience of nothingness*. New York: Harper & Row.

Olson, D. H. (1977). Insiders' and outsiders' views of relationships: Research strategies. In G. Levinger & H. L. Raush (Eds.), *Close relationships:*

Perspectives on the meaning of intimacy (pp. 115–35). Amherst, MA: University of Massachusetts Press.

Onions, C. T. (Ed.) (1966). *The Oxford dictionary of English etymology.* New York: Oxford University Press.

Parks, M. R., & Adelman, M. B. (1983). Communication networks and the development of romantic relationships: An expansion of uncertainty reduction theory. *Human Communication Research, 10,* 55–79.

Pettit, P. (1975). *The concept of structuralism: A critical analysis.* Berkeley, CA: University of California Press.

Philipsen, G. (1982). The qualitative case study as a strategy in communication inquiry. *The Communicator, 12,* 4–17.

Phillips, G. M., & Wood, J. T. (1983). *Communication and human relationships.* New York: Macmillan.

Piaget, J. (1970). *Structuralism.* (C. Maschler, Trans.). New York: Harper & Row.

Planalp, S., & Honeycutt, J. (1985). Events that increase uncertainty in personal relationships. *Human Communication Research, 11,* 593–604.

Planalp, S., Rutherford, D. K., & Honeycutt, J. M. (1988). Events that increase uncertainty in personal relationships II: Replication and extension. *Human Communication Research, 14,* 516–47.

Polansky, N. A., Weiss, E. S., & Blum, A. (1961). Children's verbal accessibility as a function of content and personality. *American Journal of Orthopsychiatry, 31,* 153–69.

Railsback, C. C. (1983). Beyond rhetorical relativism: A structural-material model of truth and objective reality. *Quarterly Journal of Speech, 69,* 351–63.

Raush, H. L. (1977a). Orientations to the close relationship. In G. Levinger & H. L. Raush (Eds.), *Close relationships: Perspectives on the meaning of intimacy* (pp. 163–88). Amherst, MA: University of Massachusetts Press.

____. (1977b). Paradox, levels, and junctures in person-situation systems. In D. Magnusson & N. S. Endler (Eds.), *Personality at the crossroads: Current Issues in interactional psychology* (pp. 287–304). Hillsdale, NJ: Erlbaum.

____. (1981). Logical force, not quite logical people, and the pragmatics of change. *Communication, 6,* 99–116.

Rawlins, W. K. (1983a). Negotiating close friendship: The dialectic of conjunctive freedoms. *Human Communication Research, 9,* 255–66.

____. (1983b). Openness as problematic in ongoing friendships: Two conversational dilemmas. *Communication Monographs, 50,* 1–13.

Richardson, H. W. (1969). Three myths of transcendence. In H. W. Richardson & D. R. Cutler (Eds.), *Transcendence* (pp. 98–113). Boston: Beacon Press.

Ricoeur, P. (1971). The model of the text: Meaningful action considered as a text. *Social Research, 38,* 529–62.

Rychlak, J. F. (1984). Relationship theory: An historical development in psychology leading to a teleological image of humanity. *Journal of Social and Personal Relationships, 1,* 363–86.

Saint-Exupery, A. de (1942). *Flight to Arras* (L. Galantiere, Trans.). San Diego, CA: Harcourt Brace Jovanovich.

Saussure, F. de (1959). *Course in general linguistics* (W. Baskin, Trans.; C. Bally & A. Sechehaye, Eds.). New York: Philosophical Library.

Schein, E. H., & Bennis, W. G. (1965). *Personal and organizational change through group methods*. New York: John Wiley & Sons.

Schrag, C. O. (1980). *Radical reflection and the origin of the human sciences*. West Lafayette, IN: Purdue University Press.

Scott, M. B., & Lyman, S. M. (1968). Accounts. *American Sociological Review, 33*, 46–62.

Seung, T. K. (1982). *Structuralism and hermeneutics*. New York: Columbia University Press.

Sheehy, G. (1974). *Passages*. New York: Dutton.

Sieburg, E. R. (1969). Dysfunctional communication and interpersonal responsiveness in small groups. *Dissertation Abstracts International*, 30/06-A, 2622.

Sillars, A., & Parry, D. (1982). Stress, cognition, and communication in interpersonal conflicts. *Communication Research, 9*, 201–26.

Sillars, A. L., & Scott, M. D. (1983). Interpersonal perception between intimates: An integrative view. *Human Communication Research, 10*, 153–76.

Simmel, G. (1950). *The sociology of Georg Simmel* (K. H. Wolff, Trans., Ed.). New York: The Free Press.

Simons, H. W. (1978). In praise of muddleheaded anecdotalism. *Western Journal of Speech Communication, 42*, 21–28.

Simpson, J. A., & Weiner, E. S. C. (Eds.) (1989). *The Oxford English dictionary* (2d ed.). Oxford: Clarendon Press.

Smith, D. H. (1972). Communication research and the idea of process. *Speech Monographs, 39*, 174–82.

Stinnette, C. R. (1968). Reflection and transformation: Knowing and change in psychotherapy and in religious faith. In P. Homans (Ed.), *The dialogue between theology and psychology* (pp. 83–110). Chicago: University of Chicago Press.

Stokes, R., & Hewitt, J. P. (1976). Aligning actions. *American Sociological Review, 41*, 838–49.

Taylor, C. (1971). Interpretation and the sciences of man. *The Review of Metaphysics, 25*, 3–51.

Thibaut, J. W., & Kelley, H. H. (1959). *The social psychology of groups*. New York: John Wiley & Sons.

Trenholm, S., & Jensen, A. (1988). *Interpersonal communication*. Belmont, CA: Wadsworth.

Tschann, J. M. (1988). Self-disclosure in adult friendship: Gender and marital status differences. *Journal of Social and Personal Relationships, 5*, 65 81.

Wallace, A. F. C. (1956a). Mazeway resynthesis: A biocultural theory of religious inspiration. *Transactions of the New York Academy of Sciences* (2d Series), *18*, 626–38.

____. (1956b). Revitalization movements. *American Anthropologist, 58*, 264–81.

____. (1957). Mazeway disintegration: The individual's perception of socio-cultural disorganization. *Human Organization, 16*, 23–27.

Warnick, B. (1979). Structuralism vs. phenomenology: Implications for rhetorical criticism. *Quarterly Journal of Speech, 65*, 250–61.

____. (1987). A Ricoeurian approach to rhetorical criticism. *Western Journal of Speech Communication, 51*, 227–44.

Watzlawick, P., Beavin, J. H., & Jackson, D. D. (1967). *Pragmatics of human communication*. New York: Norton.

Watzlawick, P., Weakland, J. H., & Fisch, R. (1974). *Change: Principles of problem formation and resolution*. New York: Norton.

Welty, E. (1984). *One writer's beginnings*. Cambridge, MA: Harvard University Press.

Wheeless, L. R. (1976). Self-disclosure and interpersonal solidarity: Measurement, validation, and relationships. *Human Communication Research, 3*, 47–61.

_____. (1978). A follow-up study of the relationships among trust, disclosure, and interpersonal solidarity. *Human Communication Research, 4*, 143–57.

Wheeless, L. R., Wheeless, V. E., & Baus, R. (1984). Sexual communication, communication satisfaction, and solidarity in the developmental stages of intimate relationships. *Western Journal of Speech Communication, 48*, 217–30.

Whitehead, A. N. (1929). *Process and reality: An essay in cosmology*. New York: Macmillan.

Wilmot, W. W. (1987). *Dyadic communication*. (3rd ed.). New York: Random House.

Wilmot, W. W., Stevens, D. C., & Miller, K. M. (1988, May). *Rejuvenation in personal relationships*. Paper presented at the meeting of the International Communication Association, New Orleans, LA.

Wilson, G. L., Hantz, A. M., & Hanna, M. S. (1989). *Interpersonal growth through communication* (2d ed.). Dubuque, IA: William C. Brown.

Witteman, H., & Fitzpatrick, M. A. (1986). Compliance-gaining in marital interaction: Power bases, processes, and outcomes. *Communication Monographs, 53*, 130–43.

Wood, J. T. (1982). Communication and relational culture: Bases for the study of human relationships. *Communication Quarterly, 30*, 75–83.

Wright, P. H. (1978). Toward a theory of friendship based on a conception of self. *Human Communication Research, 4*, 196–207.

_____. (1989). The essence of personal relationships and their value for the individual. In G. Graham & H. Lafollette (Eds.), *Person to person* (pp. 15–31). Philadelphia: Temple University Press.

Index

affect, 90; and relational transition, 28, 29, 32, 35, 36
affective exchange, 100
againness, 116
alienation. *See* relationship alienation
alienation phase, of relational transition, 123–24
anticipation, 26, 27, 33, 36
arenas of action, in relational development, 15–16
ascription, 85
assumption(s): of power, 115, 117, 128, 129, 139, 144–45; of recognition, 116, 117; of recourse, 115–16, 117, 127, 128; of release, 116, 117, 127, 128, 139, 144–45; of uniformity, 115, 117
attribution theory, 94, 133
autonomy, 71, 137
autonomy-connection, 150
avoiding, 12
awareness, 98

benign alienation, 127–28
binarism, as essential to transformation, 50
binary features, of language, 46–47
bonding, 12; as instinctual, 134

buildup, 98

causality, emanationist view of, 43–44
change, 70; dynamics of, 71–72
circumscribing stage in relationship, 12, 62, 63, 97
classical structuralism, 42
closed contradiction, 137
cognitive consistency theory, 133
comfort model, 81–87
communication, in personal relationships, 131
communication studies, theme of process in, ix
communicative action, areas of, 15–16
confirmation, 124–25
confirming messages, 142–43; dimensions of, 139
conflict, role of, in relationships, 64
conflict model, 87–90
conflicts management, studies of, 4
conjunction, 103
connection, 137
constructivists, 94
context, and disintegration, 107–08
continuation phase of relationship, 59, 98
contradiction, 70; dynamics of, 71–72

critical interpretative approaches to social theory, 42
cultural regeneration, 74

deconstruction, relationship of, to structuralism, 8
deconstructionists, 7–8
deferring conversational act, 66
depenetration, 64
detachment, in dialectical relationship, 11
detachment-intimacy, 70
deterioration, 98
determinism, 108–09
dialectical relationships, characteristics of, 70
dialectical interaction, 69–70
dialectical relationships, 10–11; intimacy and detachment in, 11
dialectical theory, 10–11
dialectics, 69–72
Diane, case of, 160–61; alienation in, 128; disintegration in, 110; resynthesis in, 146; security in, 90; structural analysis of, 29–33
différance, 6–9, 19–20
difference, x, 150–51; and dialectical theory, 10–11; as différance, 6–9, 19–20; as a given, 4–6; in interpersonal communication, 2; as key issue in self-disclosure, 3; in language, 6–9; normality of, 5; in personal relationships, 8; as problematic, 93; in relational stage models, 12–16; in relationships, 9–12, 19–40; role of, in relational transition, 28–29, 32–33, 36–37; and social class, 5; ubiquity of, 1–17, 28, 83–84; and uncertainty reduction theory, 2–3
differentiating stage, in relationship, 12, 62, 97
disconfirmation, 125
disconfirming messages, 142–43
discovery, 27, 33
discovery: language, 27
discovery: self, 27
disengagement, 119, 122
disintegration. See relationship

disintegration
disintegration-resynthesis, 150
disjunction, 103
dissolution, 98
divorce, confirming and disconfirming messages in, 143
domineering conversational act, 66
dyadic action, 16
dyadic effect, 65, 108
dyadic phase of relationship, 63, 102–03
dyadic relationships, 41

emanationist view of causality, 43–44
ending, 98
episodes: arranging, in structural analysis, 24, 26, 54–56; creation of, in structural analysis, 23–24, 53–54
equivalence conversational act, 66
exclusivity, 119, 122
expected commitment state (ECS), 136
expected termination state (ETS), 136
experimenting, 12, 13
exploratory affective exchange, 100
expressiveness, 71
expressiveness-protectiveness, 70

facilitative communication, 139
fidelity, 52
first-order change in relationship, 73
friendship, 142; confirming and disconfirming messages in, 143
frustration, 27

gaining formal recognition, 124
ggeneric divisiveness, 4
getting away, 124
Get-to-Know-Time, 119, 121–22
given, difference as a, 4–6
grammar, distinction between speech and, 46, 50
grave-dressing phase of relationship, 16, 59

helical model, 145; development of, 72–77
hermeneutical theory of textual-philological analysis, 149
homeostasis, 88

Howard and Judy, case of, 162–72;
     disintegration in, 110; alienation in,
     128–29; resynthesis in, 147; security
     in, 91; structural analysis in, 33–37
human action, as language, 44–51
human association: infant-practice
     argument for, 135; safety and
     security argument for, 134–35;
     transcendence argument for, 135;
humanized structuralism, 51–57

implicit helix, 63–69
individual, normalizing of, as different,
     5–6
infant-practice argument, for human
     association, 135
information deprivation, conditions of,
     101–02
initiation, 12, 98
in kilter, 80–81; comfort model of, 81–
     87; conflict model of, 87–90
integrating stage of relationship, 12, 59,
     62
intensifying stage in relationship, 12, 13,
     62
interconnectedness of opposites, 70
interdependence, 71
interpersonal communication:
     developmental perspectives on, 3; in
     dialectical analyses, 69–70; difference
     in, 2
interpersonal reflex, 108
interpersonal solidarity, 68–69
interpretation in structural analysis, 26,
     56–57
intimacy, 90; in dialectical relationship,
     11; dimension of, 27; and relational
     transition, 28–29, 30, 32, 35–36;
     stages of, 97–98
intimate relations, 101
intrapersonal action, 16
intrapsychic phase of relationship, 63,
     102
investing, 142
isomorphism, 103–04

joy, 26, 27

Keller, Helen, case, 157–59; alienation
     in, 128; disintegration in, 109–10;
     resynthesis in, 146; security in, 90;
     structure in, 23–29

language: binary features of, 46–47;
     difference in, 6–9; functions of, 52;
     invisible rules of, 45–46; orthogonal
     dimensions of, 47–48; semantic
     transformation of, 48–51; structural
     analysis of, 20–21
Lévi-Strauss, Claude, 7, 42, 45, 46, 48–
     49, 51–53
life cycle, relationships during, 101
life cycle metaphor, 101; strength of, 104

maintenance, 98
making up, 119, 122
marital development, model of, 62
marriage, 142; confirming and
     disconfirming messages in, 143
marriage relationships, evolution of, 98
material reality, and rhetoric, 52
mazeway, 74–75, 118–19
mazeway disintegration, 75–76
mazeway resynthesis, 75–76
Mein Kampf, analysis of, 49
memories, 64–65
mental maps for relationship, 102
mindfulness and disintegration, 106–07
mutuality of relationship, 67–68, 98
myth, 48–49, 86; monitoring power of,
     89
myth analysis, 52–53

neutralization, 137–38, 138
nonmutuality of relationship definition,
     67
nonmutuality crises, 10, 14–15;
     relationship in, 11

openness, 5–6, 116
openness-closedness, 70
open systems analogy, 88
order, pursuit of, 43–44
organizational identification, effect of
     turning points on, 124
orientation, 100

orthogonal dimensions of language, 47–48

otherworldliness of emantionist view, 44

Palo Alto group, 140

paradigmatic dimension of language, 47–48

partner dynamics in relational development, 13–14

partner perspectives in relational development, 14–15

passion, 119

perceptual congruity, 68

perceptual incongruity, 68

perpetual deferral, 7

personal constructs theory, 133

personal relationships: attributes of, 41; difference in, 8; narratives on, 41–42; stabilization of, 79–92

positive psychic change, 122

postmarital relationships, 143

power, assumption of, 115, 117, 128, 129, 139, 144–45

praxis, 51

process: in communication studies, ix; relationship as, ix, 59–63; relationship development, 72

radical individualism, 5

receiving informal recognition, 124

recognition, assumption of, 116, 117

reconciliation, 33, 35, 36

recourse, assumption of, 115–16, 117, 127, 128

redefinition, as form of resynthesis, 136

reframing, 137

relational adjustment, 108–09

relational communication categories of, 66

relational culture, 85–86

relational outcomes, 95

relational regeneration, 105

relational satisfaction, turning points associated with, 122

relational school of interpersonal communication, 47

relational stage model, 150–51; difference in, 12–16

relational transition; and affect, 30, 32, 35, 36; alienation phase of, 123–24; helical model of, 145; and intimacy, 30, 32, 35–36; role of difference in, 28–29, 32–33, 36–37; structural analysis of, 41–57; structure of, 20–23; and time, 30, 35–36

relationship(s): circumscribing stage in, 62, 63; continuation phase of, 59; cycles in, 65–67; developmental stages of, 68–69; difference in, 9–12; differentiating stage in, 62; dyadic phase of, 63, 102–03; first-order change in, 73; grave-dressing stage of, 59; integrating stage in, 59, 62; intensifying stage in, 62; intrapsychic phase of, 63, 102; mental maps for, 102; mutuality of, 67–68; problems in defining, 131–32; as process, ix, 59–63; re-forming, 119–27; role of conflict in, 64; second-order change in, 73; stagnating phase of, 63; transition and difference in, 19–40

relationship alienation, xi, 38, 39, 73–74, 113–29, 151; and benign alienation, 127–28; cases in, 128–29; and deformation of sociality, 115–19; meta-dialectic of, 114; and re-forming relationships, 119–27; in structural helical model, 76, 113–29

relationship crisis, 10

relationship deterioration, model of, 102

relationship development as process, 72

relationship disengagement, 21–22

relationship disintegration, xi, 38, 39, 93–111, 122–23, 151; cases in, 109–10; and context, 107–08; and determinism, 108–09; and gathering of forces in, 94–95; and mindfulness, 106–07; relevance to social penetration theory, 100; in structural helical model, 76, 93–111; ubiquity of, 96–106

relationship dissolution, model of, 15–16, 62

relationship repair, studies of, 3–4

relationship resynthesis, xi, 38, 39, 131–

47, 151; process of, 135–38; in structural helical model, 76, 131–47; cases of, 146–47; origins of, 133–35; process of, 135–38; promptings of, 138–46

relationship security, xi, 37, 38–39, 39, 73–74, 79–92, 151; cases in, 90–91; comfort model of, 81–87; conflict model of, 87–90; in structural helical model, 76, 79–92

relationship termination, 102

relationship turning points, 119–7

release, assumption of, 116, 117, 127, 128, 139, 144–45

repetition, 62

representing the organization, 124

resynthesis, 39. See relationship resynthesis

reunion, 122

reward dependability, 84–85

rhetoric, 52; and material reality, 52

role-action, 115; attenuation of, 133; conditions of, 115–16; debilitating effects of interrupted, 144; manifestation of, 118

role-identity, 105

role-taking, 115–16; dependence on relational partners, 118; operation of, 125, 127

romantic relationships, evolution of, 119–27

Room with a View, A (Forster), 19–20

sacrifice, 122

safety and security argument for human association, 134–35

sameness, 116

schismogenesis, 66, 108

second-order change in relationship, 73

security. See relationship security

security-alienation, 74, 114, 132–33, 150

selection, 137, 138

self-concept, 141–42

self-disclosure, difference as key issue in, 3

semantic transformation of language, 48–51

sense makers, vision of persons as, 94

separateness-connectedness, 70

separateness-reconciliation, 70

separation, 33, 34, 35, 36, 138

serious commitment, 119, 121

shared schemata, 86

social action, 16

social class and difference, 5

social comparison theory, 133

social depenetration, 99–100

social exchange theory, 99

sociality, deformation of, 115–19

social penetration, stages of, 100–1

social penetration theory, 99; relevance to disintegration, 100

social theory, critical interpretative approaches to, 42

speech, distinction between grammar and, 46, 50

stable exchange, 100

stagnating, 12

stagnating stage of relationship, 63

staircase model, 62

structural analysis, x, 150; arranging episodes in, 24, 26, 54–56; in case of Diane, 29–33, 160–61; in case of Howard and Judy, 33–37, 162–72; creating list of episodes in, 53–54; interpretation in, 26, 56–57; naming episodes as step in, 23; of relationship transitions, 41–57; steps in, 53–57

structural helical model, x, 15, 98, 149, 150–51, 152; alienation in, 76, 113–29; disintegration in, 76, 93–111; resynthesis in, 76, 131–47; security in, 76, 79–92

structuralism, x, 42–43; classical, 42; criticisms of, 44, 51; and human action as language, 44–51; humanized, 51–57; and pursuit of order, 43–44; relationship of deconstruction to, 8

structuralist goals, 45

structure of relational transitions, 20–23

structuring conversational act, 66

subjective existence, 51

submitting conversational act, 66

Symbolic Interactionist School, 140, 141

syntagmatic dimensions of language, 47–48

temporal relationships, 41
terminating, 12
time, 90; passage of, and difference in relationships, 9; and relational transition, 28, 30, 35
togetherness-autonomy, 70
togetherness-expressiveness, 150
transcendence argument for human association, 135

transformation: binarism as essential to, 50; concept of, 50–51
transition in relationships, 19–40

uncertainity reduction, 133–34
uncertainity reduction theory, 2–3, 94, 152
uniformity, assumption of, 115, 117
ubiquitous, difference as, 28
unity, of opposites, 70

vowel triangle, 45

About the Author

Richard L. Conville is Professor of Speech Communication at the University of Southern Mississippi. He has taught in the field of interpersonal communication since 1972, and his research has appeared in such journals as *Human Communication Research,* the *Journal of Social and Personal Relationships,* the *Quarterly Journal of Speech,* and *Communication Monographs*. Professor Conville has served on the Board of Directors of the International Communication Association and on the editorial boards of the *Southern Communication Journal* and *Communication Theory*.